W9-AQF-221

TOWARD A CONTEMPORARY CHRISTIANITY

BRIAN WICKER

Toward a
Contemporary
Christianity

80286

ST. JOSEPH'S UNIVERSITY

3 9353 00289 3459

BR
115
C8
W5
1967

UNIVERSITY OF NOTRE DAME PRESS

FIRST AMERICAN EDITION 1967
UNIVERSITY OF NOTRE DAME PRESS
NOTRE DAME, INDIANA

FIRST PUBLISHED 1966
AS CULTURE AND THEOLOGY BY
SHEED AND WARD LTD.
LONDON

© BRIAN WICKER

Library of Congress Catalog Card Number: 67-11836

Manufactured in the United States of America

Contents

Foreword

This book is an attempt to pursue some of the themes which I touched upon but did not have time to amplify in my earlier book, *Culture and Liturgy* (London 1963). In some respects that book took on the character of a manifesto. In it I tried to state a cultural and theological position, together with some of its implications in the field of literary criticism and political commitment. But I did not have the space to argue out everything that I had in mind. The book probably raised as many difficulties as it solved. Some of the ideas to which I alluded, and which I used obliquely, were not clear enough properly to illuminate the topics I discussed. Not all the connections were adequately made. Yet subsequent comment has convinced me that a good deal of what I said made sense, to a fairly wide range of readers, and that there would be some value in trying to present in more detail certain of the premisses upon which my argument was based, but which I did not fully state or defend. In the present book, I have tried to work out the philosophical argument upon which my conclusions were founded. In doing this I have decided to leave on one side the political thesis which was an essential feature of *Culture and Liturgy*, and have not attempted to take that part of the argument further. This is not because I think it any less important or valid than when *Culture and Liturgy* appeared: it is partly because I do not wish to complicate what is already a difficult argument, but it is also because I do not feel at present adequate to the task of filling out in detail that aspect of my position.

However, the following pages are not just an amplification of an earlier draft. The argument I have tried to sketch here—and I have done no more than that—exists in its own right. Very little of it is original, except perhaps the bringing together of ideas and themes from a number of different disciplines, no one of which seems to me complete by itself. I have raided the work of philosophers, theologians, literary critics, and students of comparative religion. Of course, to try to master the intricacies of all these fields is impossible, even within a single main line of interest. The choice of what I have included and what I have omitted may appear arbitrary, and the criteria for so doing inadequate. My defence is that I can only write about what I know, and that there must be others who can fill in the obvious gaps. What I have tried to show is that there is a certain coherence to be observed between the leading ideas of a number of independent thinkers, and that this coherence can be seen to reveal a concerted dissatisfaction, both with what I have called the "secular philosophy" on the one hand, and with much of what lies behind the "new theologies" on the other. But this is not because most of the thinkers I have in mind are particularly concerned with problems of a theological kind. They offer us, not theology, but the raw materials with which the theologian must work. They are part of the "creative centre"[1] of our culture, of which the theologian must

[1] The term "creative centre" is that of Charles Davis, "Theology and its Present Task", *Theology and the University* (ed. John Coulson), London 1963, 107ff.

For full details of this and all other books cited or quoted in the text, see the bibliography on pp. 259–71 below.

be constantly aware. There are certain common intellectual positions which can be discerned in the work (to name those whose writing has most occupied my attention in this book) of Mircea Eliade, Ludwig Wittgenstein, Maurice Merleau-Ponty, and Karl Marx. If I am right, this consensus is important because it constitutes a bridge between the value given by the contemporary logical empiricist to the qualities of hard-headedness and clarity, and the imaginative excitement and comprehensive humanity of the existentialist experience which lies behind much of the new theological exploration. It seems to me that both these qualities are essential for any creative theology—or, for that matter, for any worthwhile intellectual enterprise. But they have not often been present in equal measure in the theological debates of the past few years, at any rate in England.

I think that a Roman Catholic is in a fortunate position in this respect. For he is in a tradition which, on its philosophical side, is deeply agnostic and suspicious of large metaphysical abstractions. The Thomist, for example, is able, for this reason, to argue with the modern philosophical sceptic on his own terms. (At the philosophical level it is noticeable how often the Catholic theologian finds himself agreeing with the linguistic analyst, but at a loss when talking to those theologians who have given up the attempt to build a rational philosophical prolegomenon to theology.) On the other hand he is also in exceptionally close contact, on the theological side, with colleagues (particularly in France, Germany, and Holland) who have been deeply and creatively influenced by existentialist philosophies, and the rise of phenomenology. These continental theologians do not understand the *angst* of modern man just from books: they know of it, like their atheistic friends, from having had to confront a transcendental evil in their own midst, in the heart of Europe. The theological renewal among Catholics has much to do with the experience of occupation and resistance. Here, in Catholic theology, there is perhaps a unique opportunity to combine the values of the detached academic scholar and those of the committed partisan.

It would be absurd to claim more for this book than that it has tentatively and perhaps obscurely suggested a number of crucial components for building a bridge between those commitments and disciplines. A living theology must always begin, it seems to me, from a confrontation between an accepted body of tradition and a contemporary culture. This book is simply a discussion of certain themes, and a presentation of certain regularities, which I think have an important place in the modern cultural landscape. In this sense it may be regarded as an attempt to provide a necessary prolegomenon to a new theology. But I hope that the ideas I have discussed will seem as relevant to the reader of Dickens, or Wittgenstein, as to the reader of Newman or Aquinas, though in my experience those in the first group are not very likely to have much familiarity with the preoccupations of the second, or vice versa.

In this sense, despite the fact that I have, for reasons of space, had to assume some knowledge of the elementary facts concerning the topics I have discussed, I regard this as a work of popularisation. It is an attempt, very necessary in our specialised and fragmented world, to bring together for discussion ideas from a variety of sources. It would be quite easy for anyone in England today to get a perfectly respectable university degree in any one of the disciplines which I have raided without having read a page of any book from any of the others.

If the attempt to make some sense of this diffused collection of ideas is deemed to have failed, I shall not be particularly surprised. It was worth trying.

Perhaps I may be allowed at this point to record a few special debts of gratitude. I am particularly grateful to Stanley Windass, Walter Stein, and Fr Laurence Bright, OP, who have read this book in typescript and made very many valuable suggestions for its improvement. I would also like to acknowledge a debt to Herbert McCabe, OP, with whom I have discussed many of the philosophical themes, and who, as editor of *Blackfriars*, has given permission for me to reprint, in a revised form, a paper on George Orwell first published in the June 1962 issue of that journal; and to Fr Charles Davis for permission to quote part of an article first published in the *Clergy Review* of September 1964. In addition, I would like to pay a debt of thanks to the many circles of the Newman Association, and other interested groups, up and down the country, who have invited me to talk to them, and who have thereby helped me to formulate my thoughts. Thanks should go, too, to Mrs Doreen Leigh for typing the original version of this book, and to my wife and family for help with the index and the bibliography, and for their tolerance during a difficult period. Finally, I should like to acknowledge a debt to Allen Parker, Director of the Department of Extramural Studies at Birmingham University, for arranging a term's study leave to write the book.

I have added a bibliographical list at the end in order to enable the reader to follow-up himself the work of the thinkers to whom I am most indebted. Details of all works referred to are also given there.

BRIAN WICKER

February 1966.

Introduction
Secular, modern,
or radical ?

There are three conditions which often look alike
Yet differ completely, flourish in the same hedgerow.
[T. S. Eliot, *Little Gidding*, III, 1ff.]

If it is taken for granted—as I think it must be—that
the old, familiar expressions of institutional Christianity
are dying, if not already dead, the question arises: What
is to be put in their place? One answer is, of course,
nothing. But that is too easy a reply, even for the atheist.
For Christianity has served crucial cultural purposes
which cannot be dismissed even by the non-believer.
Indeed, it is interesting to see that, now we are faced
with some fairly basic reassessments by the most conservative of all Christian traditions—that of Roman
Catholicism—many agnostics are beginning to be
alarmed for the state of Christianity. While never having
seriously considered the possibility of acknowledging
Catholic claims for themselves, they have nevertheless
seen the Catholic tradition as an essential conserving
element in Western culture. This conserving element
has given intelligent expression to a necessary pessimism about the human condition, and, it is felt, ought

not to be lost in the frantic search for a new image. The loss of belief in the West has not been an unequivocal gain for human freedom. The old humanist confidence is as dead as the old religion it tried to confound. It is therefore a real question, for believer and non-believer alike, how to replace the religious and cultural tradition of institutional Christianity which has died on us. There is a void in the heart of Western culture which has got to be filled, and this is a task confronting anyone who belongs to that world.

Apart from the purely reactionary responses which come from an insecure but still smouldering ecclesiasticism, and the shouts of dismay from moral rearmers and other authoritarian conservatives, it is possible to distinguish three main kinds of answer. These may be conveniently labelled: secularism, modernism, and radicalism. It is one purpose of this book to try to give some intellectual underpinning to the radical position.

Much of the attention given to those who want to secularise Christianity has focused upon their attempts to reinterpret the gospel in the terms of the characteristically twentieth-century philosophies: in the case of Bultmann, that of Heidegger; in the case of Paul van Buren, that of positivistic linguistic analysis; in the case of the Bishop of Woolwich, elements drawn eclectically from many sources. But behind the din and smoke which rises from the battles being fought by and for these men, there is discernible one main concern common to all. This is the attempt to make Christianity intelligible and relevant to a world which puts almost all its emphasis upon the conscious, adult commitment of the individual person. The secularist Christian sees the essential movement of modern culture as the rejec-

2

tion of conventions, codes, habits, and traditional sanctions as the basis of life, and their replacement by the efforts of the individual, self-consciously working upon data which have been personally brought home to him. History indicates to us, the secularist believes, that we are being brought ever more decisively to the point at which every action must be undertaken responsibly in the light of our knowledge. He does not see depth psychology, for example, as revealing to us uncontrollable forces which determine us, but as a new knowledge which, ultimately, gives us new control over ourselves. Knowledge is power, self-knowledge is therefore also self-determination. Morality is essentially concerned with the exercise of those capacities which make us more self-aware, and so more in control. The objective of moral action is the attainment of "maturity" or "adulthood", which signifies just such a maxim of self-determination. Sexual morality particularly is to be governed by this ideal of maturity. A good sexual relationship is one in which I attain a greater maturity, am more capable of adult growth and the development of a responsible concern for others. If such a relationship is possible for a particular individual only outside marriage, or if it is only attainable in a homosexual context, well and good.

Faith, too, is a conscious, adult commitment to God. It is not something that can be given without response, or at any rate it is of little value until the moment of response. Faith is *my* decision, concerns *my* relationship to God. The church may have at its disposal numerous symbolisms and encouragements to my faith, but its value is ultimately to be judged by the extent to which these help to bring its members to maturity in their own lives.

The secularist position as outlined here is not just a Christian phenomenon. It is a response to the secularism of the world as the believer sees it. But it is not the only response, and it is not without its limitations. These derive from the particular view which the secularist takes of the world in which he finds himself and of the agnosticism which characterises it. There are certain natural concomitants of secularism which need to be brought to light in order to make clear the nature of these limitations. First, secularism is an individualistic approach to the problem. It is a response to agnosticism, or atheism, conceived as a personal and deliberate choice against God. It is no accident that it is the atheism of Sartre and Camus, rather than the atheism of Marx or Lenin, which is the starting-point of the secularist's journey—an atheism, in other words, of the lonely man bred in a Cartesian tradition, brooding over his stove or engaging in a heroic, nihilistic struggle in a situation of isolation. Secularist Christianity, like the atheism it is trying to grapple with, is a-historical and even a-social in its primary emphasis. Its martyr is Bonhoeffer, writing in his cell and dying without any companion. Its artistic inspirations are those of Kafka and Beckett, not those of Brecht or George Orwell. Its historical vision (such as it is) is that of Teilhard de Chardin, not that of Marx. Politically, it is possible to be a secularist Christian and a conservative, or a liberal, or a Wilsonian socialist, or indeed to have no political orientation at all. For secularism rests in a detachment from all those elements in experience which are politically important. The human community is, for the secularist, just the getting together of autonomous individuals for certain ends—characteristically, for the attainment of that amount of social cohesion which is necessary for the wants of the individual to be reconciled with those of his neighbours, and no more. The political philosophy of secularism is, at bottom, that of utilitarian liberalism, as has been well shown by D. L. Munby in his book *The Idea of a Secular Society*. Today this philosophy can, with equal ease, be made to fit into the party programmes of any of the main parties in Britain or America. That is the measure of its sterility.

These are the main limitations upon the secularist position. They follow naturally from its strength—the emphasis it gives to the individual person and his personal responsibility for everything he does. To become what I am is the first duty of a man, and secularism is primarily concerned to underline this truth. It also underlines the concomitant truth that what I ought to *do* is subservient to what I ought to *be*. It emphasizes rightly that moral action is fidelity to *myself*; is based upon the attempt to realise my own real wants. What *I* really want (which is not always what I think I want) is necessarily good, the secularist says; for though he is an individualist, he does not deny the goodness of the individual nature (as an older, specifically Protestant, individualism did). But the weakness of secularism is that it contains no basis on which to form a criterion by which I can consciously decide (as I must) what it is I really want. The very distinction between these two levels of wanting rests, finally, upon some notion of the solidarity of mankind which it is hard to fit into the secularist position, with its background of positivist empiricism or Cartesian dualism. For what I really want can only be necessarily good as long as it serves my fundamental needs. But how are these fundamental needs to be distinguished from my immediate and conscious wishes, or the drives I am already aware of in myself? Does not such a distinction rest upon a more fundamental human need which outruns my individual and fleeting wishes? It is here that secularist individualism puts to itself a problem it cannot solve on its own terms, and points to something beyond itself.

Secular Christianity, like utilitarian liberalism and positivistic empiricism, has flourished mainly in countries with a Protestant tradition. It is essentially a Protestant growth. It is not surprising to find that its main alternative—*modernism* or *modernisation*—has been the concern of the Roman Catholic renewal in recent years. The Vatican Council is, basically, concerned to modernise the church. But modernisation, as an ideology, is by no means a Latin or "Catholic" concept. It has deep roots in other places as well, and this is one of the reasons for the complexity of the present situation, and for the crossing of the wires which we find in almost every part of the debate. There is, for example, an extremely interesting connection between the ideology of modernisation espoused by Wilsonian socialism in Britain and the ideology of the Catholic hierarchy in the same country; and I suspect that similar connections could be clearly discerned between the other moderately "progressive" Catholic hierarchies in the West and the non-Marxist political progressives in the various countries. (The approval by the Vatican of the Centre-Left coalition in Italy is only one obvious example.)

The great strength of modernisation, as opposed to secularism, is its sense of a community and its history. Just as the Labour Party is able to draw upon the history of the labour movement, and of the trade unions, and point to some kind of continuous communal life linking the world of Chartism to the world of the

6

modern TUC, so the Christian moderniser can point to a continuity within history of a community which has borne the Christian tradition upon itself. The moderniser is one who sees the renewal of Christianity in terms of the renewal of an empirical community within history, whether he is a Roman Catholic or— like Dr Robinson, who is as much a moderniser as a secularist—a member of some other visibly structured Christian body. The starting-point for the Christian moderniser is the church as given to him. It is there before he starts, and it will be there after he has finished with it. His task is to renew it from within. For outside it there is no Christianity at all. (Whether anyone can be wholly outside it is, of course, questionable, as the Vatican Council's *Constitution on the Church* shows. But at this point modernisation tends to mingle with secularisation, for both are here asserting the primacy of the individual's fidelity to himself as the fundamental Christian demand.)

This assumption of a community which envelops the individual—which pre-exists him, into which he is incorporated, which he does not constitute by his own deliberate, conscious commitment—is the first thing which distinguishes the moderniser from the secularist. Modernism is a communal movement, concerned with the renewal of a community life, in which alone it sees any hope of the renewal of the life of the individual. Freedom and community are not opposed, but complementary, demands. If the secularist emphasis is to say that without personal freedom there can be no community, the modernist emphasis is to say that without a community there can be no true personal freedom. While he does not deny that the world is moving towards an ever greater degree of self-awareness, and of control of his own destiny by the individual, the moderniser sees this progress as achieved only by a communal effort. It is not an individualistic probing into the soul which will bring this control, through self-knowledge; but rather a common technological undertaking which, in the first place, will provide control of the environment for the community. Only if this is attained will any fruit be won from the self-knowledge gained by individualistic pursuits. Modernised morality, therefore, is concerned as much with a self-dedication to the concerns of the community as it is with a growth in maturity or self-knowledge. Or rather, the latter is only possible through the former, which must be recognised as a basic and inescapable first priority. Thus, the stable marriage, as a basic community of persons who see their fulfilment in each other, is the primary emphasis in sexual morality, rather than the growth of awareness gained by sexual experience considered as the satisfaction of an individual need.

Faith is something which comes to the individual from the community in which, first of all, it exists. My commitment is to the community which offers it to me from its own profound historical experience. Before I choose to believe in it, it has already formed the belief which I have either to accept or reject. The community is something which makes me. I do not make it by my own initiative towards others.

But if modernisation has these insights which secularism lacks, it also has limitations. In some ways these are even more severe than those attaching to secularism. The moderniser accepts, as his starting-point, a certain concrete condition of the community he is concerned to modernise. He begins where this community is. But, in order to make any progress, he needs to distinguish, within that situation, those elements which are essential to its continued life from those which are open to change, or are even wholly superfluous. Yet within his own ideology he has no firm set of criteria, no values for making this distinction. There is nothing in the empirical community he wishes to modernise which has labelled itself either "essential" or "expendable". The moderniser has to decide whether he is to try to keep this and abandon that, or vice versa. But where are the principles to come from by which he can decide? The past is of some help here: the tradition he has received points along certain guidelines into a short-term future. But in a world changing at an accelerating rate these guidelines from the past are getting shorter all the time. They soon vanish into an infinity of open choices. Because he has no theoretical model of the future, and only accepts the past because it has brought the community to its present condition, which is where he starts from, the moderniser can only fumble about, trying one thing and then another, hoping that he is doing the right thing.

The moderniser is primarily concerned with the present. We must not be too academic, or spend too much time discussing the exact nature of the tradition we have received, he says. What matters is what we do with it now, in the light of practicalities. Politically, his aims are (say) a 4% per annum increase in productivity, comprehensive schools for all, new towns to solve the housing problem; the distant future is a matter for Marxists or Utopians to discuss. Our job it to get on with clearing up the mess which lies on our very doorstep. So speaks the Wilsonian moderniser. And the call from the Christian moderniser is the same. Do not bother too much about the population explosion; the

9

important thing is to bring St Augustine up to date by issuing people with thermometers and charts, and so to relieve the immediate problem of sexual fulfilment in a starving world. Do not bother too much with a theology of the people of God as community; what matters is the reorganisation of parish and diocesan life so that the pastoral priest can get on with his job of saving souls. Do not worry about whether there is any sense in the notion of a Christian education; let us get on with the job of improving the standards of the institutions we already have, and which have done such good service in the past.

By taking the principle of "practicability" as his first criterion, the moderniser tries to evade the very problem which in fact faces him. How are we to know where we ought to be going? Taking the short-term guidelines as the only ones we have, modernisation seems to render superfluous the need for a theoretical analysis of the future. Just as the Marxist vision is anathema to the Wilsonian, eschatological theology is anathema to the ecclesiastical moderniser. In practice, he insists, Christianity is concerned essentially with how to conduct our lives in this world, for it is here that we have to work out our salvation. Thus, the church looks after the problem of death, not by looking death in the face, but by providing an institutional framework for it: "extreme unction" and the whole apparatus of requiem masses, prayers, and candles. The resurrection proves that death's sting has been drawn, so we have no cause to worry. As long as I am in a state of grace there is, in fact, nothing to worry about—and in any case I cannot do anything about it. It will just happen. The main thing is to lead a good and holy life here, loving God and my neighbour. But this anti-intellectual pragmatism does not really solve the problems which face the moderniser; it merely shelves them. Worse still, having no secure grounds for distinguishing between the essential and the inessential, between the right and the wrong way into the future, the moderniser is constantly being trapped by his own assumptions into an unintended conservatism. He spends his ingenuity in solving problems which, on a more radical view, would simply disappear.

Christian modernisation, by taking the empirical church as its starting-point, and finding so much there that is in need of repair, never gets to grips with modern atheism at all. Despite all its advocates, and all the publicity it has had, the Vatican Council has scarcely said anything which is really relevant to the modern agnostic in his intellectual or moral life. Irrelevance is not only a danger.[1] It is a fact.

The potentialities of the modern church—as a repository of ideas about the life of the human community, of moral ideals, of protest against tyranny, injustice, and violence, and of a tradition of high culture preserved against extreme odds—have not been realised, despite the efforts of thousands of highly gifted individuals within it, and the tolerance or even the encouragement of those outside. The reason for this is that the ideology of modernisation has been taken as the basis for the renewal of the church. It need not have been so. Despite their traditional colouring, Pope John's encyclicals did reveal something different which could have been developed in a new direction. For, unlike most of his predecessors, Pope John saw that Christianity was concerned with the attainment of what everybody really wants. He did not see the Christian life as the business

[1] See Charles Davis, *The Study of Theology*, London 1962, 13–26; and Geoffrey Preston, "The glory has departed", *Slant* 7 (February–March 1966), 10–13.

of doing what God—through the mouths of bishops and curial officials—has told us to do, whether we like it or not. He saw it as the fulfilment of our own deepest hopes springing from the acknowledgement of the goodness of our own desires. This idea of Christianity as the satisfaction of our basic human wants, which he saw as common to the whole of humanity (and which he therefore expounded to the whole world, and not just to his own fellow Catholics) was founded upon just that concept of human solidarity which the secularist needs but cannot admit.

This is where the Catholic tradition is at its strongest —in the endorsement and exploration of the idea of the unity of mankind, and hence of the universality of basic human wants. On such a basis it is possible to see the Christian life as satisfying us, not in spite of our ordinary desires, but because of them. But it is impossible to take this conception very far as long as it is stated merely in terms of the ideology of modernisation. For to limit it in this way is to identify it, and to try to contain it, within the structure of the empirical church, the church as we have known it, whereas its real significance is that it demands a breaking out from that bondage. By resting upon a criterion of what is, in truly theological and traditional terms, the essential character of the Christian community, it is able to see the expendable character of much that the moderniser believes to be important. To understand this is to see that there is no satisfaction to be gained for our basic human needs within the framework of Christian modernisation,[1] any

[1] For a further discussion of modernisation, in both theological and political terms, see the present author and Stuart Hall, *The Committed Church* (edd. Laurence Bright, OP, and Simon Clements), London 1966, 253–79 and 3–25 respectively.

more than there is in the terms of Christian secularisation. The two approaches point, in the end, to the one solution: *Christian radicalism.*

Radicalism takes seriously the secularist acknowledgement of the ever-increasing area of human self-determination, and the moral consequences of this in terms of the supremacy of fidelity to myself as the basic Christian demand. From modernism it takes the emphasis on the communal, the historical, the traditional. As a corollary, it also takes from modernism the emphasis on the satisfaction of the community needs as a moral demand equal to that of individual self-determination. As a consequence of these assumptions it takes up a position which, as a matter of political theory and political orientation, is frankly socialistic, and in which Marx, rather than Methodism, is the driving intellectual force. The rest of this book is an attempt to argue, in more detail, what the philosophical foundations of such radicalism are, and where they might lead.[1]

It may be helpful at this point, however, to indicate briefly the course of my main argument, so that the connection between its various parts may be easily discerned. If theology is always an encounter between an accepted tradition and a contemporary culture, it follows that the theologian requires an adequate and at the same time contemporary philosophy at his disposal as a framework within which he can work. There is no escape from the need for an adequate philosophical

[1] Sociologically, radicalism can be seen as dialectically combining the insights of Weber and Durkheim, using Marxist categories. See P. Berger and S. Pullberg, "Reification and the Sociological Critique of Consciousness", *New Left Review* 35 (January–February 1966), 56–71.

framework for the discussion of any important set of problems, and in the case of theology the need is perhaps more pressing than anywhere else. Now, the philosophical tradition with which most of us in the Anglo-Saxon world have grown up is that brand of empiricism which I have labelled "secular": and it is the purpose of the first section of this book to show that this tradition is (a) inadequate as an account of the general features of human experience, and (b) obsolete as a basis for the discussion of the distinctively modern problems which face us, whether we are religious believers or not. It is therefore insufficient as a basis for the construction of a contemporary theology, and we must look elsewhere for our foundations. To put it very crudely, I think that the "secular" tradition imposes a pattern of dualities where, in fact, we experience unities and connections. It drives a wedge between word and thought, between soul and body, between perceiver and what is perceived, between man and his world, and between the individual and the society which nurtures him. It is possible, at a number of critical points, to show that the "secular" philosophy is involved in radical logical incoherences; but these are no more than the outcroppings of a pervasive way of thinking which underlies a great deal of our cultural life. But it is not only that the "secular" philosophy is logically incoherent at certain critical points: it is also obsolete as a framework for the formulation of the problems we in fact face—problems which come to the surface most obviously in the discussion of great moral issues, such as the nature of personal relationships or the inviolability of human life, or of great political issues like the nature of individual freedom *vis-à-vis* the modern industrialised community. In particular, the problems with which art or religion tries to grapple—the fact of evil, the mystery of death, and all the other inarticulable presences which lie so close to us that we cannot see them clearly or walk round them to take a complete view—pose to us questions which cannot be expressed in the terms of the "secular" philosophy. We are being forced by the very weight of contemporary experience to return to an older set of presuppositions, or unconscious assumptions (which are, at the same time, for us startling and new as well) for a philosophical framework in which to articulate to ourselves the experience we all know. In the second section of this book I have tried to sketch out such a framework of presuppositions, as it is presented to us in the work of three significant figures of the modern world: Maurice Merleau-Ponty, Ludwig Wittgenstein, and Karl Marx. These may seem, at first sight, to constitute an unlikely, even eccentric, collection: but I have tried to show that, behind their obvious differences of method, expression, and background, it is possible to discern a certain common preoccupation with the reintegration of those elements which, in the secular tradition, have been too sharply separated. For Merleau-Ponty, perceptual experience presents us with a world which is not something standing over against us, but is first of all that in which we inhere, and which gives us our own identity as individuals. From this position it is possible to go on to show (with Wittgenstein) that this world is more than something given in perception: it is a world structured, to its very roots, by our own capacity for, and use of, language. We live in a linguistic world: and it is this world which gives us our own humanity. Finally, Marx adds to this insight the understanding that the linguistic world becomes ours only because we are trying all the time to transform it, to humanise it, in the process of ensuring our survival in it —that is, by the economic process. We live in a world which we make by our own labour: and it is in this labour that we come to understand our union with each other in society.

The historical process by which the philosophy of secularism as a framework for the description of our experience has begun to collapse, is extremely complex. But it can to some extent be understood in its inner nature through the critical examination of forms of art, and especially of literature. For art is, at one level, philosophy come to consciousness and brought home to concrete life. In particular, the period in which the collapse has taken place is the period of the novel; and the development of the novel may perhaps be regarded as the most sensitive register we possess of the development of the cultural process I have tried to describe. For this reason I have attempted to examine the dimensions of the problem of the secular philosophy, both in its strengths and in its weaknesses, by discussing, in some detail, the work of four English novelists who, for one reason or another, may be regarded as typical of a trend in cultural life. But it would be a mistake to think of this section merely as illustrating a theme. To use imaginative literature merely as documentary evidence in cultural or social history is to abuse its real nature, as the dramatisation of experience. It is only by understanding the novel on its own terms, and exploring it with literary-critical tools, that its significance as the register of an historical process can be understood. I have tried to show how the difference between the way man's encounter with the world is envisaged by George Eliot, and the way it is envisaged by Dickens, marks a distinction between two sets of presuppositions which corresponds with the distinction I have tried to make at the philosophical level—that is, between the secular philosophy, and the alternative offered in the work of the thinkers already mentioned. This difference is interesting precisely because it has little to do with conscious beliefs of an explicitly religious, or irreligious, sort. The kind of encounter men have with the world in a George Eliot novel is determined, not directly by her avowed agnosticism, but by the whole drift of her sensibility and her imagination. The same is true of Dickens. But, with them, the rift between the secular philosophy and its opposite is only visible beneath the surface of a seemingly consistent high-Victorian world-view. By the time we come to our own epoch, however, the breach has become apparent, and has led to the collapse of any concerted way to the world. George Orwell and William Golding—the two novelists whose work I have discussed as representative of this recent period—stand on opposite sides of a great gulf, which separates (in Stephen Spender's terms) the "contemporary" from the "modern". The nature and extent of this gulf is a mark of the breakdown of the secular philosophy itself.

In order to understand why it is that the work of three non-believers—Merleau-Ponty, Wittgenstein, and Marx—should be of crucial importance to the contemporary Christian, it is necessary to see that what they have in common is an interpretation of man's commerce with the world which is much older than that of the secular philosophy itself. It goes back, indeed, in essence, to the "sacred" world-view of unsophisticated religious man.[1] It can be seen as the modern development of a mode of understanding which is that of "participation". Religious man does not confront an alien world, but participates in a familiar one: and this concept of participation in the world is present, in a modern sophisticated form in the concern, exhibited by all my three philosophers, with the analysis and description of perceptual, linguistic, and social experience. Such analysis is a necessary preliminary to the formulation of explanatory or unifying theories. The first concern of the contemporary philosopher is therefore to return to experience, without the burden of secular hypotheses, and to understand its features as they present themselves to him. And, most notably, this concern with the analysis and description of experience is common to the philosopher and to the student of "religion in its essence and manifestation" (to use the phrase of Gerard van der Leeuw).

Just as the phenomenology of perception and of language leads naturally to a corresponding concept of human society as the locus of these activities, so the phenomenological study of man's religious experience leads, inevitably, to a religious concept of society and its internal structures. And so primitive man lives in a religious world, and his social and religious experience are different ways of referring to the one, single way of life. This fact leads us naturally to examine the modern

[1] The theory of "primitive" man's radically distinctive religious mentality is, of course, largely obsolete anthropologically speaking. But the *insights* of armchair theorists like Lévy-Bruhl and van der Leeuw are still relevant to a general phenomenology of religion, though their *theories* are outdated. See E. E. Evans-Pritchard, *Theories of Primitive Religion*, Oxford 1965 (esp. chapter 4).

Western religious community—the church—and its structures, as offering or failing to offer a way of life correspondingly valid for us in the light of modern experience. Here we find the church—the religious community—in a condition so far removed from its true centre, as the heart of life, that it is now scarcely recognisable for what it really is. The task of theology, therefore, is first of all to examine this empirically given structure, not only in its actual manifestation but also in its inner essence, and see what is needed for its renewal as the fundamental community of mankind. In order to do this, we have to distinguish, in the light of fundamental principles and also in the light of an unbiased, critical analysis of its contemporary reality, the essential from the expendable, the theologically valid from the historically conditioned. The theological sections of this book are attempts to suggest an approach to this task in the light of the understanding attained in the foregoing discussion. They centre upon two primary problems: firstly, the nature of the community of the church as the life of Christ in the present world, and secondly the relationship of this community to the resurrected, eschatological, and transfigured world of the coming Kingdom. Fundamental to this second discussion is a consideration of the nature and meaning of individual death and resurrection in terms of the concepts we have at our disposal from the experience of life in the modern world. Finally, the argument returns to its opening themes—namely, the options which are open to us here and now, and which have to be chosen in the light of the total argument. Here, if anywhere, is the immediate test of what a radical Christianity entails.

1

The secular philosophy: empiricism

I have already suggested, in the Introduction, that the ideology of modernisation, which is very powerful in both our political and our religious life, is necessarily anti-intellectual and indeed anti-ideological. Secularism, on the other hand, rests upon a distinctive philosophical position, which must be examined. But since my purpose is to sketch this only in order to illuminate by contrast the position I am trying to establish instead, it will suffice to confine my analysis of it to its classical English form —the empiricism of Locke and those in his tradition. This is partly because, in my own experience, if you ask the average non-philosophical Englishman any epistemological question, you will nearly always get a Lockeian kind of answer. The study of Orwell—in this respect a representative case—shows this very clearly.[1] But it is also because empiricism usefully connects with what I have to say about the tendencies in English literature,[2] especially in the nineteenth century. For it is in the

[1] See pp. 151–69 and 237n. below.
[2] See Chapter 3, "Sacred and secular in fiction", below, pp. 102–85.

nineteenth century that the practical consequences of the secular philosophy began to appear in overwhelming force, in the shape of Victorian capitalism and "Gradgrindery". Obviously, too, the following analysis is not to be regarded as an attempted refutation of the secular philosophy from a rigorous philosophical standpoint, but simply as an analysis of those elements in it which are relevant to the main argument I am pursuing. I am more concerned to show that the secular philosophy is irrelevant to the realities of the modern situation than to show that it is incoherent in itself—although I believe that it is possible to show this incoherence as well, and the general lines of such a demonstration will perhaps emerge from what follows. Finally, I am not supposing that my analysis is a *history* of the subject—my use of illustrations from the work of particular thinkers is designed to throw light on the points being made, rather than upon the historical growth of their interconnections.

The relevant characteristics of the secular philosophy can be summed up, in a rough-and-ready way, in a series of related theses, as follows:

A. The secular theory of perception

1. All human experience originates in the reception, by a passive perceiver, of discrete items of sense experience ("sense-data", "impressions" or "ideas").
2. The world of external objects is constituted out of these discrete items by the mind.
3. The human body is an object among other objects, and is constituted like other objects from sense-data.
4. Therefore the mind, or consciousness, or perhaps

"soul", is what alone guarantees the continuing personal identity of the individual.

B. *The secular theory of language*

5. Language is (a) a collection of signs, adopted by convention as labels for the particular items of sense-experience, or for the objects constituted from them; plus (b) a set of rules (a grammar) for their use.
6. Thinking is putting mental entities (concepts, ideas), derived by the mind from sense-experience, into certain relationships to each other.
7. Linguistic communication is putting the corresponding words into an order which reflects this thinking process, so that one person can reassemble another's thoughts in his mind.
8. Logic is the systematization of the mental procedures needed to do this properly.

C. *The secular theory of society*

9. A species is just a collection of individual objects with similar attributes. These attributes are ultimately reducible to perceptible properties.
10. The human species is therefore just the collection of separate, autonomous beings which, because of their similar attributes, we have come to label "men". The general (or species) term "Man" is the label for this collection.
11. Human society exists by virtue of a surrender for the common good, by these self-subsistent individuals, of a certain amount of their own autonomy.

It is true that many of those who would want to put themselves in the secular camp do not subscribe to all these theses. Nevertheless, I think that there is a distinctive body or tradition of thought which can be distinguished as "secular", and that these theses sum it up. (Needless to say, it is also true that many of those who would want to put themselves in the anti-secular camp accept, consciously or unconsciously, some at least of these theses. For just as a person does not make his philosophy theistic by his professing to believe in God, but only by constructing a position which is, in fact, compatible with the existence of God, so a person does not prevent himself from having a secular philosophy by professing belief in religion.) Furthermore, I think it is possible to show that there is rational connection and a natural continuity between these theses, and it is this continuity which constitutes the secular philosophical position as I am discussing it.

A. The secular theory of perception

It can be agreed at the outset that the senses are our only contact with the external world. But what is characteristic of the secular philosophy is the view that this source of all our experience of the world is a *passive reception* of "impressions" (Hume) or "simple ideas" (Locke) or "sense-data" (Russell), and not an *active participation* in the world through the senses. In other words, experience is something that happens to us. *Our* contribution is to systematize, make sense of, and interpret the world. That is to say, the world, defined as the sum total of external objects, is simply "there" in its bare facticity. But in this sense, of course, we can never *encounter* the world. For in order that we may have experience of the world, it must be mediated to us through the sense impressions which it makes upon our bodily organs. It is only in these that the world exists for us.

At this point, the secular philosophy may take one of two paths. On the one hand, it may retreat into subjectivity, and ultimately into solipsism, by saying that since all that we experience is the sense impressions which register in our consciousness, it is illegitimate to posit an external world of objects as the source of these impressions. We are for ever locked inside our own minds, able to manipulate the impressions we have, but unable to go beyond them to a supposedly external world. But—the argument may go on—to say this is not to put a limit to what we might otherwise legitimately think we can do. For it makes no difference to us whether we say that there is an external source of sense-experience or not: what we experience is just the same in either case. So it may be concluded that the problem of an external world is simply senseless; it makes no difference what the answer is. Or on the other hand, we may try to show that reason, because it reveals to us that things do not happen unless they are caused by something else, proves that there must be an external cause of the impressions which we have. They cannot just occur; something must make them occur, and so there must be something outside us which is the cause of the impressions. This is what we call the "external world". (Such is the origin of the great rationalist metaphysical systems.) But a question then arises: How can we speak about the world as being, in some sense, *like* the impressions we have? For unless we can say this, there is little consolation in having the external world at all. Yet to suppose that the world is like the impressions we have is to suppose an independent knowledge of it, by which we can compare the impression and its cause and so recognise the similarity. But to suppose this is to contradict the very premiss of the argument, which is that impressions are all that we can have.

These two paths represent, of course, only the extremes of secular empiricism. Most of the interest aroused by the premisses of the argument comes from the attempt to offer a middle way. Locke, for example, tries to show that the "simple ideas" we have—that is, our impressions of solidity, extension, figure, motion or rest, and number—are real resemblances of external objects "out there", and "their patterns really do exist in the bodies themselves"; but the "simple ideas" we have of other qualities—such as hotness or coldness, colour, and so on—are simply the subjective effects of the power which the object has to affect the senses.[1] (Locke, a friend of Newton, naturally thinks of this power in corpuscular terms, as the battering of the sense organs by insensible particles.) It is not necessary to go into the attempts to resolve the problems caused by this way of thinking about perception, since I hope to show later that it is radically incoherent from the very start. (See below, pp. 48–68.) What is important is to emphasize two essential elements in it. The first is the passivity of the percipient, and the second is the distinct and separate character of each impression. Locke's *Essay* will provide a useful illustration of both assumptions, and the source references which follow in the rest of this section are all to this work.

The passivity of the percipient is implicit in the corpuscular theory of light which Locke takes from the science of his own day. The doctrine is purely mechanistic. Objects give out invisible particles which hit us,

[1] John Locke, *Essay concerning Human Understanding*, 2, ch. 8, s. 7.

and so make us "see" them; and similarly with the stimulation of the other senses. (It should be noted that the corpuscular character of the emanation is not essential to the mechanistic theory. It might just as well be held that the object gives out a wave-like ray—the main point would remain the same.) The activity is thus all on the side of the object. The sense organ is simply a collecting and registering device which, taken together with the brain, turns the stimulus into an impression—much as a wireless receiver turns electrical impulses into sounds. "The senses . . . *let in particular ideas*." (1, 2, 15, my italics.) That sentence sums up the whole doctrine in a nutshell. Locke insists that we do not initiate perception in any way:

> The impressions then that are made on our senses by outward objects that are extrinsical to the mind, and its own operations about these impressions, reflected on by itself, as proper objects to be contemplated by it, are, I conceive, the original of all knowledge. . . . In this part the understanding is merely passive; and whether or not it will have these beginnings, and as it were materials of knowledge, is not in its own power. [2, 1, 24–5.]

But the theory also necessarily involves the *particularity* of the impressions.

> Though the qualities that affect our senses are, in the things themselves, so united and blended, that there is no separation, no distance between them; yet it is plain, the ideas they produce in the mind enter by the senses simple and unmixed. For, though the sight and touch often take in from the same object, at the same time, different ideas—as a man sees at once motion and colour; the hand feels softness and

warmth in the same piece of wax: yet the simple ideas thus united in the same subject, are as perfectly distinct as those that come in by different senses. [2, 2, 1.]

It follows from this, of course, that every object, insofar as we conceive of it as a unity, has to be reconstructed by the mind from these various impressions. "As the mind is wholly passive in the reception of all its simple ideas, so it exerts several acts of its own, whereby out of its simple ideas, as the materials and foundations of the rest the others are framed." (2, 12, 1.) Thus the concept of substance (a "complex" idea) is formed by compounding several simple ideas, that is, those "as are taken to represent distinct particular things subsisting by themselves: in which the supposed or confused idea of substance, such as it is, is always first and chief". (2, 12, 1.) If we then add to this concept of substance the impressions, or simple ideas, of

> ... a certain dull whitish colour, with certain degrees of weight, hardness, ductility and fusibility we have the idea of lead; and the combination of the ideas of a certain sort of figure, with the powers of motion, thought and reasoning, joined to substance, make the ordinary idea of a man. [2, 12, 6.]

The difficulties and contradictions of this doctrine are obvious. For instance, in attributing the primary qualities to objects as they really are, Locke is tacitly assuming the existence of such external objects. But it was the very purpose of his argument to analyse experience in order to show in what sense we can speak about the external world at all. Again, in order to speak about the particularity of our distant impressions as distinct impressions of a single object, he assumes the unity of this object in reality while at the same time trying to show why it is that this unity has to be built up by the mind before we can know it as a unity. Finally, he fails to show how we can so specify (say) the degree of hardness of lead, or rationality of man, that—in combination with other equally unspecifiable qualities—we can arrive at the concepts "lead" or "man". Even harder is it to understand how we can get the admittedly "confused" idea of substance, just by considering particular things as subsisting by themselves—especially as these things are, in any case, only constituted out of particular impressions by the mind, and in that sense we have no right to speak of them as subsisting by themselves at all.

It might at this point be asked why, if the empiricist theory of Locke and similar philosophers is so patently contradictory, it is worth while to spend time discussing it. The answer is that most philosophically unsophisticated people, at least in the English-speaking world, when asked about the way we form our idea of the external world from perception, will give a reply which is, roughly, that of Locke. It is as if the whole climate of thought and culture makes this kind of empiricist doctrine seem just to be common sense. (One purpose of this book is to show that there is no need to suppose that this is because of some built-in cast of mind which determines us to think in this way. It is part of a general attitude towards experience which can be modified in the light of the more adequate insights of modern thought.)

It is a natural, and in some forms of argument a necessary, corollary of the account of perception given by Locke that the human body should be regarded as just an object along with other objects. Indeed, for Locke, my body is for me the paradigm case of an object. The only place in his *Essay* in which he distinguishes the human body from other objects is where he wishes to argue that the human hand, as an object in space, gives us an essential ingredient of our ideas about bodies in general—namely, that of solidity.

> The bodies which we daily handle make us perceive that, whilst they remain between us, they do, by an insurmountable force, hinder the approach of the parts of our hands that press them. That which thus hinders the approach of two bodies, I call *solidity*. [2, 4, 1.]

It is solidity which gives rise to the idea of space, as being that which is completely filled by a solid body, so that no amount of force can dislodge it. If we get the concept of space from our own bodily experience, it is nevertheless the experience of our bodies, or parts of them, conceived of as external objects, that gives rise to this concept. But space is not the same as solidity, for we can imagine space which is empty. Space is, therefore, just the system of co-ordinates which, uniformly throughout the world, marks out solid objects in their positions and extension.

Once it is accepted that the body is simply one object among other objects, some form of "ghost-in-the-machine" view of the human being is practically inescapable. Since it is the consciousness which alone has experience—for it alone actually perceives, and it alone is capable of the internal operations with impressions and their combinations which constitute the world for us—the problem arises of how the relation of body to mind is to be conceived, and even of how the reality of the body is to be established at all. Thus, according to Locke,

> Self is that conscious thinking thing—whatever substance made up of (whether spiritual or material, simple or compounded, it matters not)—which is sensible or conscious of pleasure and pain, capable of happiness or misery, and so is concerned for itself, as far as that consciousness extends. [2, 27, 17.]

This consciousness is co-extensive with the body but is not, of course, identical with it (for if that were so, then to lose one's little finger would be to lose part of one's consciousness). So the conclusion is that

> ... that with which the consciousness of this present thinking can join itself, makes the same person and is one self with it, and with nothing else; and so attributes to itself and owns all the actions of that thing as its own, as far as that consciousness reaches, and no further. [2, 27, 17.]

The person, then, is a "self", or consciousness joined to a body which it "owns" and which is the instrument by which it communicates with the outside world. But, of course, this "self" is also the constitutor of this world out of the fragments of sense-perception which the body offers it; and so, in a sense, all it communicates with is itself. The outside world, in its very exteriority, is metaphysically inaccessible, and exists in its own sheer facticity in a realm beyond the reach of man's awareness. It must exist in order to be the basis of all experience; but it must remain unknowable because we cannot get at it. This is the fundamental subject-object duality which is the foundation of the secular philosophy, with its premiss that experience is not a participation in the world, but merely a passive reception of messages from it. It is of course a philosophy which seems to be the natural counterpart of the scientific outlook of the Newtonian world-view. Locke is, pre-eminently, the philosopher of the Newtonian revolution in science.[1]

B. The secular theory of language

Nominalism as a theory of logic and language is a natural corollary of the empiricist theory of knowledge which I have been discussing. As before, Locke exemplifies the general tendency very clearly. Once the senses have "let in particular ideas" the mind

> ... by degrees growing familiar with some of them, they are lodged in the memory, and names got to them. Afterwards the mind, proceeding further, abstracts them, and by degrees learns the use of general names. In this manner the mind comes to be furnished with ideas and language, the materials about which to exercise its discursive faculty. [1, 2, 15.]

In Book 3 Locke goes into more detail. It would be impossibly clumsy, he says, to give a different name to every separate thing we wish to talk about, and even

[1] Nothing could more clearly express the uniformity of all our notions of space and time—which is to say, the exclusion of any possibility of that qualitative break in space and time which, as we shall see later (pp. 211–21 below), are presuppositions of the "sacred"—than the vast synthesis of Newton's *Principia*, in which the existence of God was necessary only to account for the few little inconsistencies within the physical world which Laplace was soon to claim to have overcome. On this see also Gerd Buchdahl, *The Image of Newton and Locke in the Age of Reason*, London 1961, 5ff.

if it were possible it would be useless. For whether we think of the words we use as naming particular external objects or as naming the general concepts which, on Locke's theory, we ourselves generate from combining "simple ideas", a difficult problem arises with the theory of abstraction, which is used to account for all those words in language which are not simply proper names.

The argument runs as follows. All the things that exist are particulars: that is to say, whatever view we may take of the capacity of the mind to come to any knowledge of a really external world, the materials we begin with consist of particular and distinct items (simple ideas). But it is impossible for every particular to have its own name; moreover, even if it were possible —and the impossibility of which Locke speaks is not a logical impossibility—it would not make communication between us any more practicable.

> I alone having the ideas in my mind, the names of them could not be significant or intelligible to another, who was not acquainted with all those very particular things which had fallen under my notice. [3, 3, 3.]

So we need general names, to name the general ideas which we frame "by separating from them the circumstances of time and place, and any other ideas that may determine them to this or that particular existence". (3, 3, 6.) For instance, children first have an "idea" (a kind of mental picture) of their nurse or mother, and give the name "nurse" or "mamma" to this particular idea. But when they observe

> . . . that there are a great many other things in the

world, that in some common agreements of shape, and several other qualities, resemble their father and mother, and those persons they have been used to, they frame an idea, which they find those many particulars do partake in; and to that they give with others the name *man* ... wherein they make nothing new; but only leave out of the complex idea they had of Peter and James, Mary and Jane, that which is peculiar to each, and retain only that what is common to all. [3, 3, 7.]

Thus we get general terms by a process of *systematically not attending* to the particular features of the various ideas. It is important to emphasize the negative character of this process of abstraction. A "general idea" is not, according to the theory, a positive concept, but is simply what is left over when all the particular features have been omitted. For, as Berkeley saw, if we try to frame the concept of "triangle" by actually picturing triangularity while not allowing it to become a picture of any particular kind of triangle—"neither oblique nor rectangle, neither equilateral, equicrural nor scalenon: but all and none of these at once"[1]—we soon find the task impossible. This is why many writers, trying to defend the theory of abstraction, have been at pains to point out that, as Mansel says, "abstraction is nothing more than non-attention to certain parts of an object".[2] Husserl, however, saw a difficulty here. "The peculiarities of the individuals that are collected ... must be carefully abstracted from, but at the same time their connection must be maintained. This seems to involve

[1] Berkeley, *Principles of Human Knowledge*, Introduction xv, xvi.
[2] H. D. Mansel, *Prolegomena Logica*, 36.

a difficulty, if not a psychological impossibility. If we take abstraction seriously, then the individual contents vanish, and so naturally does their collective unity, instead of remaining behind as a conceptual extract. The solution is obvious. To abstract from something simply means: not to attend to it specially."[1] Credit must be given to Husserl for seeing the difficulty which abstractionism involves. But he cannot be excused for failing to see the futility of his "obvious solution". How we can get the concept "man" just by looking at a collection of men but not paying any special attention to them, is left unexplained. Frege's comment is conclusive:

> Inattention is a very strong lye; it must be applied at not too great a concentration, so that everything does not dissolve, and likewise not too little, so that it effects a sufficient change in the things. Thus it is a question of getting the right degree of dilution: this is difficult to manage, and I at any rate have never succeeded.[2]

Nominalism is the natural, if not inevitable, theory of language for an empiricist philosophy which begins by trying to base human knowledge upon a passive, mechanistic view of sense-perception. The separation of word and thing, which is implicit in the relationship

[1] Quoted by G. Frege, *Translations*, 84, where he is reviewing Husserl's *Philosophie der Arithmetik*.

[2] Frege, 84. For a rigorous, and I think decisive, demolition of the entire theory of abstractionism, see P.T. Geach, *Mental Acts*, London 1957, 18ff. Geach shows that abstractionism is not just a dead theory of the past, but still active and influential. This is why it is necessary to discuss it here, as a characteristic element of the secular philosophy.

of naming,[1] with all its arbitrary character, is the automatic consequence of the view that the mind is itself ineradicably cut off from the external world by the apparatus of sense-perception. Perception is as much a barrier to the world as a way into it. Only particular and distinct fragments are available to the mind, which has to make up the unity of objects from these; and similarly the communication of ideas and feelings between men must also follow the same general pattern.

The unity of the concept, the unity of the proposition, and the unity of an argument all have to be constructed artificially from a fragmentary experience. Thus the *concept* "man" is a combination of ideas formed by a mental operation based on abstraction. The *word* "man" is a verbal label fixed to this mental entity for the purpose of making it publicly available. That is to say, there is a clear separation between the word—which is merely a sound arbitrarily chosen—and what the word *means*. The *meaning* as such is an idea; that is, something within the private consciousness. The word itself is simply an arbitrary symbol of this idea made available to the public world. Language is a kind of monetary currency. Thus, when I say that I am prepared to sell my car for £400, I am attaching a public label to an idea I have in my mind, which is the "value" of the car. It is true that, in order to be able to do this, I must have learnt a system of monetary currency which is already in force. But the point is that this currency only "expresses" the value of things. The value itself is an

[1] It should perhaps be pointed out here that I am referring to the act of naming as conceived in a Western, and perhaps over-rationalistic, tradition. For the religious, as opposed to the secular, way of thought, naming is much more than the attachment of a verbal label to a predetermined object. See below pp. 209–11.

idea I have of some property of the car, which I have got by abstracting all the other irrelevant features of it. Having done this, I can then put this value into publicly accessible form by giving a monetary equivalent for it. Furthermore, just as my giving the value of the car as £400 is the same as saying that it is worth 8000 shillings, or 96,000 pennies, so too the general idea of the value of the car is the same as the collection of simple ideas which go to make up this idea of value. In just the same way, according to the nominalist view, general terms stand to particular terms (that is, to proper names) as pounds stand to pennies. Thus, for any statement in which the term "man" is to be found, it would be logically, if not practically, possible to substitute "Peter and James and John and . . ."; that is, to give the names of all the men that belong to the species.[1] Such a theory obviously involves the destruction of the unity of the species. For example, it is clear that, if "man" always refers to, or denotes,[2] the complete collection of all

[1] The analogy of monetary currency is actually used by one of the editors of Aldrich's *Artis Logicae Compendium* to clarify the doctrine of how language works. Aldrich was a contemporary of Locke, but his book remained the main textbook of logic at Oxford for much of the eighteenth and nineteenth centuries, contributing heavily to the decadence of logical studies in England for the whole of that period. See John Hill's edition of Aldrich, entitled *Artis Logicae Rudimenta* (first edition 1821), 1835[5], 11.

[2] Considerable efforts were made, within the empiricist logical tradition, to distinguish the *denotation* from the *reference* of a term (or, as the Cartesian *Port-Royal Logic* puts it, the *comprehension* and the *extension* of the term). Thus, in its denotation, it is said that "man" covers "those attributes which it involves in itself, and which cannot be taken away from it without destroying it" but its reference may be restricted, as by the addition of an "indistinct and indeterminate idea of a part" as in

individual men, then a statement such as "man has thirty-two teeth" is simply false. It cannot be made sense of by any attempt to interpret "man" as referring in this case only to a definite, or indefinite, portion of this collection of individuals. The fact is that the language we use, and use intelligibly, forces us to recognise that the species is by no means the same as the set of individuals who are members of it. On the contrary, the species, at any rate in the biological sense, is a reality which, albeit divided, is at the same time a unity such that we can predicate properties of it which do not belong to most, or some, or even all of its members. In this sense the intelligibility of our language indicates to us an ontological commitment which, on an empiricist basis, is inexplicable. For, according to that tradition, only particulars exist, as we have already noted. The species, as an ontological reality, has no place within it. This is a feature of the secular tradition which is of the utmost significance for the theory of human society.

The unity of the proposition, which, as I have tried to show, cannot be accounted for in the nominalist scheme, is also destroyed by it. This has an important logical consequence. For a single word tied to an object, or to the inner "idea" of it (it makes no difference), has no meaning by itself. It can only be given meaning within a context of communication. (A piece of wood, even if it is arrow-shaped, does not "point" in a direc-

---

"*some* man". (See *Port-Royal Logic* (ed. T. Baynes), 48–50.) But many logical problems are insoluble on such a theory. For example the difference between "Every kind of food is eaten by some man" and "some man eats every kind of food" is thereby rendered inexplicable. (See Peter Geach, "The doctrine of Distribution", *Mind*, (1956), 70.)

tion, unless within a system of rules in which such pieces of wood are accepted as "pointers".) Likewise a concept is not an idea held privately in the mind, which just happens to be given linguistic expression for purposes of communication. It is a capacity intelligibly to use the common language in which the word for this concept occurs. Manifesting that capacity is a sufficient condition for ascribing the possession of some concept to a person. "If somebody knows how to use the English word 'red', he has a concept of *red*; if he knows how to use the first person pronouns, he has a concept of self; if he knows how to use the negative construction in some language, he has a concept of *negation*."[1] But these words only exist in use in the context of statements, questions, arguments, musings, etc., in which meaning is given, in the first place, to a linguistic structure such as a proposition, which is grasped as a whole.

If the unity of the proposition is lost in the nominalist view, the unity of an argument is lost as well. For in the decadent tradition exemplified by Aldrich, the syllogism, instead of being regarded as an implication, is treated as if it were a set of separate propositions. Once the syllogism is so regarded, the problem arises of how the mind is able to link these three different propositions into a single inference. Inferring itself then becomes a problem. For it is now a psychological process, and logic becomes the art, or science, of showing how it is to be carried out. A complete mythology of mental operations has to be invented to account for the simplest logical problem. The confusion which lies behind this development is best understood by noticing the difference between the way Aristotle had conceived the syllo-

[1] Geach, *Mental Acts*, 12f.

gism and the way it became distorted in the so-called
Aristotelianism of later empiricism. For Aristotle a
syllogism was a single proposition—an implication of
the form:

If B belongs to all A, and C belongs to all B, then
C belongs to all A.[1]

But for Aldrich, and those like him in the psychological
tradition, a syllogism was a set of *three separate propositions*, of the form:

All A is B;
all B is C;
therefore, all A is C.

While the latter could plausibly be considered as a
written report of a set of linked mental operations, each
of which is expressed by one of the propositions, no
such theory is either necessary or plausible in the
former case. For there the syllogism is simply a formally
true proposition, as free from direct reference to any
mental process as a proposition of pure mathematics.
It is just an empty schema, and it can be made to apply
in the real world only by our giving values to the
variable symbols A, B, and C. And that is a purely
arbitrary procedure. The *truth* of the proposition does
not depend upon whether we give values which correspond to some external reality or not. The syllogism
is true necessarily, by virtue of its purely formal character. Now it is essential to recognise that this formal
truth of the Aristotelian syllogism is not to be interpreted as a self-evident fact about the way our minds
actually work. For such a view would suggest that we
might be able to imagine another kind of world than

[1] Jan Lukasiewicz, *Aristotle's Syllogistic*, Oxford 1951, 20f.

40

this one, in which our minds worked along different logical lines. And to imagine that is to suggest that we can conceive the inconceivable. No: the formal truth of the proposition lies simply in its being part of a system built upon certain axioms which are not, themselves, self-evident truths about the world, or about our minds, but are simply taken as data for the system. They are like the data assumed, for the sake of argument, in a Euclidean theorem.

The importance in the present discussion of this point about the nature of logic is that it reveals the irrational consequences of the empiricist tradition particularly clearly. But the difficulties which this tradition presented to any thinker once he accepted its fundamental epistemological premisses were not so clear in the past as they are now.[1] It is largely because of the development of mathematical logic that we have been able to free ourselves from the snares of logical psychologism. The work of Wittgenstein, to be discussed at greater length below, would have been impossible without this work in logic and mathematics. Mathematical logic and philosophical empiricism are not, in fact, natural bedfellows.

C. The secular theory of society

I have said that the secular philosophy characteristically refuses the ontological commitment involved in the doctrine of the reality of the species. It finds the idea

[1] An outstanding example of the way a philosopher or theologian could still, in the middle of the nineteenth century, be trapped by the difficulties of reconciling a psychological logic with a non-empiricist view of knowledge is to be found in the work of Newman. I have dealt with this point at some length in my article, "Newman and Logic", *Newman Studien*, Folge 5 (1962), 251–67.

of a reality which is both objective and yet present only in a divided state untenable on its own principles. The fact that the denial of the species involves insoluble problems does not suffice to convince the secular empiricist of the inadequacy of his principles. Perhaps one of the most important reasons for this is that, to him, it appears that his doctrine of the absolute priority of the individual over the collectivity is the only one which is capable of yielding a theoretical basis for human freedom within a secular society. The sense of the solidarity of the species as the ontological basis for the supremacy of moral over positive law having been lost, the autonomy of the individual has to be asserted as the first principle of any society which could consider itself the master of its own destiny and the shaper of its own laws. The autonomy of the secular order and the sovereignty of the individual were essential bulwarks against the rule of the absolutist monarch claiming all power from on high to deal with his subjects as he thought fit.

This practical secularism was shared by thinkers as different as Hobbes and Locke. What marks the difference between them is their estimate of the basic attributes of the human individual who, they both assume, is the autonomous self-subsistent molecule out of which the social order is made. The individual, for both of them, is essentially complete in himself. One of the attributes of this self-subsistent individual is, of course, an orientation towards social life with others. But this is precisely an orientation on the part of a being who, in his own life, is already sufficiently complete to be counted a fully developed human being by himself. For Hobbes, this individual man in the state of nature is a savage creature at the mercy of his own disordered and destructive energies. For Locke he is a rational creature well able to see what enlightened self-interest demands of him. Hobbes thinks of the only tolerable society as that of an absolute monarchy in which a single person, whose power has been vested in him by the rest, is able, by his unchallenged authority, to create an order out of the prior human chaos of the life of nature. Locke, on the other hand, sees the individual as capable of reason, and therefore as able freely to see that, in his own interest, he must surrender some part of his personal freedom for the sake of the common good. If Hobbes is a secular monarchist, Locke is a secular democrat. Hobbes takes a pessimistic view of human nature, while Locke takes an optimistic view. But the basic presuppositions about the nature of the human species as such are the same in both cases. Both subscribe to the "rabble hypothesis" (see below, p. 246) which, as Elton Mayo insisted, is still a prevalent concept of the human community in the industrialised secular world.

The consequences of the different emphases of Hobbes and Locke are important. For Hobbes, man in the presocial state of nature is living in a condition of anarchy. There is no such thing as a natural law, for nature is precisely a state of lawlessness. It is true that Hobbes speaks of laws of the natural condition of men, but for him these are "but conclusions or theorems concerning what conduceth to the conservation of themselves; whereas law, properly, is the word of him that by right hath command over them". (Leviathan, I, 15.) That is to say, natural laws are simply empirically established generalisations about what men must do if they are to achieve that individual security which, as a matter of empirical fact, they all demand

Natural laws oblige only in the sense that, until they are accepted and followed, man's desires cannot be fulfilled. Those who disregard them are stupid, but they cannot be called immoral. The only laws (in the strict sense of the term) are those which are formed within society by the sovereign. All true law is positive law. For Locke, however, there is a continuity between man as we know him in a social state and his natural presocial condition. Society is not designed to abolish a presocial anarchy, but to perfect a natural state which is itself rational. Thus it is possible to discern empirically, by a study of man as we know him, certain basic natural rights and duties which belong to him in his essence as a presocial, autonomous individual. The most fundamental of these rights is that of private property, which is given to an individual by virtue of the fact that he has mixed his labour with the thing. His having taken water from a stream, or picked an apple from the ground, is what makes something that was formerly common property to be now his own.[1]

The basis of this assertion of natural rights is Locke's ethical theory of natural law. For him, the natural moral law is to be ascertained, just as it is in the case of the laws of science, by the power of the mind to form general ideas from the discernment of similar qualities in a range of particulars. But, in the case of morals, as in mathematics, the particulars from which we begin are not "nominal essences", as in the empirical sciences (that is, the "ideas" we have of external objects, which are always at one remove from their external reality as it actually is), but the "real essences" of ideas themselves which exist only in the mind. That is to say, although ultimately the "ideas" which it connects together come

[1] See Locke, *Second Treatise of Civil Government*, ch. 5, 29.

44

from sense-experience, a moral law as such concerns only the relationship of ideas, and is true even if the ideas in question do not, after all, correspond with reality. For example, to say that murder is wrong is to connect the two ideas of "murder" and "moral badness", and this relationship may be the correct one (that is, the statement may be true) even if our observation of what goes on in life does not bear out this asserted relationship (that is, even if murder goes uncondemned). Thus it is theoretically possible to arrive at a moral law which is as certain and free from all doubt as a truth of mathematics. The natural law, then, is a set of truths about the relationship between ideas, but these ideas themselves derive from particular instances of human behaviour. As with every other generalisation, the general truths of the natural moral law come, eventually, from the observation and comparison of particulars derived from experience.

For Hobbes, disobedience to natural laws is a kind of stupidity, resulting from an inability to understand the true needs of the individual. It is based on an inadequate level of self-knowledge. For Locke, it is a disregard of the mathematically certain truth of a moral proposition. In neither case can the specifically moral evil of disobedience to natural law be admitted. Neither view explains the specific character of a *moral obligation*. Now it may well be that moral obligation is *sui generis* and inexplicable in any other terms—that the so-called "naturalistic fallacy" would be operative in any attempt to explain it in other terms. But, be that as it may, it is still worth while to distinguish a view of morality which sees its field of operation as that of obedience (or disobedience) to our own deepest common needs and inclinations, from a view which sees it as that of disobedience to some external law, whether positive or revealed. The former view will insist that there can be a discrepancy between what I really want, and what I merely think, at the present moment, I want. Because my nature, as a member of the species, is something which I am capable of betraying (for the species is not just definable as the collection of individuals who are members of it), I have a moral obligation to live in accordance with it. The achievement of a moral life *is* the fulfilment of what I really want; and the way towards it is through my being able to conform what I think I want to what I really want. It is morally wrong to defy my nature because to do so is to destroy myself.

Newman saw this clearly:

I am what I am, or I am nothing. I cannot think, reflect, or judge about my being, without starting from the very point at which I aim at concluding. My ideas are all assumptions, and I am ever moving in a circle. I cannot avoid being sufficient for myself, for I cannot make myself anything else, and to change me is to destroy me. If I do not use myself, I have no other self to use. My only business is to ascertain what I am, in order to put it to use. It is enough for the proof of the value and authority of any function which I possess, to be able to pronounce that it is natural. What I have to ascertain is the laws under which I live. My first elementary lesson of duty is that of resignation to the laws of my nature, whatever they are: my first disobedience is to be impatient at what I am, and to indulge an ambitious aspiration after what I cannot be, to cherish a distrust of my powers, and to desire to change laws which are identical with myself.[1]

[1] *Grammar of Assent*, p. 347.

In that statement, which expresses the essence of the religious approach to morality, Newman combines what is valid in both the Hobbesian and Lockeian theories. He agrees with Hobbes that natural law has to do with the attainment of self-knowledge, and that all deviation from it is a kind of blindness to the fact of one's own, and others' predicament. Immorality *is* stupidity, and that is part of its badness. And he agrees with Locke that natural laws are truths in the moral, not just the empirical, order. Disregard of them is always *wrong*. But it is only possible to make this combination by rejecting the concept of society from which both Hobbes and Locke begin. Of course, as Newman himself makes abundantly clear, this is not the end of the matter. The question still arises as to whether we can elucidate the specific quality of moral *obligation*. For Newman, this was only intelligible if the sense of our being under an obligation, and even a judgement (brought home to us through that particular quality of feeling and understanding which we call conscience), was referred to an external judge over us who has the sovereign power to *oblige* us—that is, to God. To say this is not to commit the "naturalistic fallacy", but to confess that it constitutes a barrier to all *explanation* of the unique character of moral feeling.[1]

[1] For an important discussion of the philosophical problems concerning natural law and the "new morality", and the foundation of the latter in the secular philosophy, see Herbert McCabe, OP, "The Validity of Absolutes", *Commonweal*, 14, January 1966. See also Columba Ryan, OP, "The Traditional Concept of Natural Law", *Light on the Natural Law*, ed. Illtyd Evans, OP, London 1965, 13–37.

2

The end of secularism

I have analysed the secular philosophy under three main
headings: the theory of perception, the theory of language, and the theory of society. I now want to show that
in each of these areas there is already available a different, and more coherent, philosophy. In the field of
perception, the secular philosophy has been effectively
attacked by Maurice Merleau-Ponty. In the field of
language, the same may be said of the work of Ludwig
Wittgenstein. And in the social field, the early philosophical work of Karl Marx reveals the same basic preoccupations.

A. Perception as a way to the world:
Maurice Merleau-Ponty

Merleau-Ponty begins his study of the phenomenology
of perception by looking at the phenomenon of "sensation" itself, and in doing so, with the help of Gestalt
psychology as well as of philosophical argument, he
comes to the conclusion that the sharp distinction
drawn by former thinkers between subjective consciousness and the external world is simply a rationalisation.
The fact is that the bare atoms of visual, tactile, and
other sense-impressions which, according to the empiricist tradition, we actually experience, and from which
we build up unified objects, and ultimately a whole

world, are themselves rationalisations, constructed because of a certain "prejudice in favour of an objective world". But in fact the world, so far from being something constituted by the mind from atoms of sense-experience, is already present to us before any analysis starts. It is, indeed, what we *perceive*. That we are already inserted into the world, before even our most primitive concepts of subject and object arise, is the basic condition on which all our knowledge and understanding of the world itself rests. In saying this, we are not just making a dogmatic assertion, but studying the experience as we actually have it.

Merleau-Ponty argues, in opposition to empiricists such as Locke, that the impressions we have through the different senses are not, from the very outset, of radically distinct kinds, as the empiricists asserted. Thus a red, woolly carpet is not "constituted" by the twin experiences of "red" (sight) and "woolly" (touch). The red of a woolly carpet is not the same, to our *sight*, as the red of another kind of surface.[1] It is simply a rationalisation to think that we can break down all the distinctive perceptual experiences into a limited number of identical ingredients out of which all perceptual objects can be constituted.

Again, we tend as empiricists to think that, in seeing an object, we somehow know it from all points of view at once—that it is present to us, as a result of our having built it up from various perspectives, not in any particular spatial relationship to us, but simply "in itself". But this is intellectual self-deception. We are never out of our bodies, and so are never present to a physical

[1] M. Merleau-Ponty, *The Phenomenology of Perception*, London, 1962, 5.

object except from a particular perspective. Familiarity does not abolish this perspective, or enable us to know a thing from all sides, inside and outside, at once. For instance, it is a mistake to suppose that depth, or distance away from us, is actually experienced as "breadth seen from the side", as a person obsessed with ideas drawn from Euclidean geometry would have us believe. If we consider the problem of the apparent size of an object which is receding from us, we begin to realise that what happens is that the object occupies less of the visual field, not that it becomes "smaller" in itself. But "to say that an object takes up only a smaller part of the visual field is to say in effect that it does not offer a sufficiently rich configuration to absorb completely my power of clear vision". (Merleau-Ponty, 261.) If I am asked *how big* it appears to me I have to take some standard of measurement, such as a pencil held at arm's length, and compare it with that; and to do this involves a deliberate effort to isolate the object from its context. That is to say, I try to cling to the object as it recedes from me, and focus attention upon it. All experience of relative distances depends upon this capacity to cling to one thing and lessen the visual grip upon the rest. There is this kind of *intentionality* at the heart of every visual experience.[1]

[1] The word "intentionality" is here being used, as normally in phenomenological writing, in a somewhat unusual sense. It does not connote the ordinary distinction between intentional and unintentional actions, as when we speak of the intended and the unintended effects of something we have done. It refers to the pervasive, pre-reflective movement towards the world which we undertake in all experience. For the phenomenologist, all experience is an *active movement towards the world*, which "tests out" (*ex-perior*) that which is perceived and gives it a structure by which it can be assimilated. This "stretching out" towards

Perception, then, always presupposes the body. (But it is presupposed not in a logical, but in an existential, sense.) For the body is the base from which the stretching out towards the world, which is the active element in perception, takes place. My body is not one object among other objects, but is the support from which I stretch out to the world, and is the subject to which the world is given as a perceived structure. It is not itself, in the first place, a perceived structure; it is that which structures a perception. "My body is wherever there is something to be done." (250.) Just as there is no such thing as a sense-experience which is unrelated to the physical situation of the body which perceives it, so there is no sense-experience which is unrelated to a "project" or meaning which is sought and found in it.

How does perception relate to conceptual thinking about the world? Perception stands between the qualities of external objects and the intellectual analysis which gives us conceptual knowledge of them. Intellectual knowledge comes about by the effort to take apart the unity of the original perception. That is, it arises by the removal of the "intentional tissue" from the object in an act of judgement which gives "objective" knowledge by conceptualism. (53.) But this is not the old doctrine of perception as a bridge between two prior, given points, subject and object. It is the recognition that the primordial experience of perception, which is the source of all experience, and which is always orientated towards a "project" and a meaning,

the world in perception (*in-tentio*) is always a response to some need which is fulfilled in it. The fulfilment of this need is the "project" which the perceiver has before him at every moment of perceptual experience.

is dissolved by the reflective intelligence into object and subject at a subsequent stage—that of judgements. Objects, therefore, with their qualities, always exist *for me* already, prior to any work of my "constituting" intelligence. Not that they are merely subjective entities with no exterior reality, but in the sense that what is first of all given is an "object-related-in-a-certain-way-to-me", not some object conceived of as wholly free from all relationships or meanings. Such an object cannot, indeed, be part of direct human experience. "Intellectualism and empiricism do not give us any account of the human experience of the world; they tell us what God might think of it." (255.) But this relationship *to me*, which is the primordial structure of experience, is not just an "intellectual" relationship to me as a conscious mind; it is, ineradicably, a relationship to me as a physical body. The body is what relates me to the world. To be a person is to be "thrown into a nature", to be in a relationship to the world from the very beginning, to exist as a "being-in-the-world" directed towards objects from the inescapable perspective of this body.

By stripping away the "intentional tissue" inherent in perception, conceptualisation involves both loss and gain, both approach and withdrawal. It gives us a completer knowledge, but at the expense of a thinner texture, and a less "active" realisation of the qualities of objects. (52.) This element in our experience corresponds, I think, to what is said later about the development of myth and magic in religious cultures. (See pp. 206ff. below.) They too represent a necessary widening of horizons at the expense of the richness of the primordial experience in which man participates without analysing it. Insofar as myth and magic indicate the beginning of a profanation of what is originally thought and felt to be sacred, Merleau-Ponty's analysis of perception may be seen as revealing the profane character of the intellectualist and empiricist tradition in philosophy, and perhaps as pointing the way forward (which is also, as always, a way back) to a renewed conception of the "sacred". But that is a step which he personally does not take.[1]

If the analysis of perception so far given is correct, even if only in outline, then it is possible to consider in its light our experience of other people, and how we are related to them. If objects were constituted by the intelligence from atoms of perceptual experience which, in themselves, had no meaning, but were simply bare "appearances", then the problem of the existence of other people would become even more insoluble than the problem of physical objects. For if what we are given is simply the bare sense-data, out of which we "construct" the body of another person, why should we suppose that it is the body *of another person*? What reason have we for thinking that this collection of sense data is inhabited by another "I" like mine? Indeed, since "I" am the one life of this body, and therefore unique, how is it possible even to conceive of another "I" at all inhabiting quite a different body? How can "I" be

[1] It must be emphasized that the process of conceptualisation here sketched by Merleau-Ponty is not just a modern version of the doctrine of abstraction already condemned in the work of the decadent logicians. For it is a theory based upon the evidence of empirical psychology, not upon an *a-priori* doctrine of how the mind necessarily *must* work. It is not simply the automatic process posited by Lévy-Bruhl, according to which the intellectual concept simply arises once the emotive and intentional elements in a collective representation disappear. See pp. 200-05 below.

transposed into a wholly different mode, that of "Thou"? How can there be any basis for such a transposition? Are we not here involved in that notion of an "I" detached from its inner relationship to its own body, and therefore somehow available for inspection in the public world, which has already been rejected as untenable?

According to Merleau-Ponty, the solution is to be found (insofar as there is one) by rejecting the basic notion which lies behind the posing of the problem in these terms. What tends to be assumed is that what I perceive, as I look at another person, is a body in the sense that the physicist or the physiologist thinks of it; that is, as a collection of organs, a mechanistic system of physio-chemical processes. If that is what the body of another is for me, then it is simply another object, standing over against me, presenting itself to me in the form of various sense-data, and which I constitute as a unity from these. But this is not, in fact, what I *see* at all. What I see, it has already been established, is not to be discovered just by an intellectual analysis of the sense-data given by external objects, but first of all, and fundamentally, by returning to what *my* body gives *me* of the world. "My body and the world are no longer objects co-ordinated together by the kind of functional relationships that physics established" (350)—relationships, that is, between separate autonomous entities intelligible in themselves without reference to anything outside. On the contrary, without the world "I" am incomplete and even unintelligible. "I" *exist* only in my relationship to the world; and "I" *have* this relationship only because my body *gives me* my world. My personal existence is always a presence in and to the world. "My body is a movement towards the world, and the world my body's point of support." (350.) So, because my consciousness is not a separate entity inhabiting a body as conceived by physics, but is rather an awareness of inherence simultaneously in my body and in the world, I can posit another awareness of another inherence in the world: which is to say, another person. This positing is not an analogical inference, but is simply what is *perceived*. Just as I perceive only because my body *is itself expressive to me* of what is in the world, so I can perceive another intrinsically expressive object alongside myself. In its expression I see that it too is perceiving the world—in other words, that I can see that here is another person, who shares the world with me.

A baby of fifteen months opens its mouth if I play-fully take one of its fingers between my teeth and pretend to bite it. And yet it has scarcely looked at its face in a glass, and its teeth are not in any case like mine. The fact is that its own mouth and teeth, as it feels them from the inside, are immediately, for it, an apparatus to bite with, and my jaw, as the baby sees it from the outside, is immediately, for it, capable of the same intentions. "Biting" has immediately, for it, an intersubjective significance. [352.]

Yet the condition for this immediate awareness of our sharing the world is that we do not completely know even ourselves. For if we did find ourselves completely self-transparent, then the lack of similar transparency in our knowledge of another person would be an obstacle to our common sharing. "You" would not be quite another "I" if I had an experience of myself which was of a completely different order of clarity from my

55

experience of you. My own inability to see myself clearly is, therefore, an intrinsic ingredient in the situation we both share.

But this is only another aspect of the fact that, in any case, perception is never finally clear or absolutely defined. What we perceive is rather a field, in which one part or another may come into focus while the rest remains as background; but the background is always there as part of what is perceived, even though it is not clearly perceived. Clarity and obscurity go together at every point of our perceptual life. Everything we perceive clearly is constantly being outrun by a total perceptual experience which we can never grasp entirely. This is the "ambiguity" of experience. Perceiving is always exploration of a field, and there can never be an end to the possibilities which lie before us. In perceiving another person—that is to say, in perceiving another person's expressive body in action—I also, at the same time, see the world in which he is acting, the "cultural objects" surrounding him, in the light of the action he is undertaking among them. Language is, pre-eminently, the form of this world we share. It is not something either of us has created, but is a pre-existent world which we both inhabit. (354.) In understanding your thoughts as yours, I escape my own subjectivity, and you yours, while we meet in the common world of the language we both possess.

In children, the recognition of others as inhabiting a common world is automatic and unreflecting. When two people are gazing at the same thing, the child will wonder why the two gazes do not break upon each other, so "materialistic" is its view of things. According to Jean Piaget, this is but an undeveloped stage, the "mistakes" which are corrected when the child reaches the understanding which conceptualisation gives.[1] But Merleau-Ponty denies this.

> In reality it must be the case that the child's outlook is in some way vindicated against the adult's and against Piaget, and that the unsophisticated thinking of our earliest years remains as an indispensable acquisition underlying that of maturity, if there is to be for the adult one single intersubjective world. My awareness of constructing an objective truth would never provide me with anything more than an objective truth for me . . . if I had not, underlying my judgements, the primordial certainty of being in contact with being myself, if, before any voluntary *adoption of a position* I were not already *situated* in an intersubjective world . . ." [355.]

In the understanding of how we actually meet others we can, perhaps, begin to see the meaning of the *sacred*, not as a corner of the world which is privileged to be free from profane intrusion, but as the basis of the whole intersubjective situation which is the reality of our community together. But the problem of our relationship to other people is not yet solved. Indeed, for

[1] Piaget's tacit assumption of the truth of his own "intellectualist" view over that of the child's is paralleled by Lévy-Bruhl's similar assumption about the primitive mentality. (See pp. 201–05 below.) In both cases a Cartesian intellectualism is confronted with data that it cannot consistently accommodate. But here, in Merleau-Ponty, we can see the outlines of a return to the "prelogical" mentality of Lévy-Bruhl's "primitive", for whom the "law of participation" is something taken unconsciously for granted as the basis of his relationship to the world, and which is gradually undermined by the development of the myth-making or magic-using attitude of the dominating, objective intelligence. (See pp. 206–09 below.)

Merleau-Ponty there is a deeper level at which it remains for ever problematic. For despite the fact that perception itself provides me with a shared world which is *there*, and does not have to be constructed, it is only there *for me*. If my perception gives me a way into you, it is all the same *my* perception and not yours. There is no perception which is not an act by a particular person; and one person cannot share *his* perceptual act with another, even though what it is a perception *of* may be a shared world. This is a final limitation to the expressibility of our social experience, despite the "social atmosphere" which envelops us on every side. Here we run up against an absolute boundary to reflection, which is a kind of forerunner of the boundary of death:

> Being established in my life . . . I feel destined to move in a flow of endless life, neither the beginning nor the end of which I can experience in thought, since it is my living self who think of them, and since thus my life always forestalls and survives itself. Yet this same thinking nature . . . opens the world to me through a perspective, along with which there come to me the feeling of my contingency, the dread of being out-stripped, so that, although I do not manage to en-compass my death in thought, I nevertheless live in an atmosphere of death in general, and there is a kind of essence of death always on the horizon of my thinking. In short, just as the instant of my death is a future to which I have not access, so I am neces-sarily destined never to experience the presence of another person to himself. And yet each other person does exist for me as an unchallengeable style or setting

of co-existence, and my life has a social atmosphere just as it has a flavour of mortality. [364.]

A number of points arise from this phenomenological analysis of human experience which are important for the present purpose. The first is that the dualism of subject and object which is set up in the intellectualistic and empiricist tradition is not so much abolished as transformed. For now we have a distinction drawn between the world of reflection and the world of perception. The world of reflection, which is based upon our effort to arrive at "objective" understanding, arises, as we have seen, in the effort to take apart, in conceptual judgements, the inextricable complexity of perception itself. It separates out the "object" as such from the aura of intentionality, and the orientation towards meanings and "projects", which surrounds and envelops it in the act of perception. The body, which is intrinsically expressive of purposes and actions, and which can only be defined for perception as "where there is something to be done", becomes for reflective analysis a system of relationships between measurable objects and properties placed in a space which is itself conceived of objectively as a system of homogeneous co-ordinates. Space is just the unbroken continuum in which the objects of science and measurement are placed. But this is not the space which perceptual experience gives us.

For example, Merleau-Ponty shows, by discussion of experiments with subjects wearing glasses by which the retinal image is inverted, or subjects whose only vision is through a mirror placed at a sharp angle to the "vertical", that notions like "top" and "bottom" or "upright" cannot be given uniform objective sense just by reference to the physical situation of the body or its geometrical relationship to the objects around it. The psychologist, in studying the way a person wearing "inverting" spectacles gradually gets used to the world he perceives with them, will tend to say that, while he began by having his visual images disconnected from his tactile and other sensations, he soon learns to associate them in the new setting to the point where they once more form a coherent whole. Thus, one not only sees people's legs at the "top" of the visual field, but to *feel* them to be at the "top" of the whole perceptual field. Or rather, once this has happened, it ceases to be thought of as "top", and reverts to the "bottom" because feet are always, somehow objectively, at the bottom. But such an explanation begs the question. For it begins by taking one set of sense-contents (in this case, the non-visual ones) as standard for the rest. But there is no way in which to establish such a standard simply among sense-contents. They have no direction in themselves. They do not come to us labelled "this way up". We do not come to understand that, say, a chin is at the bottom of a face because we are always presented with faces which are "upright". We see faces from all sorts of angles indiscriminately, both with reference to other things and to ourselves. And yet we have a concept of facial up-and-down; and we can tell when this concept is being tampered with.

The experiment with a slanted mirror reveals that the subject tends after a time to establish a new spatial level, and a new perception of the "vertical". This new "vertical" remains, objectively, at an angle with that of his own body, but is nevertheless somehow demanded by the visual spectacle. He somehow "needs" a vertical axis, and establishes one even when this conflicts with the axis of his own body. This is because the body, considered merely as a set of given sensations, has no objective orientation in space, but only arrives at one by the prior establishment of a level. It is this independent establishment of a level which has to be explained. (Merleau-Ponty, 243-9.) The conclusion to be drawn is that

> ... what counts for the orientation of the spectacle is not my body as it in fact is, as a thing in objective space, but as a system of possible actions, a virtual body with its phenomenal "place" defined by its task and situation. [250.]

The subject establishes a new level because he "wants" to enter the room seen in the mirror. So it can be said that, prior to the establishment of a notion of objective space occupied by bodies considered in the scientific sense, a space is defined by what is to be done —by a "certain possession of the world by my body, a certain gearing of my body to the world". This spatial orientation, which is established by what is to be done, for ever precedes, and makes possible, its objectification into an absolute space. We are always in a situation, and hence the orientation of space to the project we have in view is not just a beginning, but is a pervasive element in experience.

The analysis of time follows a similar general course. Merleau-Ponty finds it necessary to reject the concept of time as a flowing stream, on the grounds that it tacitly assumes a fictitious observer who is somehow able to be present at all the various events which make up the stages of the flow. It thinks of an "I" who, in seeing these events in the flow of time, compares *his* successive views. But this chopping up of the flow into separate events presupposes a certain position which is taken up, and from which the events are viewed.

But the world is simply one and indivisible. It is we who divide it up into events. "Time is, therefore, not a real process, not an actual succession that I am content to record. It arises from my relation to things." (412.) But this does not mean that time can be constituted by any system of bodily traces in myself of the past, or by any system of memories, any more than objects can be constituted from separate sense data. For my present memory of the past to be recognisable by me as precisely a recollection *of the past*, I need to have a concept of the past already. For without that, what I am now recalling would not be able to impress itself on me as anything other than something present to me now. And if memory cannot give us the concept of the past, because it presupposes it, *a fortiori* anticipation cannot give us the concept of the future. "Let us no longer say that time is a 'datum of consciousness'; let us be more precise and say that consciousness unfolds, or constitutes time." (414.) If, however, temporal succession is not wholly objective, but is rather a relationship to a consciousness which is enmeshed, of its very nature, in a world with a past, present, and future, then time cannot be conceived as wholly unfolded and open to view, not even by an "absolute" eternal consciousness. For such a consciousness *excludes* time and cannot enter into an awareness of it.

It is indeed the dream of philosophers to be able to conceive of an "eternity of life", lying beyond permanence and change ... [for a] consciousness *of* time which stands above it and embraces it merely destroys the phenomenon of time. If we are in fact destined to make contact with a sort of eternity, it will be at the core of our experience of time, and not in some non-temporal subject whose function it is to conceive and posit it. [415.]

As we have argued already, visual perception of space is rooted in a field, within which some things come into focus while others form a background according to the "project" which I have at the moment in question, so that spatial relations are present to me immediately as elements of the visual experience itself. Similarly, I have a "field of presence" in the temporal dimension.

I do not pass through a series of instances of now, the images of which I preserve, and which, placed end to end, make a line. With the arrival of every moment, its predecessor undergoes a change: I still have it in hand, and it is still there, but it is already sinking away below the level of presents; in order to retain it I need to reach through a thin layer of time. It is still the preceding moment, and I have the power to recapture it as it was just now; I am not cut off from it, but it would not belong to the past unless something had altered. [Similarly, in the case of the future,] ahead of what I can see and perceive, there is, it is true, nothing more actually visible, but my world is carried forward by lines of intentionality which trace out in advance the style of what is to come . . . [416.]

But, like the visual field, my field of temporal presence is not something detached from myself. It is that through which I constitute time. "The passage from one present to the next is not a thing which I conceive, nor do I see it as an onlooker, I perform it." But if I constitute time, then, as subjectivity, I am myself not "in" this dimension which I constitute. But neither am I one who stands outside it as an onlooker. Rather I *am* time. The justification of the river metaphor is not that I am something flowing down the river, nor that I am a watcher on the bank, but that I am the river, considered not as a flow, but as a permanence which is one with itself. But this is not to suggest a roundabout return to a concept of eternity as a subjectivity which lies beyond time altogether; for this permanence which I am, and which makes a synthesis of time, is

> ... the action of a life which unfolds, and there is no way of bringing it about other than by living that life ... The feeling for eternity is a hypocritical one, for eternity feeds on time. The fountain retains its identity only because of continuous pressure of water. Eternity is the time that belongs to dreaming, and the dream refers back to waking life, from which it borrows all its structures. [423.]

It follows from these analyses of time and space that it is a mistake to think of time or space as merely undifferentiated dimensions which are uniformly present as the setting for the objective world. Perceptual time and space, so far from being uniform, and "objective", are the changing accompaniment of our differing perceptions and actions, and it is only by abstraction from this "intentional" time and space that we arrive at the concepts which we find in the thought of the geometrician or the physicist or the physiologist. Perceptual time and space define "where there is something to be done". Now this distinction between "perceptual" and "rationalised" space and time corresponds in certain ways, as we shall see later (see pp. 212ff. below), to the distinction drawn by religious man between sacred space and time on the one hand, and, on the other, profane space and time. For religious man the profane world is felt as a uniform and unbroken continuum; but the sacred world breaks into this homogeneous continuum with its own conception of space and time. Sacred space and time give the setting for action which presents us, not with a dream (or ghostly) world, but, on the contrary, with a much more solid and real world than that of "ordinary" experience. For it is the world of power which comes from the very beginning of things. Profane space and time are a kind of chaos, or formless (because homogeneous and unstructured) expanse surrounding sacred space.

A second point arises from the first. Sacred space and time, as I have said, are the setting of actions which cut across the unbroken continuum of profane space and time. Within this sacred world, sacred power is manifested, and made available to those who live within it. Similarly, Merleau-Ponty's analysis reveals that perceptual space and time are also a setting for the manifestation of action. For they constitute, precisely, "*where* there is something to be done", and they are defined by relationship to the body which is geared for action. All bodies—both mine and another's—are "manifestations of behaviour". (352.) That is to say, my body is not just an object for you, or yours for me; both are ineradicably expressive. Expressiveness is the mode of being of bodies in perceptual space and time.

The thing and the world . . . are offered to perceptual communication as is a familiar face with an expression which is immediately understood. But then a face expresses something only through the arrangements of the colours and lights which make it up, the meaning of the gaze being not behind the eyes but in them, ... expression is the language of the thing itself and springs from its configuration. [322.]

But expression is not just a configuration. The configuration is rather a manifestation of something, of a power for action. If the body is, for perceptual experience, a manifestation of power for action, then we can take the parallel with mankind's religious consciousness further. For just as the sacred is a manifestation of power, so too is the human body; and so also are all the other objects of perception insofar as perception is always geared towards action. Every perception, then, is a perception of a power for action: and it is only the taking apart of this "intentional tissue" by the self-conscious intelligence which reduces objects which manifest "power" to objects defined solely by measurement and analysis. But this "power" is now not some specialised force, located in a special realm, that of the "sacred"; it is a power for action in our ordinary transactions, and reveals itself in every moment of existence. It is the universal power of the ordinary to point to what lies beyond itself.

But it would be a mistake to interpret the phenomenology of Merleau-Ponty as atavistic in tendency. Despite his dissatisfaction with the tradition which has enthroned the autonomous intellect, and its abstract objectivism, he acknowledges that rational knowledge is the characteristic, and indeed triumphant, achievement of humanity, even though that intellectualism has led us in the past along false trails of empiricism and idealism. He is too good a Marxist to pretend that the "religious" is anything but a beginning from which man *had* to explore the world of the intellect and of science, although this meant at the same time a loss of direct participation with the world as understood in the religious way. However, we are now at the end of a phase in which intellectualism has been dominant, and are able to return to a certain participatory mode of understanding. For phenomenological analysis has shown that the effort of man towards an ever greater degree of clarity and conscious control itself leads to a recognition that the reflective opens on to the unreflective. There is discovered, at the limit of rational consciousness itself, a necessary obscurity, which is not that of confusion or of mysticism, but a certain opacity in the concept of the self. This obscurity is at the very centre of the search for clarity and controlling consciousness. Here we find a barrier which is not of our own making, but which is built into the very scheme of things. This barrier does not block off vision, but is an opening into something which we cannot wholly grasp. It is a challenge, rather than a source of a new self-satisfaction. For

> ... knowledge imposes a pattern, and falsifies,
> For the pattern is new in every moment
> And every moment is a new and shocking
> Valuation of all we have been. We are only undeceived
> Of that which, deceiving, could no longer harm.
>
> [T. S. Eliot, *East Coker*, II.]

The effort towards clarity and control, which is the triumph of the rational intelligence, is in no way abandoned or even impeded by this recognition; for it is simply a recognition of the character of reason itself, an undeceiving of reason about its own ambition for total self-transparency.

This short summary of some of the main points in Merleau-Ponty's analysis of perceptual experience is enough, I hope, to show that, simply on philosophical grounds, the secular philosophy in its traditional form will no longer satisfy us. There is a distinctively modern objection to the secular search for total uniformity and transparency in our view of the external world, and this is enough to make possible once more the accommodation of that non-transparency and non-homogeneity which is a precondition of the sacred. This is not to say that this is a conclusion which Merleau-Ponty himself accepts. Indeed, his own analysis seems to involve new difficulties in the way of any restoration of theological concepts. But it also has enough in common with modern theological ideas to make it worth while considering whether these difficulties are as fundamental or final as Merleau-Ponty himself seems to think.

B. Language as the form of communal life: Ludwig Wittgenstein

Just as Merleau-Ponty's phenomenological examination of perception has led to a new understanding of the opacity of our perceptual experience, so Wittgenstein's examination of the structure of language leads to similar conclusions about the limits of our ability to speak about the world into which we are thrown. In his first published work, the *Tractatus Logico-Philosophicus*, Wittgenstein undertook to push to their furthest limits the secular Newtonian presuppositions. For the early Wittgenstein the Newtonian world was the only world, not because empiricist epistemology was the only true theory of knowledge, but because a mathematically uniform and unambiguous language was the only medium we have in which to describe it clearly. Of those features of experience which fell outside the scope of this utterly clear, purely factual, and value-free language, we could say nothing at all. And if we tried to go beyond this iron rule of our very existence, we only fell into a mire of confusion and absurdity.

The interest of Wittgenstein's early work, for the present study, is that by pushing secularism to its furthest possible limits, with the utmost possible logical rigour, he found a way through the impasses he had himself thought to be impenetrable. The very cogency of the argument exposes its manifest and intolerable absurdity. That is to say, the movement of Wittgenstein's thought from the *Tractatus* to the *Philosophical Investigations* is a reflection of the movement I am trying to discuss in other contexts: a movement away from an acceptance of the secular, on through an understanding of its own inadequacy, to a new recognition of the possibility of the "sacred".

But in order to understand this movement, it is necessary to grasp as clearly as possible the inner core of Wittgenstein's secularism itself. This means grasping the basic ideas of the *Tractatus* firmly. For while Wittgenstein later discarded many of these ideas, he did not wholly repudiate them. Rather he went through them to something on the other side; and to understand what this new conception was, it is necessary to see why he felt it was impossible to remain where the *Tractatus* had left him. And if this is a difficult process, it is because his thought is itself difficult.

It is a commonly held notion that Wittgenstein's philosophy, especially the *Tractatus*, is a manifesto for an anti-metaphysical positivism. That is to say, it is taken to be a systematic statement of the position outlined by Hume's famous remark at the conclusion of his *Enquiry Concerning Human Understanding*:

If we take in our hand any volume; of divinity or school metaphysics, for instance; let us ask, Does it contain any abstract reasoning concerning quantity or number? No. Does it contain any experimental reasoning concerning matter of fact and existence? No. Commit it to the flames. For it can contain nothing but sophistry and illusion.

Hume's scepticism is, of course, the final stage of the secular tradition which I have outlined above. Having begun by taking for granted the empiricist presuppositions of Locke, he admits the incoherence of the attempt to construct on this basis an external world and all the features of it which Locke tried to establish. Logical positivism was, in all essentials, a restatement of this position in a modern form, in the light of twentieth-century developments. Ayer, in his famous book *Language, Truth and Logic*, made this explicit: "What is this [Hume's conclusion] but a rhetorical version of our own thesis that a sentence which does not express either a formally true proposition or an empirical hypothesis is devoid of significance?"[1] The basis of this position, both for Hume and for the logical positivist, is that all our factual knowledge of the world comes from the registration by the mind of sense-impressions, or sense-data. All significant propositions can be built up from

[1] A. J. Ayer, *Language, Truth and Logic*, London 1936, 34.

a combination of the truths of logic (which are true simply by virtue of their formal internal relationship) and statements which report the observations made by sense-perception. Thus one account of Wittgenstein's *Tractatus* asserts that, according to it, "all genuine (or meaningful) propositions were truth-functions of the elementary or atomic propositions which described 'atomic facts', i.e., facts which can in principle be ascertained by observation".[1] Another account claims that the *Tractatus* "does not appear to leave any claimants to the title of empirical fact other than what Hume would have called impressions and ideas, and more recent thinkers had described as sense-data".[2]

Now these views are not just wrong; they are completely beside the point. For Wittgenstein's central interest was in a question which, on logical-positivist assumptions, was meaningless. His early philosophical influences were those of Schopenhauer, not Descartes or Hume. And his principal obsession, which led him towards the *Tractatus*, came from the study of mathematics and mathematical logic, not from problems in the theory of knowledge. Because of this, the tendency of his thought was to proceed from the nature and structure of language (including both mathematical language and ordinary language) to what language entailed about the world. Unlike the secular empiricist, he did not proceed from a conception of the world, derived from perception, to a theory about the nature of language and what could be said in it. On the contrary, he proceeded, from an analysis of the nature of logic and

[1] Karl Popper, *British Philosophy in Mid-Century*, London 1957, 163f.
[2] D. J. B. Hawkins, *Crucial Problems of Modern Philosophy*, London 1957, 61.

language, to construct the only kind of world which seemed to him to fit in with it.

However, there *is* a sense in which the *Tractatus* is a "secular" book. For it is an attempt to give an account of what can be said, in all possible contexts, in terms of a single, clear, and absolutely final set of principles which themselves cannot be controverted. It is, so to speak, a Newtonian account of what can be said, in which no relativity, no obscurity, no shades of meaning, no mystery is left. "Everything that can be said can be said clearly." (Preface.) It takes human discourse into a kind of Orwellian Room 101, in which there is no shadow, the light is always on, and everything is exposed for analysis into its perfectly simple and separate parts. However, this does not mean that this philosophical Room 101 is a complete exposure. It is only what can be *said* that is held to be utterly clear-cut and without any obscurities. There is much left over that cannot be said, but which is nevertheless *shown* by the structure of what is said. This includes the whole of ethics, aesthetics, and religion—everything that is of "value".

This idea of values that can be shown but not stated is fundamental to the *Tractatus*, although it is itself very difficult to understand. Indeed, dissatisfaction with the distinction was one of the reasons which led Wittgenstein to reject the whole argument in his later work. One may distinguish the *Tractatus* from the later *Philosophical Investigations* in the following way. According to the former, everything that can be said can be said clearly, but there is nevertheless much that can only be shown and never be said. But according to the *Investigations*, there is much that is obscure and puzzling about what we do say, or can say, but there is nothing which *completely* transcends what can be said. What was, for the *Tractatus*, a transcendent "mystical" realm of values which manifest themselves but cannot be stated, has become in the *Investigations* an immanent puzzlement about what is, or can be said, in the bewildering variety of "language-games" which make up our actual discourse.

As has already been said, Wittgenstein's approach is to show the structure of reality by showing the structure of language. This is the opposite, as we have seen, of the approach of an empiricist like Locke, who tried to establish the structure of reality from an analysis of the various disparate items of experience which register in our consciousness and which, he held, are somehow informative of the reality of which they are the product. For Locke, language is just a system of conventions we consciously adopt to *express* this reality of which sense-experience tells us. We do not need language in order to have contact with the world, but only to communicate what we already know about it to other people. But for Wittgenstein, the given structure of the ordinary language which we already have tells us about the world. By showing, from the inside, what can and what cannot be said, we are able to show what the world can and what it cannot be like. Of course, both for Locke and for Wittgenstein, there is an assumed relationship between language and reality, in virtue of which what we say somehow applies to the reality of which it is said. But if Locke takes, as the more basic and self-evident side of this relationship, the external world of which we speak, and infers from this what language must be like, Wittgenstein thinks of language as the clearer and more accessible element, from which the nature of the world can be inferred.

Ordinary language, despite its variety and its vagueness, is the starting-point of Wittgenstein's analysis. It is this which tells us about the world. But if we think about it we will realise that, as it stands, it presents a highly complex structure which needs to be analysed into something much simpler. All ordinary languages are reducible into a single, structurally much more simple language which lies beneath them. Now the reason why, according to Wittgenstein, there must be this simple language is that, without it, it is impossible to explain why the propositions of pure logic or pure mathematics should be both absolutely certain in themselves and yet apply to the world. If, say, the theorem of Pythagoras is absolutely true only *because* it is independent of all actual triangular objects in the world, how is it that it has anything to do with the triangular objects that are in the world? The existence of the utterly simple language is Wittgenstein's answer to this question.

The basic idea is that the propositions of logic are not just statements *about* reality, but actually represent or "picture" reality in their own structure. Thus in a proposition such as "Smith is to the left of Jones", what makes it to be a statement of something-that-is-the-case is, ultimately, the fact that the relationship of the symbols to each other is a "picture" of the relationship that holds in reality. There is somehow a correspondence between the relationship in "real space" between the *men* Smith and Jones and the relationship that holds in "logical space" between the *names* Smith and Jones. Of course the picturing relationship is here obscure and tenuous. This is because all ordinary languages include a great deal of confused emotional and evaluative material. But in the completely simple language which has to be postulated to account for the success that these actual languages have in picturing the world truly, there are only "elementary propositions", and these picture reality in a wholly unambiguous way.

It follows from this that the totality of all such "elementary propositions" would be a complete picture of the world. For since the pictures correspond *exactly* with that of which they are the pictures, the pictures and the world reproduce each other perfectly. Therefore the picturable *is* the world. There can be no discrepancy between what *is* and what is pictured; and hence each is definable in terms of the other. But it also follows that, because there is no discrepancy—that is, because language "reaches right out to reality and is laid alongside it" (*Tractatus*, 1.1511–12), the relationship between picture and reality cannot itself be stated, for obviously it cannot itself be pictured. If you lay a ruler alongside an object to measure it, you cannot also measure with that same ruler a distance between it and the object. The relationship of perfect correspondence between the picture and the reality therefore "manifests itself", but cannot be stated.

If the picturable *is* the world, then it can also be said that the world *is* the picturable. Now, the elementary propositions, or pictures, of which the perfectly simple language consists, are pictures of elementary, or "atomic", facts. All our ordinary knowledge is reducible in theory to these atomic facts. Therefore, since the totality of these atomic facts is the totality of what can be pictured, or *said* in the elementary language, the totality of atomic facts *is* the world. Hence "the world divides into facts, not things". (1.1.) By "things" Wittgenstein here means those purely external objects in themselves, knowable from all points of view at once, which the secular empiricist philosophy thinks of as the constituents of the world. On the contrary,

75

Wittgenstein says, to be an object *is* to be that which can be a constituent of an atomic fact. And this is the same as saying that an object *is* that which corresponds to a term in an elementary proposition, or to a piece of the "picture". This is the only conceivable way in which we can speak about objects: namely, as constituents of "facts" and never as "things in themselves". So just as Merleau-Ponty insists that we cannot perceive objects purely in themselves, but only from the perspective of our bodily position in perceptual space, Wittgenstein insists that we cannot speak about them except from within the perspective of our position as language-users. Language is a perspective from within which we speak, and it is as inescapable as the perspective which is given us by our bodiliness.

The last point leads Wittgenstein to say that "the limits of my language are the limits of my world". We need to see the precise force of this remark. It says more than that language is the limit of what can be said about the world, and is therefore the limit of what we can suppose the world to be. It also emphasizes that this is a limit placed upon *me* through the limits of *my* language. Now my language is not the elementary language of which we have been speaking; for that language is only a postulate, forced upon us by the consideration of the capacities and deficiencies of our ordinary language. Nor is it to be thought of as a kind of "primitive" language, from which our known languages were originally derived. Nor, again, is it an artificial language we could construct by a process of analysis and simplification of known languages. It is rather the substance of language as such—a concept forced upon us by philosophical analysis, but never encounterable by itself in experience. But "my lan-

guage" means just: the language as I use it. And it is
this which Wittgenstein says is the limit of *my* world.

Here he is simply taking up the logical consequences
of his own theory. That theory is of value only if it has
some relevance to the actual situation of the real person.
It follows from Wittgenstein's own premises that if, by
a consideration of the very substance of language *per se*,
we are compelled to admit that the limits of language
are the limits of the world, then the limits of ordinary
language in its ordinary use by me and others is necessarily the limit of *my* world. If something is unsayable
in the very substance of language then, *a fortiori*, it is
unsayable in my language. It therefore cannot be a fact,
or part of the real world as I know it. But there is a
danger, it must be noted, in the phrase "*the* real world".
Such an expression looks empiricist, suggesting as it
does a world which is independent of the perspective
of the language-using person in his unique linguistic
situation. For me there is only *my* world, which is what
is picturable, or sayable, in *my* language. For language,
together with my body, *gives me* my world. "I am the
limit of my world." But the "my" which is stated here
is not the "empirical self"; for insofar as that self is *in*
the world, it is an object only describable as a constituent of "facts". And the self in this sense cannot be the
user of language, for this is itself "generated", so to say,
in the very act of using language. The self of which
Wittgenstein is talking, therefore, is just that absolute
self which generates the language, but which is incapable of being named or described in it. Therefore, it
is not *in* the world. But neither is it outside the world.
I *am*, simply, that through which my world *is*. Just as
the eye is neither within the visual field nor outside
it, but generates the field, so that self is neither within

the world nor beyond it. It is the limit of the world. "I am my world." (5.63.) Hence solipsism is correct, though of course its correctness cannot be stated: it can only be *manifested*. But this means that it cannot be stated even by Wittgenstein in the *Tractatus*. To understand the *Tractatus* is therefore to realise that what it tries to say cannot be said. The *Tractatus* is itself senseless, and its use is merely that of a ladder by which we climb up to a new vantage-point, and which we throw away as soon as we get there.

It follows from all this that the world is independent of my will. (6.373.) For all events in the world which can be described are "merely accidental". (No picture can, by itself, necessitate the existence of another picture.) As we have seen, every proposition which has a sense is either a picture of an atomic fact or a picture of a possible state of affairs which, as it happens, is not the case. (And in respect of the particular state of affairs in question, these alternatives are exhaustive; so that if a certain possible state of affairs is not the case, it follows that the contrary of this state of affairs must be the case.) But to say that I did something *voluntarily* is to try to say more than that it is simply the case that it happened. That is, it goes beyond what can be said. Thus the realm of the will is never to be found in the world where events take place. It is part of the transcendant realm which can be "shown" but never stated. My willing cannot be properly regarded as an intrinsic element in an action. "The facts all belong to the task set, and not to the solution." (6.4321.) Hence my act of the will, which of course is the bearer of ethical value, and is what makes an action "mine" and not just "accidental" to me, has no logical connection at all with what happens.

If the good or bad exercise of the will does alter the world, it can alter only the limits of the world, not the facts—not what can be expressed by means of language. In short the effect must be that it becomes an altogether different world. [6.43.]

Here we see, more clearly than anywhere else in the *Tractatus*, the logical consequences of the relegation of the human agent to the limits of the world, his total displacement from the centre. Any human action which is free, and therefore capable of being regarded as good or evil, is outside the world. It is as if every tiny movement of the seeing eye, instead of slightly changing the contents of the visual field, displacing some and bringing others into view, automatically destroys the whole of the old field and replaces it with a completely new one. But to say this is not to speak about anything happening *in* the visual field. The eye can do nothing to affect what is in the field. All it can do is destroy one field, and create another. What this doctrine amounts to is that, in the realm of the ethical, as in the realm of the visual, all we have is a set of "frames" (as in a ciné-film), and the impression we seem to have of continuous movement is due to our failure to analyse the situation down to its ultimate constituents. We cannot induce the movement we think we see before us because there is none.

Now it is here, as Elizabeth Anscombe says,[1] that the most intense feeling of dissatisfaction with the doctrine of the *Tractatus* emerges. She notes that, in the notebooks written before the *Tractatus* was composed, Wittgenstein had a somewhat different conception of the will,

[1] G. E. M. Anscombe, *An Introduction to Wittgenstein's Tractatus*, London 1959, 171–3.

but rejected it on the grounds that it seemed to conflict with the inexorable logic of the *Tractatus* doctrine.

> The consideration of willing makes it look as if one part of the world were closer to me than another (which would be intolerable). But, of course, it is undeniable that in the popular sense there are things that I do and there are things that are not done by me. In this way the will would not confront the world as its equivalent, which must be impossible.[1]

But so far from continuing to see it as impossible, Wittgenstein, in his later work, took it as the basis for a completely new start. The hint for this, perhaps, lay in his admission in the *Tractatus*: "In fact, all the propositions for our everyday language, just as they stand, are in perfect logical order." (5.5563.) It was precisely this that made possible the search for the *substance* of language which is the purpose of the *Tractatus*. But if everyday language is in perfect logical order, there is another approach which becomes immediately available, namely the detailed study of the infinite variety of this everyday language. Philosophy could now become the phenomenological study of empirical language, and hence of its implications. It is this approach which is adopted in the *Investigations*. But, of course, unlike the search for the substance of language, the study of everyday language and its ramifications will automatically bring back, into the centre of the study, the human individual who uses it, and—perhaps even more emphatically—the community whose language it is. So far from my "self" being regarded as merely the limit of the world which language gives, I am now the focus of the whole enterprise, because I

[1] Anscombe, 172.

am the speaker of the actual language we use. The self who was only the limit of the world was absolute, certainly, but was also as metaphysically remote as the essential language which presupposed him merely as its limit. But the self who is the user of our everyday language is the full flesh-and-blood individual, with all his social commitments and orientations, and it is this being which is now under scrutiny.

This shift of emphasis, however, does not mean that all the presuppositions of the *Tractatus* have been abandoned. In the *Philosophical Investigations* Wittgenstein is no more in the tradition of English empiricism than he was in the *Tractatus*. Indeed the implication of what he says is, I think, a decisive refutation of the empiricist, or "secular", position as I have sketched it. This is, indeed, its special significance.

We may begin to understand the new approach by considering what Wittgenstein says about voluntary action in the *Investigations*. According to the *Tractatus*, the will seemed to be something the existence of which, and the activity of which, could not be stated. This is, of course, very different from the position of those thinkers who have supposed the will to be some kind of interior faculty, which necessarily has to be exercised *before* any action itself is performed. According to that view, one difference between my raising my arm voluntarily and, say, its going up because of some electrical stimulus given by a surgeon, is that in the former case I performed an "act of will" which caused my arm to go up, whereas in the latter case I did not. It is this difference, they argue, which marks off the voluntary character of my action: every voluntary action has to be preceded by an appropriate act of will, every attempted action by an act of trying, and so on. This view fits in well with the empiricist philosophy, which is based upon the radical dichotomy between the subjective consciousness and the external physical world. But of course, it is not the view which Wittgenstein held in the *Tractatus* and came to repudiate in the *Investigations*. For, according to the *Tractatus*, the empiricist account was precisely an attempt to speak about acts of will, when these could not in any circumstances be spoken about significantly.

In the *Investigations*, then, Wittgenstein is not asserting that there are such things as acts of will in the empiricist sense, but rather that what we ordinarily say about voluntary actions is, despite its obscurities, a rough guide to the truth of the matter—that when we speak of an action as having been performed by someone we are rightly asserting *both* that it is an event in the world *and* that it is a personal willed act. To say: "I raised my arm", is to affirm both that something has happened in the world, and that I, the personal subject, voluntarily brought it about. It was just the conjunction of these two things which the *Tractatus* view ruled out. (Either "A happened" *or* "I willed A", but never "I freely did A".) But now Wittgenstein looks at our everyday language, and notices that, for instance, "I don't need to wait for my arm to go up—I can raise it." And, he goes on, "Here I am making a contrast between the movement of my arm and, say, the fact that the violent thudding of my heart will subside." (*Investigations*, 612.) The general conclusion follows, that:

> In the sense in which I can ever bring anything about (such as stomach-ache through over-eating), I can also bring about an act of willing. In this sense I

bring about the act of willing to swim by jumping into the water. Doubtless I was trying to say: I can't will willing, it makes no sense to speak of willing willing. "Willing" is not the name of an action; and so not the name of any voluntary action either. And my use of a wrong expression came from our wanting to think of willing as an immediate non-causal bringing about. A misleading analogy lies at the root of this idea; the causal nexus seems to be established by a mechanism connecting two parts of a machine. . . . Willing, if it is not to be a sort of wishing, must be the action itself. It cannot be allowed to stop anywhere short of the action. If it is the action, then it is so in the ordinary sense of the word; so it is speaking, writing, walking, lifting a thing, imagining something. But it is also trying, attempting, making an effort—to speak, to write, to lift a thing, to imagine something. etc. [612–15.]

Here we have a typical example of an argument from a study of our everyday language to a philosophical conclusion. It is just one of those cases of the philosopher "letting the fly out of the fly-bottle"—the bottle in this case being the trap of taking it for granted that the word "will", as a verb, must refer to some action (for that is how its grammar suggests it works: Are not verbs words of "doing"?), and the noun "willing" being the name of a species of action. And behind this trap is another—that of the picture of man as a kind of machine. But, having disposed of the myth of these purely private, interior, inaccessible actions, Wittgenstein then goes on to show that, in this case as in all other cases, "nothing is hidden". Talk about willing, far from being about the purely private, is part of a language which has to do with a variety of visible, public actions—speaking, writing, lifting things, jumping into the water. All the things which we do "in our heads"—such as imagining things—are nevertheless *learnt*, from others, in a communal setting. If it is no longer true that everything that can be said can be said clearly, it is now true that everything that can be, can be said.

But, when we say that, we must not be led astray into supposing that there is basically only one way of saying things—that is, that language works, ultimately, in the same way in all instances. The "substance" of language is itself a chimera. The absolutely unambiguous "yes or no" of the *Tractatus*' elementary propositions, strung together in an absolutely uniform way in a single logical space, led us up a false trail. There is an almost infinite variety of "logical spaces", which share no one substance in common. In fact Wittgenstein drops the metaphor of logical space altogether, and substitutes for it the concept of a family of different "language-games". (65ff.)

The significance of this metaphor needs to be understood clearly. Wittgenstein is not now saying that our everyday language is in perfect logical order, but that on the contrary, as we have seen in the case of willing, we are often tempted by what we say to transgress the logical order which our own language implies but does not guarantee. To say that the language, say, of some part of ethics is a "game" is to suggest: first, that it is governed by rules, without which it could not be played, and which indeed, *are* the game (one might say that they give the game its structure; they are the equivalent in this terminology for the spatial terminology of the *Tractatus*); and secondly, that games constitute a *family* of activities. That is to say, there is no single feature common to all games. One game is not simply a projection of another into a different kind of space. That various activities are all games does not consist in that kind of similarity. Hence there is no point in looking for some single, essential feature about language which will give the key to its nature, and enable us to take a short cut to the philosopher's goal—which is, as I have said, to let the fly out of the flybottle. There must be patient analysis of every case, with no attempt to force one kind of game into the category which is occupied by the next one.

How a person uses a certain language is not an infallible guide to its proper use. One cannot deduce the rules of football just by watching football matches, for one needs to have some prior criterion for deciding which pieces of behaviour are in accordance with the rules and which constitute an infringement of the rules. The rules are, in this sense, prior, and constitute the game. This is why the philosophical analysis of language-games is not just the study of how language is used, but must be normative—must be a discovery of the rules which alone allow the game to be played properly, that is, without deviation into illegitimate (senseless) activity.

The game analogy also emphasizes that the language is something played by a human community. It is not something to be determined by the autonomous individual player. On the contrary, if he wants to play it he must accept the rules which are already laid down in advance. Although the rules are determined by human action, they are not valid just because those who play them make them so. *This* particular football-match is not constituted by the consent of *these* individual players to abide by the rules. For one becomes a footballer by being brought into the footballing community and playing football in it—not by sitting alone and inventing the rules by oneself and then going out to find some others who happen to have been doing the same thing.

Thus, in the *Investigations* Wittgenstein says that a language is a form of life. So far from relegating the person to the edge of the picture, he now implies that the community of persons whose language it is are at the centre of interest. How they behave and speak is itself the starting-point for any philosophical analysis. But these are not persons conceived of as constituted objects, let alone machines, about which language can speak (as in the empiricist tradition); but neither are they simply absolute consciousness at the limit of the field, about whom nothing can be said. The concept of the person, or tribe, or community, seems to be taken by Wittgenstein in the *Investigations* as more or less basic. This is why he does not directly tackle the philosophical problem of personality, or community, at length. In analysing what people do and say, he is not trying thereby to elucidate the notion of a "person". He is using the person as a primitive, and even unanalysable, datum from which to begin analysis of personal speech and action in the world.[1] To say that "I raise my arm" is to presuppose an "I", which is indeed the simple, and fundamental, genesis of the entire enquiry. To speculate, in this context, whether (say) the person is composed of body and soul, and if so how these two are to be related, would be completely beside

[1] For a further development of the idea that the concept of "person" is a basic datum presupposed by all philosophical discourse, see P. F. Strawson, *Individuals*, London 1959, especially pp. 103ff.

the point. For that would be to put the person back into the world as an object. Yet to refuse to do this is not to leave the person where he was (or rather where he was not) in the *Tractatus*. For it is now possible to speak about persons, if not in themselves, at any rate in their actions in the world. Here we begin to see why it is that Wittgenstein's preoccupation with language takes him to a position comparable to that of Merleau-Ponty. For both, it can be said that "being-in-the-world" is the basic situation, out of which all philosophical analysis starts.

For Merleau-Ponty, as we have seen, the emphasis is, first of all, on the bodily character of our being-in-the-world. The body is itself intrinsically expressive of this being-in-the-world. It is not to be thought that we *use* our bodies for the physical expression of some "personal" meaning which is hidden behind this bodiliness. There is no "essential" personality hidden behind the body at all. On the contrary, the body just *is* our mode of being in the world, considered in the framework of time and space. Our temporal and spatial being-in-the-world *is* our body in its intrinsic expressiveness. To ask: What do our bodily actions, gestures, etc., *express?* is to ask for some hidden meaning behind the meaning which lies before us on the surface of our bodily life itself. What we express in our bodily gestures and expressions is just those gestures and expressions themselves, which carry their meaning in their faces. This meaning which they carry *is* what we express.

Similarly, for Wittgenstein, language is a mode of being-in-the-world. The characteristic thing about language in this connection is that it has to do with our communal being-in-the-world, as distinct from our individual mode of being-in-the-world which is what our bodies express. The body is what divides me from you. (Matter is the principle of individuation, to use scholastic terminology.) But language is something which transcends this individuality, and gives us the form of a community. Just as the body is, for Merleau-Ponty, intrinsically expressive, and not just a vehicle for something else to express itself through, so too with language. Language is not, for Wittgenstein, the vehicle for some set of meanings which we all have in common but which in themselves cannot get out into the public world of expression and communication. Language is intrinsically expressive of what it says. The meaning of a sentence, as long as it is formed within the rules of the particular language-game of which it is part, lies open to view. It bears its meaning in its own face.

Language, then, is the form of community life, in the sense that it makes us present to each other, not as separate individuals, but precisely as members of one another. For language is what we all share, whereas the body is precisely what is not shared. In sharing the language—not sharing it out, but each possessing it wholly—we share each other's being in a single common life.

C. Participation in the transformation of nature: Karl Marx

There is a third mode of being-in-the-world which gives us ourselves in a way not so far discussed. This is the activity which we undertake in the economic transformation of nature, and in which we make not only our individuality expressive (in our bodiliness) and our common life meaningful (in language), but even turn the natural environment itself into something which becomes expressive. The insight of Marx, more than of any other thinker, has made us aware of this idea.

I have already noted that one of the characteristic features of the secular philosophy is that it denies the ontological reality of the natural species. According to this way of thinking, only individuals exist. Everything else is a pure constitution by the mind. This individualism lies behind the social contract theories of human society which are characteristic of secular thinkers, whether they be pessimists like Hobbes or optimists like Locke. It may be useful to begin, therefore, by pointing out that one difference between the secular outlook and that of Marx lies in this matter of species-life. For Marx, men did not just create human society in the first place; nor can we say that, if we abstract all that belongs to man's social life as such, what is left is the bare individual human being. On such an assumption there would be no human being left at all. For man only exists within a community setting. He becomes human by becoming capable of social relationships. Society creates men, and man creates himself in the development of social life. There can be no separation here. The wholly autonomous human individual is an abstraction from the complex of which he is a part. But this is not to deny man his freedom, or his transcendence of the natural world. For it is in the particular characteristics of the complex in which he lives that man's uniqueness rests.

Even when I carry out *scientific* work . . . I perform a *social*, because *human*, act. It is not only the

89

material of my activity ... which is given to me as a social product. My *own existence* is a social activity.[1]

But to say this is not to make the individual merely an element in an anonymous collectivity.

It is above all necessary to avoid postulating "society" once more as an abstraction confronting the individual. The individual *is* the *social being*. The manifestation of his life—even when it does not appear in the form of a social manifestation, accomplished in association with other men—is, therefore, a manifestation and affirmation of *social life*. Individual human life and species life are not different things, even though the mode of existence is necessarily a more *specific* or a more *general* mode of species-life, or that of species life a *specific* or more general mode of individual life. In his *species-consciousness* man confirms his real social life, and reproduces his real existence in thought, while conversely species-being confirms itself in species consciousness, and exists for itself in its universality as a thinking being.[2]

Now, the species-life of man, like the species-life of other animals, is concerned with those things which are necessary for survival and health. They include not only those activities which are essential for the individual's survival as such, but also those things which are neces-

---

[1] K. Marx, "Private Property and Communism", *Economic and Philosophical Manuscripts* (written in Paris in 1844). Quoted from T. B. Bottomore (trans. and ed.), *Karl Marx: Early Writings*, London 1963, 157f.; extracts, including this passage, also available in T. B. Bottomore and Maximilien Rubel (edd.), *Karl Marx: Selected Writings in Sociology and Social Philosophy*, London 1963², 91f.

[2] Marx, "Private Property and Communism", in Bottomore, 158 (this passage also in Bottomore and Rubel, 91f.).

sary for the survival of the species. The things which are necessary for the individual's survival are what Marx called "material life".

> Life involves, before everything else, eating and drinking, a habitation, clothing and many other things. The first historical act is thus the production of the means to satisfy these needs, the production of material life itself.[1]

But Marx well understood that this attention to the individual's particular needs is not all that is required for the survival or the health of the human animal. There are also things which have to be done for the sake of the species; and if these are denied, in the name of individual freedom of action, the result is that estrangement, or alienation, which distinguishes all our present-day social relationships. In a society which has lost its primal communist innocence, and has not yet regained it in the mature form which still belongs to the future, labour

> ... alienates (man) from the species. It makes *species-life* into a means of individual life. In the first place it alienates species-life and individual life, and secondly, it turns the latter, as an abstraction, into the purpose of the former, also in an abstract and alien form.[2]

Here Marx reveals his understanding of the way individualism has come to dominate our social problem, forgetting the prior needs of the species-life from which we, as incarnate beings, can never escape. The frustra-

[1] Karl Marx and Friedrich Engels, *The German Ideology*, London 1938, 16.
[2] Marx, "Alienated Labour" (Bottomore, 128).

tion of this species-life is automatically the frustration of individual life. For I can only be fully myself by being faithful to *what* I am—that is to say, a man. This species-life of mine defines me and determines the limits of what I can personally become.

But for Marx, this historic frustration of the whole life of the individual was inevitable in man's case. It was but a condition of his attaining humanity and turning mere animal existence into history. Furthermore, it was destined to disappear with the emergence of man's maturity in a non-alienated world. It marked the beginning of all characteristically historical development.

Now, the discovery of that consciousness and freedom which mark the human, and which was conditional upon the estrangement of individual life, was made, according to Marx, in the process of "working up" external nature. By working upon nature, and seeing it as capable of surrendering to human purposes, primordial man achieved the transition from a merely passive animal awareness to the awareness of the external world as objective.

It is just in his work upon the objective world that man really proves himself as a *species-being*. This production is his active species-life. By means of it nature appears as *his* work and his reality. The object of labour is, therefore, the *objectification of man's species-life*; for he no longer reproduces himself merely intellectually, as in consciousness, but actively and in a real sense, and he sees his own reflection in a world which he has constructed.[1]

[1] K. Marx, "Alienated Labour", *Economic and Philosophical Manuscripts* (Bottomore, 127).

Labour was the process by which man became capable of reducing the chaos of the world,[1] which was at first merely present as the contents of a sensuous field, to the order of a world now *understood*, as something over against man, in a dialectical relationship with him. But, of course, to see the world outside as structureless or "chaos" is already to have a certain "intellectual" consciousness, and is not therefore quite the most primitive human condition. Before the conceptualisation which makes it possible to see the world even as a chaos to be ordered, one must allow a consciousness which is

... merely an awareness of the immediate sensible environment and of the limited connection with other persons and things outside the individual who is becoming self-conscious. At the same time it is a consciousness of Nature, which appears to men as a completely alien, all-powerful, and unassailable force,

[1] In speaking of this presence of the world, at the pre-human stage, as "chaos", I have deliberately added a religious dimension to Marx's thought. For to put it in this way links the Marxist analysis with that of the historian of religions. In primordial religion, as Mircea Eliade has shown (see pp. 211–16 below), the first necessity of man is to create a sacred time and a sacred space. In myths and rituals which are concerned to consecrate a space—as, for example, by the institution of an *axis mundi* or world tree which gives a centre and an orientation to the life of the community around it—man gives himself a sense of direction in the otherwise wholly relative and formless chaos. But he also understands this human consecration of time and space as an act of creation. To make sacred is to make real and intelligible. It is a participation in an act of divine world-making. The profane, on the other hand, is the pre-existent, the merely potential, the void. This void encompasses the sacred world, which is now real—because it is not just passively perceived, but understood and grasped as an objective environment surrounding the human community.

with which men's relations are purely animal, and by which they are overtaken like beasts. [Yet even this level of consciousness is social, not individual.] Here, as everywhere, the identity of Nature and man appears, in that the limited relation of men to Nature determines their limited relation to each other, and their limited relation to each other determines their limited relation to Nature. . . . This beginning is as animal as social life itself at this stage.[1]

Now Marx held that the process of labour, which is part of what gives us an external world over against ourselves, was inseparable from the development of language.

Language is as old as consciousness, language *is* practical consciousness, as it exists for other men, and thus as it first really exists for myself as well. Language, like consciousness, only arises from the need, the necessity of intercourse with other men. Where a relationship exists, it exists for me; the animal has no "relations" with anything, has no relations at all. For the animal, its relation to others does not exist as a relation. Consciousness is therefore from the beginning a social product, and remains so as long as men exist at all.[2]

Not only is language intrinsically social, then. It is the very form of society in the human sense of the term. Language is not something we *use* in order to communicate. It is the ether in which we communicate— that is to say, in which our community lives and mani-

[1] Marx and Engels, *German Ideology*, 19f.
[2] Marx and Engels, *German Ideology*, 19.

fests itself. Linguistic communication is the activation of the communal ether and gives us our shared world. Here Marx and Wittgenstein are at one.

Language transcends mere species-life because it enables us to think and act in a *representative* way. It belongs to Fido to have canine life, and therefore sometimes to do things which are more for the dog species than for himself, to act in a species-directed way. But he cannot *represent* the species. To say this is to say that he cannot consciously take upon himself the interests of the species. This is part of what is entailed by the divided character of species life. It is language which enables us to transcend this divided state, because it enables *me* to possess *in toto* something that *you* also possess *in toto*. What divides me from you is our bodiliness. But what makes us capable of community, is language. I cannot, bodily, be in the same place, or have the same sensation as you. But in appropriating the language which we share I come to possess, wholly, something which you too possess wholly. This is why it is possible for a human being to represent, in his language, the whole community. For as a language-bearing creature I can bear within myself that which also lives in my fellows, and so manifest to the world something which is not just characteristic of them, but actually makes them present in my action. Fido can act in a characteristically dog-like manner. But I can act in a way which is not just characteristic of humanity, but which somehow makes present, symbolically, humanity itself. For my words are not mine, but belong to, and are defined by, the entire linguistic community; so that, when I utter them, I reveal the community of which they are the form.

Though man is a *unique* individual—and it is just his particularity which makes him an individual, a really *individual* communal being—he is equally the *whole*, the ideal whole, the subjective existence of society as thought and experienced. He exists in reality as the representation and the real mind of social existence, and as the sum of human manifestations of life.[1]

The significance of this Marxist analysis is that it sees, in the interaction of man and nature which is the basis of our species life, a process of transformation from chaos to meaning. Nature itself now becomes meaningful, expressive in its own right. This *humanisation* of the natural world is a process which begins at the very instant when the concept of the natural world itself becomes available to man. It is what Marx has in mind when he observes that:

Animals produce only themselves, while man reproduces the whole of nature. The products of animal production belong directly to their physical bodies, while man is free in face of his product. Animals construct only in accordance with the standards and needs of the species to which they belong, while man knows how to produce in accordance with the standards of every species and knows how to apply the appropriate standard to the object. Thus man constructs also in accordance with the laws of beauty.[2]

Once more, then, in Marx as in Merleau-Ponty and Wittgenstein, we find a rejection of the idea that mean-

[1] Marx, "Private Property and Communism" (Bottomore, 158; Bottomore and Rubel, 92)
[2] Marx, "Alienated Labour" (Bottomore, 128).

ings are hidden behind the veil of the things that express them. For Marx, nature, as transformed by man's labour, carries a meaning, and indeed an aesthetic value too, in its face, just as do the significant sentences of our everyday language and the gestures of our bodies. The humanisation of the world by which natural chaos is transformed into a structure of meanings, is therefore the religious process as such. For, as we shall see later (see pp. 230ff. below) religion is concerned with exactly this structuring of the world into something meaningful. But the humanisation of the world can also become somehow very different: namely, an idolatrous imposition of human meanings which, instead of structuring the world, merely reflects man's own conception of himself. This happens when man's task of humanising the world is distorted into something different: namely, the *secularisation* of the world according to the norms of a "secular" philosophy.

D. *The concept of community*

Our being-in-the-world, then, is given in three modes: the mode of individual physical embodiment (the body as expression); the mode of linguistic presence (languages as expression); and the mode of social labour, in which we do not just have our being-in-the-world, but transform our environment into something which is itself expressive—a human world. These three modes of being-in-the-world together give us the concept of community. For they all, in their characteristic ways, reveal a structure which consists of a going-out and a bringing-home, and hence a sharing in something beyond the self. They are all dynamic relationships to something which is both other and yet accessible, held at a distance but also capable of being taken in and transformed.

The body has a kind of dialogue with the objects which surround it, and which support it. "I do not so much perceive objects as reckon with an environment; I seek support in my tools, and am at my desk rather than confronting it", says Merleau-Ponty. (416.) Similarly, man as speaker is not merely giving out and taking in messages in words; he is giving himself to the other person, and taking that person into himself also, so that the bodily distance which lies between them is annihilated by a community of personal presences. This is not just a sharing of ideas, but a true sharing of personalities. And man the worker is not just manipulating nature but is, at the same time, being shaped by it and is given to himself, incarnate as he is and dependent on nature's gifts for his survival, by the world which supports him and gives him its own meaning. The world becomes a human world, intelligible and capable of entering into him, just as he is able to leave the stamp of his own personality upon it in return.

The human community exists in all these dialogues. Indeed it *is* just these dialogues and their mutual interactions. Having understood this, we can now see that it is useless to attempt to prescribe the ideal community. For the community is not, as a secular mode of thought would tend to suggest, some hidden essence which lurks behind, and is expressed by, these three modes—some "community feeling". It just *is* these modes, in their interaction. It is indeed part of the secularist illusion that a genuine community life is something which is over and above what we do as physical, linguistic, and working beings—that is to say, something which these can give, but which itself is not in them as they are.

Assertions about community which take this form—namely, that the difference between a mere contiguity and a "genuine" community, is that in the latter a meaning is *expressed* through these outward and visible signs—are always futile. Community is not something which a physical environment, a culture, and a common economic effort together express; they are themselves, in their intrinsic expressiveness, the community of life itself. There is not, in a "genuine" community, some hidden common purpose, or belief, or attitude to life, which these things simultaneously hide and reveal. The physical, cultural, and economic activity *are* our community, for they themselves bear the meaning of human life in their faces. This means that it is only in the modification and enhancement of these modes of being-in-the-world that a genuine "sense of community" can be formed if it is not already there. But to say this is, of course, to point to the fact that the creation of this community is not a matter of artificially imposing some inner common purpose or belief—some ideal of a Christian, or communist, or humanist society—but simply the business of tackling the quality of physical life, cultural life, and economic life as they now exist. In other words, it is not a task which is over and above all particular contemporary social and political attitudes and policies; it is only obtainable through them.

This is something which has not always been understood by those numerous groups of people who, in some way or other, have deliberately gone about the creation of a "community life", as though this were some special kind of life which is in a realm apart from the "dirty" work of running democratic institutions and making social commitments. They have been taken in by the secular myth of a community life which lies altogether hidden behind the forms of the community as it already exists. In their best forms, they have, inevitably, had to "express" this inner community in some special and usually relatively artificial way—by the creation of small isolated agricultural groups, say, or by artistic or literary institutions which give a form and focus to the community life. In their worst forms, they have taken, as the inner meaning of community, some secular myth, and tried to impose it upon society as a whole. And this is fascism. All of this is bound to end in failure and disillusionment. For it is impossible to prescribe for something which is not, itself, a subsistent entity, but is a mode of being-in-the-world. Community is not meaning given to a certain way of life, but is simply the way of life we have. The way we bear ourselves to each other bodily, linguistically, and economically *is* our community life. The only way in which we can improve it is by improving these modes of being-in-the-world, not by doing something else which is felt to *be* the meaning they carry. They carry their own meaning and there is no community other than the meanings they carry. What this means in practice is the tackling of the evils we face in the quality of our physical life and health, the quality of our culture—that is, the whole range of communications and their media—and the quality of our social, political, and economic relationships, by every means at our disposal.

This is the task of the Christian as well as of the humanist. But, in addition, the Christian has the task of relating his social and political commitments to his commitment to the community of mankind considered specifically as the people of God, that is the church. For him, the recovery by the church of its true structure and orientation, in the modern world, is an essential part of the process of creating an adequate community life. The provision of the theology necessary for this task is, therefore, as crucial a need as is the creation of a viable political philosophy. The two are, indeed, aspects of the one undertaking. This is why, as I have said in the Introduction, the approaches of the seculariser and of the moderniser are both inadequate. A radical theology of the church is a necessary element in a Christian understanding of the needs of the modern political community.

It is important to insist that, in saying that community can only be created through actual policies and decisions, I am not making a concession to the "modernisers" as defined in the Introduction. (See pp. 2–12 above.) For the difference is that, to the moderniser, an actual political policy for society as a whole is simply a collection of individual suggestions, decisions, and reforms. Taken as a sum, these are his political commitment. Whereas the view that I am putting forward is that a real policy, though it is not a commitment to anything apart from these separate solutions, is not just a collection of ideas arbitrarily put together, either. They have a real coherence, and belong naturally in a single view. Just as the human species is not merely the collection of individuals, but is a divided reality which we all share, so a political or social policy is a coherent commitment, in which all the separate measures and objectives belong, and in which they find their meaning. If the argument I have put forward so far is valid, it will be obvious that for the Christian such a coherence can only be found in the tradition of socialist thought. And, furthermore, this must be a socialism which fully acknowledges the insight of Marx; that is to say, it will in an important sense be a revolutionary ideology.

3

Sacred and secular in fiction

If we cannot prescribe the ideal community because it is, as it were, too close to ourselves, too much involved in every thought and action we undertake, perhaps we can still begin to understand the concept of the human community by standing back from it in imagination. This is one activity of art, in which we hold up a mirror to nature in which to see ourselves. In the world of literature especially we shall not be surprised to find revealed the contrast between the secular and sacred, as ways of trying to understand our being-in-the-world. By considering the contrast as acted out in fiction, we may be able to see more clearly certain features which, in the real world, are more elusive. Because literature concentrates attention, and focuses it by eliminating the complications which beset us in life, it may offer us a clearer conception of the problem that I am trying to elucidate than is possible in a purely philosophical discussion.

The following remarks claim to be no more than a brief sketch of the way such an understanding might be attained. Of course, to deal with the contrast between the sacred and the secular in fiction coherently, let alone adequately, would require a book in itself. Since that is impossible here, I merely pick out one or two obvious moments in our own literature at which the distinction can be illustrated clearly. In the first of these "moments" I shall contrast the greatest of English secularist novelists—George Eliot—with her greatest near-contemporary, Charles Dickens.

It may seem strange to insist, in this particular context, upon a contrast between George Eliot and Dickens. Are they not equally limited by a concern with the human world in all its autonomy and bewildering variety, and equally unconcerned with questions of an ultimate reality beyond nature? The answer to this question must, in one sense, be: Yes. Dickens is concerned with human society as an object of study, analysis, and criticism in its own right, and he is only peripherally interested in any more "ultimate" world than the one he sees before his eyes. But the point I am trying to make is that it is not a concern with another kind of world, of a more ultimate order, which distinguishes the secular philosophy from its opposite: it is first of all a question of how this empirical world itself, in which we find ourselves, is perceived and understood—that is to say, whether it is seen simply as an environment, held at a distance from us as the passive context of human life, or whether all our experience consists of an exchange, or commerce, between ourselves and the external world, in which the world gives to us its own immanent meanings, revealing its latent sacramentality, and we, in turn, are able to enter into this world and with our humanity light up a significance it already latently possesses.

One of the most notable points of contrast between Dickens and George Eliot lies exactly at this point. For George Eliot, man lives in a *human* world, to which material objects are simply a background. For Dickens, man lives among, and even in, material objects themselves. He is in continual commerce with them. Things take on a human aspect when we encounter them; and people take on the aspect of the things they enter into. There is no absolute barrier between the human and the material world which surrounds us. Man lives in a world which is either alive or dead, not according to some fixed distinction between the kinds—the animate and the inanimate—but according to whether a person is morally alive or dead in himself, and can therefore animate, or is deadened by, the life of the material world around him. The good person is one who transcends his given nature, and in so doing transcends his circumstances and the drag of the external world upon his energy. Nature is not sovereign, because nature is not itself immutable. There is a sense in which nature itself can go awry, so that the whole order of things is reversed, and chaos rules where it should not. The order of things is not unchallengeable, but is liable to be inverted by evil in the actions and wills of men, until the whole world seems to be disrupted, almost as Lear sees it disrupted.

Moral goodness, for Dickens, is measured by human actions in themselves, rather than by their place in a process of moral growth. Individual moral growth is, indeed, a comparatively rare feature of the Dickensian world. People are mostly as good or as bad at the end as they were in the beginning. We know them better, of course; but this knowledge shows us only that our first impressions were, on the whole, correct. This is not because Dickens is blind to the fact of the human capacity for growth in understanding and sensibility, or for the compassion with which we need to understand moral weakness. It is because, for him, the subject of growth and change is society itself, rather than the individual. For George Eliot, the individual changes against the background of a static social world (this is why she chooses to write mostly about the past, when things seemed to be more permanent, rather than about the shifting world of the present). In Dickens, society itself is in a turmoil of change and upheaval, of growth and decay. The extent and significance of this process is measured by the eternally valid moral positions of certain absolutely good or bad people who transcend the change which is going on all around them, and give a point of view by which the emerging values can be judged.

A. George Eliot

The basis of George Eliot's secular world-view is the sovereignty of nature. Nature for her is not contingent, but absolute. It is that beyond which we cannot go, and outside whose orbit it is useless to speculate. If she took this belief from her rationalist agnostic friends,[1] like Charles Bray, she gives it a colouring of her own, and humanises the impersonal tendency that was latent in such a view when put into the hands of many of her scientific contemporaries. For she understands nature as the common basis of different kinds of life, and does not try to interpret the whole of experience in a single scientific or mathematical spirit. "Human beliefs, like all other natural growths, elude the barriers of system." (*Silas Marner*, Chapter 17.) Each kind of life has its own specific nature, and it is this which is unassailable

[1] See Humphry House "George Eliot's Unbelief", *Ideas and Beliefs of the Victorians*, London 1949.

and absolute for all its members. Now the special characteristic of human life is self-knowledge. The growth of a capacity to achieve an understanding of one's own character and actions, and their effects on others within the great interlocking system of human relationships into which we are born, is the mark of a mature human being; and it is his chief task to perfect this capacity and bring it to fruition. As David Daiches has said about Dorothea, in *Middlemarch*, she

> ... is educated by life into a fuller knowledge of herself and her relation to her environment. Self-knowledge, and the development of a sense of true vocation, are for George Eliot the proper object of all questing, and characters are judged by the degree to which they achieve them. One might say that the grand theme of Middlemarch concerns the problem of self-knowledge and vocation in the context of society at work.[1]

But it is important to see that for George Eliot this process is an unfolding, or growth, of something that is latent, never an assertion of a freedom in the individual altogether to transform himself, or to transcend the limitations set by his own original gifts and endowments. This is how the sovereignty of nature makes itself felt in her world. While we are free to act in this way or that, according to choice, on the short-term view, and at the particular moment, we are not free either to control the consequences for good or evil of what we choose to do, or to transcend completely the circumstances of birth and temperament and the social situation into which we are plunged. In the *Mill on the*

[1] David Daiches, *Middlemarch*, London 1963, 10. One might say that it is the grand theme of all her novels.

Floss she shows how Tom felt immovably harsh towards Maggie because he "like every one of us was imprisoned within the limits of his own nature". (Book VII, Chapter 3.) "Character too is a process and an unfolding", George Eliot insists in *Middlemarch*. (Chapter 15.) There is a tension between the freedom of our everyday actions and the destiny which governs us in the long run. We are free to grow to maturity or to stunt ourselves, but we are not free to become a wholly new being, or to become the bearer of a transcendent good or evil. People are divided into those who achieve more or less what they are capable of, and those who fail to do so. We are all either good, or immature and stupid. (In seeing the moral problems of man in these terms George Eliot connects herself with the pessimistic but profound secularism of Hobbes.) Of course, we are all mixtures of goodness and stupidity:

> If we had a keen vision of all ordinary human life, it would be like hearing the grass grow and the squirrel's heart beat, and we should die of that roar which lies on the other side of silence. As it is, the quickest of us walk about well wadded with stupidity.
> [*Middlemarch*, Chapter 20.]

Human goodness, then, is the attainment of full growth and sensibility. The worst people are those who have most signally failed to grow up, and remain in a stunted, self-enclosed world of insensibility towards others. In failing to grow up, however, they fail to become properly human, like Rosamund, who seemed to Lydgate "as if she were an animal of another and feebler species". (*Middlemarch*, Chapter 65.) There is no such thing, in George Eliot's world, as an outright self-commitment to evil.

What damns Rosamund is that she is incapable of moral growth. That kind of culpable immaturity which she evinces is the only form of damnation there is in George Eliot's scheme of things. Thus, unlike Rosamund, Silas Marner is redeemable because, despite the stunted life that his bitter experience has forced upon him, he is still capable of growth, once the latent power for it is reawakened. When he cures Sally Oates with his mother's herbal recipe he feels "a sense of unity between his past and present life, which might have been the beginning of his rescue from the insect-like existence into which his nature had shrunk". (Chapter 2.) When, after the robbery, he comes to the Rainbow Inn and speaks to his neighbours for the first time, George Eliot comments that this "strangely novel situation ... had doubtless its influence on Marner, in spite of his passionate preoccupation with his loss." And she goes on to remark, "Our consciousness rarely registers the beginning of a growth within us any more than without us; there have been many circulations of the sap before we detect the smallest sign of the bud." (Chapter 7.) As Eppie grows up physically, so Marner correspondingly begins to grow with her. "As the child's mind was growing into knowledge, his mind was growing into memory; as her life unfolded, his soul, long stupefied in a cold, narrow prison, was unfolding too, and trembling gradually into full consciousness." (Chapter 14.)

These last two quotations are typical of the whole George Eliot world view. Not only is moral goodness something that grows, and is to that extent determined by what is given in the seed, and cannot go beyond it; it is also governed by an unconscious, slow, unobserved natural process. This gives man's capacity for moral growth a continuity with that of nature. It is the achievement of a harmony with nature in this wider sense that marks the greatest human maturity. (Caleb Garth.) The supreme human value is a static condition of peace and rootedness, won by a long moral struggle, in which all but the minor irritations and blemishes, which for George Eliot are never absent, have been burned away by a suffering which has been endured.

It follows, of course, from her own premises that, if we can never find a person wholly committed to evil, if there is no possibility within us of such a transcendence of the natural order, then there is no perfectly complete commitment to good either. It may be possible to speak of the "growing goodness of the world" (last paragraph of *Middlemarch*), but there is no actual example of a completed personality to be found in human history. Not only can there be no wholly good or wholly bad characters, then; there is no place even for any symbol of such a condition, as an ideal to be aimed at or avoided at all costs. Moral completion is not merely incredible in this world of change, growth, and decay; it is inconceivable, a contradiction in terms. Moral goodness consists in undergoing the growth-process, which never comes to a perfect fruition. Growth in sensitivity itself is a value, the only value, just because we cannot posit any perfect completion.

History, like individual life, is a process of unfolding, of growth. In George Eliot's hands, the novel is the unravelling of a tangled mass of possibilities, and the exhibition of the connections between events in their natural context. Thus in the fifteenth chapter of *Middlemarch* she begins by contrasting the limited space she has at her disposal with the slow pace of life in Fielding's day, when "summer afternoons were spacious, and

the clock ticked slowly in the winter evenings". Unlike
Fielding, she tells us, she has "so much to do in unravelling certain human lots, and seeing how they were
woven and interconnected, that all the light I can
command must be concentrated in this particular web".
The word "lots" here has to be given its full weight.
George Eliot's purpose is to show the paradoxical
character of the tragedy of human life: that our very
freedom to act is contradicted by the determinate chain
of consequences which follow from every act, and which
involves us all in inescapable necessities. The very optimism of the "growing goodness of the world" entails
that life is tragic at the same time. We are caught in
the "web" of human, social existence, but are bound
to be defeated by what it conjures up for us. When
Lydgate chooses, at a crucial moment, to pick up the
piece of chain work which Rosamund dropped, and is
captivated in that instant by her beauty, and her
"naturalness" (which is as undeveloped as it had been
when she was five years old—this is the damning indictment in the George Eliot world) "that moment of
naturalness was the crystallizing feather-touch: it shook
flirtation into love. Remember that the ambitious man
who was looking at those forget-me-nots under the
water was very warmhearted and rash. *He did not know
where the chain went. . . ." (Middlemarch,* Chapter 21.
My italics.) The web of fate is nonetheless a trap for
being made by human beings themselves, out of their
own natural inclinations and desires. It is our fate to
catch and betray each other. That is the tragedy to
which we are condemned, and which we cannot escape.
"Young love-making—that gossamer web . . . is made of
spontaneous beliefs and indefinable joys, yearnings of
one life towards another, visions of completeness, in-

definite trust." (Chapter 36.) But completeness and indefinite trust are for ever unattainable, and the mature person is one who sees this. As Mr Irwine puts it to Adam Bede:

> There is no sort of wrong deed of which a man can bear the punishment alone; you can't isolate yourself, and say that the evil which is in you shall not spread. Men's lives are as thoroughly blended with each other as the air they breathe: evil spreads as necessarily as disease. [*Adam Bede*, Chapter 41.]

This then is the nature of human life; and the good man is one who comes to terms with it by taking full responsibility for his actions, and by understanding, to the furthest extent of his capacity, the forces which shape the actions of others.

It is in this sense, then, that nature is the unconditioned basis of human life, and cannot be challenged. The human "lot" lies in the nature of our being-in-the-world, and is our ultimate reality. Nature is not a transcendent destiny, let alone a personal providence, but is simply the immanent essence of human beings themselves, taken in their solidarity with each other and with the material world in which they are set. How then can man be free at all, in his actions? How can he be free from the environment which seems to determine his unfolding? George Eliot sees that there can be no free human action until man has erected over against himself something from which to be free. Just because there is no transcendent reality to confront man, the external world itself has to be seen as confronting him with its inexorable challenge. The continuity between man and the world cannot be absolute. The harmony with the world which can be achieved at the furthest

111

points of human growth is something wrought out of a struggle with an external world set over against man's life; it is not simply given, but has to be made. But this opposing force over against men can only be that of the material world and the human world of other individuals. It is in understanding human freedom in this sense that George Eliot's way of conceiving the material environment and the social environment, in which her characters are embedded, is brought into being.

As I have already said, nature for her is divided into kinds. The life of human beings is one kind of life, that of the organic external world is another, that of material objects and human artifacts another. Precisely because, for her, the human world is sovereign in its own order, it has to be shown as wholly different from other kinds of life. There can be no mutual interchange between the kinds without endangering the whole edifice which has been erected upon the concept of growth in human sensibility. This is why, despite the perpetual presence of a vivid sense of the organic and material environment which envelops man, the external world is always held at a distance. It does not present itself as something to be entered into. Of course human beings are *shaped* by their environment. (Consider, for instance, the magnificent analysis of the different effects of rural and industrial conditions upon social life which opens *Silas Marner*.) But there is no *dialogue* between the environment and the characters. George Eliot's great "set-piece" descriptions have a magnificent sweep, and display a unique sense of the social history which lies buried in them; but they remain descriptions, landscapes and interiors seen from outside. The characters see them, and we look at them in their company; but the landscape of, say, the borderland between Loamshire and Stonyshire (*Adam Bede*, Chapter 2), or the description of the objects in Adam Bede's workshop (Chapter 1), or of the house at Hall Farm (Chapter 6) are firmly "out there", as settings for human activity. They are not seen as the repository of a living power which in turn can exercise itself upon the characters.

The cyclic quasi-permanence of the seasonal round to be lived through in the countryside, which is always an important element in George Eliot's work, emphasizes the distance between static nature and developing man, and it is this which mutes the evolutionary optimism implicit in the concept of a continual possibility of moral growth, both for individuals and for human society as a whole. A house is the context of the life of its inhabitants, but it does not (as so often in Dickens) possess an active power to influence them. Houses are houses, chairs are indubitably chairs, and there must be no confusing one kind of thing with another. The environing objective world is mostly benign, but passive. It is never *alive* as a power to challenge and threaten the life of man.

This is true, even in *Silas Marner*, which, because of its extreme compression, has more of a "poetic" character than most of the other novels. The Raveloe peasantry may have the feeling that there is an invisible power in their environment, but this is a superstition left over from the past. However understandable such a superstition may be, and even attractive in its way, George Eliot herself, the omniscient author, puts all such power firmly where she insists it belongs—that is, in the hands of men. (Chapter 1.) Marner's loss of faith in the invisible power of God may be a benumbing influence upon his sensibility, but what releases him from it is not a rediscovery of that power, but the slow working of human activities and needs upon his own latent capacity for growth. The power he loses in the outside world he discovers in himself. It is true that, in his simplicity, he attributes his new-found joy in Eppie to a mysterious "good i' this world", and affirms that "the drawing o' the lots is dark; but the child was sent to me. There's dealings with us—there's dealings." (Chapter 16.) But it is clear from the whole context of the story that this is but a part of his becoming more integrated with the Raveloe villagers, to whom this kind of mystery is a commonplace. The weight of George Eliot's own emphasis is all upon his own self-knowledge as the source of his recovery. It is true that there is a strong element of "chance" in the story—the unlucky death of Godfrey's horse, the lucky wandering of the child Eppie into Marner's cottage. But the very point of this, for George Eliot, as she makes explicit at the end of the ninth chapter, is that what looks like chance is neither the workings of a lawless world nor that of a providential power, but is simply—as we would all understand, if we but knew more about the "cunning complexity" which we call chance—the "orderly sequence by which the seed brings forth a crop after its own kind". There is no "chance" then. Life has its own laws, according to which it functions implacably.

The material environment of human life, despite its complexity and richness, and even oppressiveness, is described on the whole in relatively flat language. It is not alive, as a power over against man, because George Eliot's language does not come alive when she describes it. She has to *tell* us what effect the external world has upon people, because for her the material world does not possess the living power to do so. For example,

Caleb Garth's dedication to manual labour is described in the following passage:

> The echoes of the great hammer where the roof or keel were a-making, the signal shouts of the workmen, the roar of the furnace, the thunder and plash of the engine, were a sublime music to him; the felling and lading of timber, and the huge trunk vibrating starlike in the distance along the highway, the crane at work on the wharf, the piled-up produce in warehouses, the precision and variety of muscular effort wherever exact work had to be turned out—all these sights of his youth had acted upon him as poetry . . . [*Middlemarch*, Chapter 24.]

The effect of this post-Wordsworthian passage, and many others like it, depends almost entirely upon its cumulative bulk; there are few striking metaphors, no memorable images, but rather a blur of activity in and among the multitudinous objects among which Garth worked. We are told about them, rather than seeing them with our own eyes.

Dorothea's return with Casaubon from their miserable Roman honeymoon to the equally miserable Lowick Manor calls forth a more striking set of images, because there is now some human contact by which the material world can be given a positive significance as a context of life:

> The very furniture in the room seemed to have shrunk since she saw it before: the stag in the tapestry looked more like a ghost in his ghostly green-blue world; the volumes of polite literature in the bookcase looked more like immovable imitations of books . . . [Chapter 28.]

But even here it is the idea, as much as the visual impact, which is remembered. The characteristic verbs are passive and flatly informative: "seemed", "looked". It is only when she is talking directly about some interior human problem or situation that George Eliot can be expected to bring about a bright memorable image:

There is a sort of jealousy which needs very little fire; it is hardly a passion, but a blight bred in the cloudy damp despondency of uneasy egoism. [*Middlemarch*, Chapter 21.] In warming himself at French social theories he had brought away no smell of scorching. [Chapter 36.]

For George Eliot, then, as for Butler, "everything is what it is and not another thing". Human life and human relationships are one kind of thing, the environment in which they come to be and in which they have their "incalculably diffusive" effects (see especially the last paragraph of *Middlemarch*) is another. A living organism is one kind of thing, a piece of furniture or a country house is quite a different one. There may be illuminating ways of speaking as though there was a real interaction between these various kinds, but it is only a manner of speaking, and does not transcend the clear, objective distinctions which are given to us. There may be ways of talking as if things happened by chance, but again, this is only a metaphor to disguise our imperfect knowledge of the laws of the world, and should not suggest to us any real power at work behind the scenes. It may be useful to speak of objects as if they could enter into a relationship with man, but it is only an artistic technique. Thus, for instance, she speaks of Silas Marner's bitterness accumulated over

the years, his "face and figure shrank and bent themselves into a constant mechanical relation to the objects
of his life, so that he produced the same sort of impression as a handle or a crooked tube, which has no
meaning standing apart". (Chapter 2.) This sentence
is interesting, not only because it is a striking metaphor,
but also because George Eliot is so emphatic that it is
only a metaphor. (For Dickens, as we shall see, there are
no such inhibitions. For him a character is liable, at
the extremity of moral and spiritual impoverishment,
actually to shrivel up into a mere thing.)

Because people are people, and can never be reduced
to things—there is no such depth of damnation in
George Eliot's world—the human community can be
adequately described only in terms strictly appropriate
to a human, that is to say, moral, kind of life. In order
to suggest to us the wider significance and typicality
of the particular social world and the particular events
she describes, it is natural to find her intervening
directly to enlarge the moral scope of her story. The
notorious moral reflections which she scatters about her
works are not the dreary Victorian sermons some critics
have taken them to be. She is not "pointing a moral",
but making clear the universal scope of her preoccupation, as an artist, with "the fusion of the particular and
the general",[1] which is the basis of all realistic art. But
by contrast with Dickens, she makes relatively little
use of a consistent symbolism for this purpose. She
does not give unity and universality to her works, and
wider significance, by a systematic use of recurrent
images, symbolic themes, or similar devices. It is true

[1] See G. Lukács, *The Meaning of Contemporary Realism*,
London 1962, 45.

that a certain number of recurrent images do occur. For example, images of water are common in *Middlemarch*. The deep feelings and life-affirming qualities latent in Dorothea, and the shallowness of feeling which she admits to herself, are suggested by comparison to deep pools or shallow streams. Casaubon's character is described by contrast in terms of dryness, and the absence of any irrigating sources of energy.[1] But these are not prominent features of the novel's orchestration, they do not stand out very far from the ordinary texture. It is far more in the deliberate plotting of changing human relationships—concerning marriage, business, employment, money, health and sickness, rank and status, class and dialect—that she gives expression to the processes of moral growth and moral decline which are the substance of the book.

But these are all distinctively human processes, and they are dealt with in terms of a distinctively human organization. For the primary reality for George Eliot is always what is *distinctively* human. The external world is the setting for human activity, and gains all its significance from that. It is incapable of entering into a relationship with man, except as a sleeping partner, and on man's terms. Even where, on a few occasions, a storm, or a winter landscape is inserted in order to enlarge the scope of some incident, the human meaning is the primary element, and gives significance · to the external world rather than the world giving a new meaning or dimension to the human activity. For everything centres upon man and his moral struggle with his own nature, which is itself sovereign. That is the ground of his existence, the only unchallengeable and changeless reality.

[1] See Daiches, 18.

B. Charles Dickens

For Dickens, society is not a web, or network, but an organism. The image of the web suggests a number of points connected by a system of extrinsic links; and then society *is* these links, formed by blood, money, status, dialect, occupation, and all the rest which go to make up the human world. Individuals interact, and grow perceptibly in their interactions; but the community as such does not perceptibly grow. But in Dickens, society is an organism, and as such is itself susceptible to changes of health or disease. If, for George Eliot, man cannot isolate himself, because "men's lives are as thoroughly blended with each other as the air they breathe: evil spreads as necessarily as disease", for Dickens the blending of men's lives *is* the breathing of the same social air, and moral evil is also a real disease. *Bleak House* is the outstanding illustration of this. What for George Eliot is still a simile between the blending of lives and the breathing of a common air becomes in *Bleak House* the real fog in which the whole of society is enveloped. It is both a real, meteorological fog, and a moral and social fog. The one element merges imperceptibly into the other, because for Dickens there is no fixed barrier between them. It is the human lot to be the victim of a single disorientation from the natural order of things, and this may manifest itself at one moment in the moral order and at another in the physical order. The pestilential fog which seeps into the lungs of sailors is the same as the fog which seeps into the legal obscurity of the Chancery Court. This fog is alive, "creeping", "hovering", "drooping", "cruelly pinching", and is one with the "foggy glory" which surrounds the head of the judge and the advocates "mistily engaged in one of the ten thousand stages of an endless cause". (Chapter 1.) What in George Eliot was a simile based upon the distinction between the various kinds of life has, in Dickens's hands, become a single continuum, the assertion of the indissoluble unity of the one social, physical, and moral predicament of humanity.

The great fog passage in which Dickens introduces *Bleak House* is not just an isolated prologue, but has its ramifications throughout the work. The fog is a pestilential filth causing "a general infection of illtemper", bringing bronchitic wheezings to the Greenwich prisoners, rolling about the "waterside pollutions of a great (and dirty) city", and is closely associated with the accumulating muck of the streets, on which people are continually tripping themselves up. But it is also a legal filth in which the lawyers, in this "most pestilent of hoary sinners", the Court of Chancery, find themselves "tripping one another up on slippery precedents, groping knee-deep in technicalities". The fog which envelops the court and the legal system is therefore one with the infection which has its origin in the slum of Tom-All-Alones, and which brings both physical and moral corruption into almost every corner of the community.

There is not a drop of Tom's corrupted blood but propagates infection and contagion everywhere. It shall pollute, this very night, the choice stream (in which chemists on analysis would find the genuine nobility) of a Norman house, and his Grace shall not be able to say Nay to the infamous alliance. There is not an atom of Tom's slime, not a cubic inch of any pestilential gas in which he lives, not one obscenity or degradation about him, not an ignorance, not a wickedness, not a brutality of his committing, but shall work its retribution, through every order of society, up to the proudest of the proud, and to the highest of the high. Verily, what with tainting, plundering and spoiling, Tom has his revenge. [*Bleak House*, Chapter 46.]

What is most remarkable in this passage is that it transcends the duality of physical and moral, individual and social, completely. It is not merely a highly wrought metaphor, but is, for Dickens, as literally true (within the realm of the story) as the Blue Book "facts", from which it takes its inspiration, were true of the real world. It is not "as if" the plague-ridden fluid of the slum could infect the moral relationship between Sir Leicester and Lady Dedlock; Dickens shows us, in the story, that it really does—the evil influence it exerts upon them is as manifest as the effects it wreaks upon Esther's pock-marked face. The infection is something which connects all the characters, and all the institutions, and gives their complex mutual interconnectedness an empirical basis. They participate in one another by virtue of their all being enveloped in the pestilential infection, which is liable sometimes to break out into actual physical disease, as when Jo escapes to spread his smallpox abroad, but which is all the time working. The complex relationships between characters—Krook as Smallweed's brother-in-law, Lady Dedlock as Esther's mother, Snagsby's copyist as Lady Dedlock's lover, and so on—are but the expression in "realistic" terms of this deeper, but tangible, unity between people which is their involvement in the infection of Tom-All-Alone's. When Krook disintegrates, what is found on the window-sill of the house is a pool of corrupt fluid from the running sore on society which is the slum itself.

What Dickens has achieved here is a vision of the whole of nature as being somehow out of joint.[1] The natural order of things has been reversed, and the structure of the human world corrupted as a result. In its own terms, it is a concept of the tragic inversion of nature as powerful as *King Lear*. Now this total corruption is, at one and at the same time, a corruption of individuals and of an entire community. The two things are not distinguishable, for the corruption of individuals defines the nature of the social disease, and the social poison is what enters the hearts of individuals. Each person bears within himself the corruption of the whole of the community, and is typical of it because he participates in it wholly. Like the capacity for language, this disease is something which defines a social world by being possessed in all its fullness by each member. It can only be by a process of intellectual analysis of this experienced and prior unity that we can try to separate the plague as a physical disease from the moral, intellectual, emotional, and social corruption which it also represents in the story. The first emphasis must remain upon the unity of this corrupting influence, and this is given to the reader, not in terms of an intellectual *composite* of the physical, the moral, and the emotional, but in the words themselves, and what they simply say. We must resist the temptation to think in separate categories when Dickens is trying to force us to recognise

[1] Dickens achieves the same thing in similar ways elsewhere. The rise of the railway where Staggs's Gardens used to be, in *Dombey and Son* (Chapter 6), and the pervasive imagery of a whole world imprisoned in *Little Dorrit*, are examples that immediately spring to mind of a reversal of nature.

that the fundamental experience which he is trying to convey is prior to those categories, and is given to us with its own intrinsic significance open to view in the words themselves. To say that "Tom's corrupted blood ... shall pollute ... the choice stream of a Norman house" is not just

a way of putting it—not very satisfactory,
a periphrastic study in a worn-out poetical fashion;[1]

it is an exact statement of the unity of the human community and of the physico-moral structure of each member of it. It does not run together physical, moral, and emotional elements which we know in fact to be quite separate; it presupposes a pre-intellectual experience of the human condition as an unbroken continuum which can only be dissolved out at different levels by the analytical intelligence. In other words, for Dickens there is an intrinsic expressiveness which is evident on the face of things. Just as George Eliot's metaphorical language suggests a hidden, "moral" life going on beneath the surface of empirical life, so Dickens's language suggests the opposite. The moral evil is not hidden, but manifest. Metaphor has become literal truth.

In each of the later novels a particular theme, or themes, is taken as a microcosm of human society as a whole, and is given wider significance by the use of controlling images and analogies connected with it. In *Bleak House*, it is the entanglement of human beings in a suffocating network of legal regulations; in *Little Dorrit* it is the imprisonment of the human spirit in a society dominated by money and status; and in *Our Mutual Friend* it is the decay and waste of human resources in a desert of mud and dust.

[1] T. S. Eliot, *East Coker*, II, 18f.

But it is notorious that, unlike George Eliot, Dickens does not show us this process of entanglement from the inside, by an exploration of the psychological perplexities of individual characters. On the contrary, his characters are known to us very largely through their appearances and their actions. One might conclude, from a superficial reading of Dickens, that his is a world of appearances lacking in depth, and that for him human relationships are extrinsic links between sharply defined, and separate individuals. For him the involvement of one person with another might seem possible only via the medium of some institutional arrangement—legal, financial, political. The psychology of romantic love, it might be argued, is Dickens's weakest point, the area which he knows least and in which he is most likely to become literary and even "novelettish". Marriage and the family are, for him, public institutions rather than expressions, in the world of action and experience, of a profound bond between persons. But to suggest this is to fail to see the role which Dickens's language plays in creating imaginatively interpersonal bonds in another way. Because he thinks of the moral life of people as always expressing itself in observable motions and gestures, he can give us the essence of this inner life by showing us what these motions and gestures express. For they are always, and intrinsically, expressive of life.

Dickens's view of man is based, at the individual level, on the idea that there is no ultimate duality between the physical being and the moral life of a person. The one cannot suffer a change without the other being at all affected. Thus, the extraordinary incident of the spontaneous combustion of Krook, in *Bleak House*, is only the most obvious example of a general recognition by Dickens that the collapse of the inner moral being is necessarily an event of the whole physical person. It is expressible only in terms of the disintegration of the individual as a whole. Again, Smallweed has so used people as objects for his own manipulation that he himself has become a mere object in a world of dead chairs, tables, and cushions. Similarly, the clothes which a man wears take on the expressiveness of the being beneath them—as with Mr Tulkinghorn, whose black clothes never shine, for "mute, close, irresponsive to any glancing light, his dress is like himself". (Chapter 2). Clothes are the living and active bearers of a person's inner character. This kind of Dickensian description is far more than caricature, or symbolic technique for giving a depth to an otherwise flat texture—or even for giving meaning to the disparate elements in a story in the light of its entire perspective. It is a way of seeing, and indeed a way of understanding, the human world itself. Man and the cultural objects which surround him are in a constant living dialogue with each other, and each helps to define the other. At the level of pure comedy this commerce with the material world is liable to explode in such fantasies as the warning of Alfred Jingle to his companions at the beginning of *Pickwick Papers*:

"Heads, heads—take care of your heads!" cried the loquacious stranger, as they came out under the low archway, which in those days formed the entrance to the coach-yard. "Terrible place—dangerous work —other day—five children—mother—tall lady, eating sandwiches—forgot the arch—crash—knock—children look round—mother's head off—sandwich in her hand—no mouth to put it in—head of family off—shocking, shocking!" [Chapter 2.]

But at the level of seriousness which is to be found in the later social criticism, the same dialogue with the material world is constantly emphasized. It is impossible to say which is the more important: the way Mr Tulkinghorn's room gives definition to the owner, or the way the owner gives definition to the room. Everything about the room, despite its gloom and silence, is latent with life, as the active verbs testify.

Like as he is to look at, so is his apartment in the dusk of the present afternoon. Rusty, out of date, withdrawing from attention, able to afford it. Heavy, broad-backed, old-fashioned mahogany and horse hair chairs, not easily lifted, obsolete tables with spindle legs and dusty baize covers, presentation prints of the holders of great titles in the last generation, or the last but one, environ him. A thick and dingy turkey carpet muffles the floor where he sits, attended by two candles in old-fashioned silver candlesticks, that give a very insufficient light to his large room. The titles on the backs of his books have retired into the binding; everything that can have a lock has got one; no key is visible ... Here, beneath the painted ceiling, with foreshortened Allegory staring down at his intrusion as if it meant to swoop upon him, and he cutting it dead, Mr Tulkinghorn has at once his house and office ... [*Bleak House*, Chapter 10.]

But it is in *Our Mutual Friend* that this commerce with the inanimate world which defines the character of individual, and even of collective, life is most richly developed.[1] This novel might be fruitfully regarded as an exploration of the depths to which men are liable to sink once they find themselves living in an entirely humanised world, without the possibility of any gratuitous intrusion from a different dimension of existence. For in *Our Mutual Friend* the only resolutions of the problems posed for the characters are gratuitous: sudden inheritances, old wills, and visitations which bring a conversion of the spirit. Without these graces, people die—morally, and often indeed physically as well. These visitations must be recognised as exactly the opposite of that social causality which we see developing slowly throughout the course of a George Eliot novel. They represent a prehuman, or superhuman, form of life, which the attempt at total humanisation seems necessarily to elicit in opposition to itself.

This total humanisation of life is perhaps most obvious in the Veneerings and the Podsnaps. Both families exist only in terms of the objects they surround themselves with. The Veneerings, as their name implies, have a superficiality which is so exclusive that they do not exist at all except in terms of their own reflections. They are simply creatures mirrored in their own furniture. They are "bran-new people" with no past to give them any depth or solidity, and consequently they exist only as a thin crust of apparent life which breaks down so easily that, when the crash occurs, they shatter into fragments. Thus at a Veneering dinner party, the entire description takes the form of flat visual impressions seen through the Veneerings' own sideboard mirror. This is

[1] I am deeply indebted, for the following paragraphs on *Our Mutual Friend*, to the remarkable chapter on that novel in J. Hillis Miller's important study, *Charles Dickens: The World of His Novels*, Cambridge, Mass. 1958.

not just a technical device, but a way of showing how they see themselves. Their furniture is so polished that they are reflected in it all the time. Only in this way can they encounter themselves. For instance, because there is so little reality behind the superficial reflection, Lady Tippins, who is one of the Veneering set, does not actually speak: the "words fall from her". (Book 1, Chapter 2.) Since she has no interior life, she cannot perform the human act of utterance. Speech is just something that happens to her.

Similarly, the appearance of weight, and reliability, of the Podsnaps is entirely the result of the ponderous furniture which defines their life.

Hideous solidity was the characteristic of the Podsnap plate. Everything was made to look as heavy as it could, and to take up as much room as possible. Everything said boastfully, "Here you have as much of me in my ugliness as if I were only lead; but I am so many ounces of precious metal worth so much an ounce;—wouldn't you like to melt me down?" A corpulent straggling epergne, blotched all over as if it had broken out into an eruption rather than being ornamented, delivered this address from an unsightly silver platform in the middle of the table. Four silver wine-coolers, each furnished with four staring heads, each obtrusively carrying a big silver ring in each of its ears, conveyed the sentiment up and down the table, and handed it on to the pot-bellied silver salt-cellars. All the big silver spoons and forks widened the mouths of the company expressly for the purpose of thrusting the sentiment down their throats with every morsel they ate. . . . The majority of the guests were like the plate, and included

several heavy articles weighing ever so much ...
[Book 1, Chapter 2.]

In both cases, however, the humanisation of the world goes deeper than just the commerce between people and objects. There is a causal connection. The reduction of things to people, and of people to things, so that at its extreme the distinction is indeed entirely obliterated, is the result of the economic activities of the families as capitalist entrepreneurs. It is in the turning of the whole of human life into money, and into that which can be expressed in terms of money, that this metaphysical obliteration of the distinction between persons and things arises. This is the profundity of Dickens's analysis of the personal degradation which is implicit in this humanised world. But Dickens is not a total pessimist at this point. He does not think that the world will submit wholly to this degree of human domination; it must, and does, fight back. Against the will towards domination and control it posits the sheer reality and weight of its own otherness and materiality, symbolized in the dust of the rubbish dumps and the slime and mud of the river. Out of these formless, unshapeable elements sometimes come mysterious and gratuitous deliverances, and the people who have not completely submitted to the humanising process are able to assimilate and make use of these for their own salvation (Eugene Wrayburn, Boffin). But at other times, these elements reveal a destructive force which swallows up all the efforts of those who wish to control and exploit them (Headstone, Riderhood, Wegg). That is to say, for Dickens, in this novel as elsewhere, the final condition of people in a world which is heading for total humanisation is either a gratuitous personal fulfilment through a kind of moral death, or complete physical obliteration. Death is either a means by which the individual, willingly giving up the eternal round of human exchanges, enters into a new dimension of existence beyond the horror, or a reduction of the person to the level of the horror itself. The damned become what they have made of themselves: objects (the Veneerings), or even mere pieces of refuse (Wegg). The saved are those who, through some kind of death in life, transcend the horror by willingly offering themselves up (Harmon, Eugene Wrayburn). But this achieved transcendence is a gift, not just the reward or the result of moral effort.

It is characteristic of this humanised world that, everything having been turned into human terms, there should be nothing hidden, or without meaning. There are no secrets in *Our Mutual Friend*. Harmon's identity is no secret, and neither is the will discovered in the dust heap. Everything is available; meanings are patent in the appearance of things. Gestures and objects are all expressive of this availability: for example, Boffin's stick (Book 4, Chapter 3); Lammles's nose (Book 4, Chapter 2). People may even have a kind of meaning emanating from themselves, like Mrs Wilfer's glare:

> A magnetic result of such glaring was, that the person glared at could not by any means successfully pretend to be ignorant of the fact: so that a bystander, without beholding Mrs Wilfer at all, must have known at whom she was glaring, by seeing her refracted from the countenance of the beglared one. [Book 3, Chapter 16.]

The result of all this is, as J. Hillis Miller says, that

> ... the human world made by the transformation of matter into utensils, values, and meanings is the

vehicle of an intercommunication which liberates all the characters from the prison of their subjectivity. Since each of the characters penetrates and possesses a material world which extends far beyond his private milieu, all the characters are in touch with each other. ... The inner self of another person is not here ... hidden behind the masks of his home, costume, or body. It is open, accessible, almost as much present as one's own consciousness.[1]

Finally, it follows from the logic of this humanised world, that there is no omniscient author who can know it as it is "in itself". The very availability and accessibility of the various views and perspectives precludes even the narrator from having any privilege in this respect. For there *is*, in fact, no world as it exists "in itself" to be described or presented in any way. There is only a world as seen from certain points of view. For example, the Greenwich pensioner has to be invented simply in order that someone may see the Wilfer-Harmon wedding. (Book 4, Chapter 4.)

In all Dickens's work there is a participation by the person in the objects which define him, and similarly a living influence is exerted by those objects upon the whole being of the person. The way in which this participation is accepted, for good or evil, determines the ultimate moral and spiritual state of the individual. This is but the rendering in art of the participation in the world which I have already discussed in philosophical terms (Merleau-Ponty), and which I shall be going on to discuss in religious terms (Lévy-Bruhl). Dickens's vision is not only a marvellous mixture of realism and symbolism; it is based upon a concept of the unity of

[1] Miller, 288.

man with the world, of his being-in-the-world, which is philosophically grounded, even if it is not consciously the product of a philosophical intelligence.

Just as the individual for Dickens exists and is defined by the dialogue between himself and the physical world around him, so also society exists as more than a set of institutional links between individuals. For Dickens, as Raymond Williams has convincingly argued,[1] the usual nineteenth-century dilemma in social reform: Must we begin with the reform of institutions or with the changing of people's hearts? does not apply. In Dickens these alleged alternatives do not offer an adequate diagnosis of the issues. Individual and society are not the opposed poles of a dilemma, but mutually necessary elements in a single historical process. For Dickens, society, like the individual, is not essentially constituted by some hidden bonds between individuals, of which social institutions are but the outward clothing, transferable at will. On the contrary, institutions are to society what the bodily gestures are to the individual person—the manifestation of an immanent direction and significance which is not arbitrarily symbolized, but naturally bodied forth in these particular forms. The reform of institutions is simply the outside of that same process of which the inside is the reform of individual wills. They are two sides of the same task. Dickens expresses the unity of all social life and progress by means of an extension of the methods he uses in the description of the individual's dialogue with his environment. In *Bleak House*, this is achieved, as we have seen, principally by the controlling image of the infection which, originating in the slum of Tom-All-Alone's, spreads to all the rest of the

[1] R. Williams, "Social Criticism in Dickens", *The Critical Quarterly*, VI, 3 (Autumn 1964), 214–27.

book's world. In *Little Dorrit*, the theme of the imprisonment of a whole society within its own false values is expressed in an even closer integration of the material, the moral, and the psychological, through the controlling imagery of the prison. Not only is the Marshalsea a microcosm of the whole world, but even those who never go near it—like Merdle and Mrs Clennam—are imprisoned souls. Mrs Clennam is a prisoner in her house, and Merdle is a prisoner of his money, his wife, his butler, and even himself. He is continually holding his hands as if "taking himself into custody". Mr Pancks is the economic prisoner of the "Rachmannite" system symbolized by Casby. He is but the steam "tug", tied to its master vessel. Pancks's life is reduced to the purely mechanistic level of economic slavery and "alienation". Daniel Doyce is the prisoner of the Barnacles and of that paralysed social will which is symbolized by the Circumlocution Office.

But this cosmic imprisonment is not quite total. It is not a vision of an eternal and necessary human condition. For this prison is not quite the whole world. It is itself poised between two transcendent principles, two freedoms of pure goodness and pure evil. Little Dorrit is free because she rejects the imprisoning forces of money and status; Blandois is free because he represents that positively evil will which creates and controls the prison into which all the other characters have entered. Blandois—a kind of devil himself, as we are continually being reminded, who arrives to the accompaniment of lightning and thunder (Chapter 29)—is the universal jailer. That is where his power lies. But Little Dorrit's power is that of an achieved inner liberation which sets her free from Blandois' will. The novel begins with the imprisonment of the travellers in Marseilles, and, more significantly, with the escape from prison of Blandois, whom no bars can hold. Blandois is the embodiment of pure will, the denial of any external limits; he seems to be everywhere at once, and exists in a world of mystery quite beyond the reach of any of the other characters. Little Dorrit, too, is free, but for the opposite reason. She has transcended all limits by accepting and transforming them. Because there are evil spirits abroad, like Blandois, we need the safety of our prison, which in one sense represents what George Eliot calls our "stupidity", or that "padding of the moral sensibility" which protects us from contact with the absolutes which must destroy all but the saints. Now, as Lionel Trilling has shown,[1] the evil character of Blandois is more particularly the spirit of absolute secularism. He is the embodiment of the absolute rationalism of the French revolutionary. His is an ardour which has lost all its idealism and become simply a cynical disregard for other people, and a readiness to sell them for the highest price. (Chapter 28.) He is, in other words, the "perfection" of a ruthlessly rational economic system which, in its various ways, has imprisoned all the world. He is the legacy of the "hard fact" philosophy. (*Hard Times.*) Though he is himself mysterious, his character rests upon a total dedication to the destruction of the imaginative, of the mysterious, of the inexplicable. This is why he can only be destroyed in his turn by something inexplicable, and mysterious. He is blotted out by the house full of weird noises which collapses upon him without warning and without mercy. So like Krook and Silas Legg, Blandois is a damned man who is reduced, in the end, to a mere piece of dead matter, a

[1] L. Trilling, in *The Dickens Critics*, ed. G. H. Ford and L. Lane, Ithaca, NY (1961).

lump of rubble tossed among the ruins of the prison he has created. But his ally, Flintwinch, escapes that fate, and so the power of evil lives on. The ending of the book is therefore a muted victory. The struggle against evil is perpetual, and the story begins all over again at the end with Little Dorrit and Clennam (the "inseparable and blessed" pair who have won their own personal struggle) being caught up in the uproar of the ordinary crowd, every member of which has his own struggle to carry on—a struggle of which the story of Little Dorrit and Clennam is but a single example.

Little Dorrit is, however, far from being an allegorical book. It is always on the plane of what Lukács calls "critical realism" that Dickens operates. Blandois is a human being, not just a symbol, not just a carrier of meanings. He is an evil human being considered in his essence, shorn of the complex deceiving features which would otherwise conceal his inner commitment to evil. He is manifestly and completely what other characters are only inwardly and partially. But this is merely to say that, for Dickens, the almost infinite gradation of moral evil which we find in human society has its limit, and it is at the limit that, finally, a person must be judged. Blandois is a man whom Dickens, his creator, has already judged, in his naked reality, and has condemned. For Dickens, unlike George Eliot, seems to believe in that kind of damnation. For him, an irrevocable and absolute commitment is a possibility for men. It is what we are growing into that constitutes our moral worth. Not just the struggle to grow in itself, but the fruition, is what we are to be judged upon. But because there is a limit, or boundary, to our capacity for growth, there is at death not just a blotting out, but rather the completion of a process of growth which implies its own termination. It is possible to conceive of a world beyond that boundary, in which everything is revealed nakedly for what it is. Blandois is one who has already, somehow, crossed into that world, and reveals to us something of its character.

There is implicit in the Dickensian view, then, a break between two worlds which are discontinuous. For George Eliot the secularist, there was a discontinuity between the kinds of life we know in the familiar empirical world, but there was no other locus for life than this one familiar nature which determines us. The natural world has no limits—it stretches endlessly before and after us, and our personal growth has no terminus. For Dickens, on the other hand, there are no absolute barriers between the kinds of life we experience in this world. Things, people, and dreams mingle into and interpenetrate each other to build up a single life. But this life has its limits, its points of perfect culmination and total destruction, its completions, beyond which there can be guessed only a world of absolutes lying in a different dimension. Dickens does not try to see beyond our limited world; but he describes it in such a way that its contingency is implied and something beyond this is pointed to by the limitations of the world he knows. Dickens's characters of completed innocence and perfect guilt are not just the products of a childish dream or nightmare (though the child's experience is valid and important, and points to something); they represent the child's world as confirmed and validated by a vivid adult experience which does not seek to deny the moral absolutes of childhood, but tries to understand them in a mature way.

Despite the fact that their difference illustrates the distance between the sacred and the secular ways of understanding experience, I do not think that we have to choose between George Eliot and Dickens. The failures and inconsistencies of one must always be balanced by those of another. The completion of our personal growth, which Dickens sees as a real possibility, still lies in the future, and meanwhile George Eliot's emphasis on responsibility and a progressive maturity must be ours too. It is the weakness of an absolute vision that it will often seem less full-bodied and actual than a less ambitious view. The characters who live at the limit, in Dickens, tend even at their best to be melodramatic contrivances who symbolize rather than incarnate their own meaning (like Blandois), or in a slacker and less acute phase they may become perfect in a sentimental way (like the Cheerybles). It is the life that lies at the centre of the picture, rather than at the edges, which occupies our interest, though this is given its special orientation by being set in a framework which has its boundaries. Hence George Eliot's emphasis on the need for growth in awareness and sensibility is not wholly incompatible with Dickens's emphasis on the final value of what is achieved. This is because the concept of growth in George Eliot is always distinctively human. She does not try to explain the human in non-human terms.

The secular philosophy, as we have seen, is dualistic. It tends to think of the human person as the composite of two entities, neither of which is fully personal: the body as a mechanical object, and the spiritual element as the interior inhabitant of this bodily object. Thus the "spiritual" is to be distinguished from the physical in such a way that what is distinctively human is always the life of the inner spirit, over against that of the external world. But for George Eliot, it is not a "spiritual" interior life, but rather the moral life of action freely entered into and chosen, which is the mark of the human. That is to say, it is the personality as a subject of moral activity—which is always expressive action in the social world—that is her concern. What is over against the dead determinacy of inanimate nature is the world of moral freedom, which is a freedom of the full person to grow in conscious awareness and to enter into social relationships. Personality, not spirituality, is the foil to materialism.

But this is not the common way of regarding the "sacred" in the nineteenth century. This becomes clear if we compare George Eliot with a more conventional writer, such as Charlotte Brontë. For the latter, the tension in living lies between the value of physical life and energy on the one hand, and the spiritual otherworldliness of the "Christian" ideal on the other. Thus Jane Eyre's resolution to keep in good health and not to die is a deliberate defiance of Mr Brocklehurst's "Christian" message of bodily self-denial. (Chapter 4.) In her battle with Rochester she has to assert herself by refusing to be regarded as an angel—she would rather be a *thing* than that. (Chapter 24.) It is in these terms, and between these poles that the struggle is fought out for her self-hood. Jane Eyre is defined, as a creature of nature, and hence as human, by the contrast between herself and Helen Burns. The latter's creed of self-denial is based upon the idea that

the time will soon come when we will ... put them [i.e., our moral faults] off in putting off our corruptible bodies; when debasement and sin will fall from us with this cumbrous frame of flesh, and only the spark of the spirit will remain—the impalpable principle of life and thought. [Chapter 6.]

Although Charlotte Brontë opposes this "spiritual" view of life, she nevertheless takes it as one of the terms within which the struggle for human growth must be waged. Behind this dualism lies the shadow of the secular philosophy of man. By contrast with this, George Eliot's moralism must be recognised as integral. Because there is no escape from bodiliness, but only growth within its terms, there is no escape from the complex unity of the human personality in action.

Dickens refuses to accept George Eliot's belief that, ultimately, our moral growth is, at the personal level, doomed to be cut short, and never completed—that is, that it is carried on, after us, only by the "growing goodness of the world" to which we bequeath our individual lives, so that they may be added to the stock of human moral improvement. But neither does he accept the dualism of Charlotte Brontë's conventional, and diluted, Christianity. His sense of individual completion is not spiritualistic. The attenuated reality of his "perfect" characters, whether good (like Little Dorrit) or bad (like Blandois), is not due to their being spirits, merely encumbered by a bodily garment; it is due to their being at the limits of the picture, and not in the centre where life is lived. They are attempts to imagine what we know. They show us that the boundary between the world of moral growth and becoming, and the world of personal completion, is not simply the boundary of physical death. There is, even in our ordinary life, something which is an anticipation of this state of completion. Eternity is already with us, in a shadowy form. But this eternity is not an escape from life, but simply its completion, the end of the unfolding, the last link of the chain. It is what our moral growth is aimed at—that eternal life which belongs to those who live in the present.[1]

C. Modernism and the contemporary

I have tried to illustrate, from the comparison between Dickens and George Eliot, how within the tradition of the realist novel in England there can be discerned some of the critical distinctions between the secular and the sacred world-views which I earlier discussed in more philosophical terms. In doing this I have, of course, tended to emphasize certain features of the two writers without paying very much attention to other, complicating factors. I think this is a legitimate procedure, since my principal object is to consider how the "critical realist" nineteenth-century literary tradition, so solid in its day, has fragmented in the twentieth, and what effect the appearance of the "contemporary" and the "modernist" tendencies of our age has had upon the course of the argument.[2]

The dangers which the novel faces today are, on the one hand, the temptation to allegory, and, on the other, the temptation to pure contemporaneity. We can see the roots of this double temptation in the breakdown of the humanist vision. The complex ambiguity of George Eliot's humanism is manifested in the hovering between the value placed on the static traditional community as

[1] Compare Wittgenstein, *Tractatus*, 6.4311: "If we take eternity to mean not infinite temporal duration but timelessness, then eternal life belongs to those who live in the present".

[2] These terms are borrowed from Stephen Spender, *The Struggle of the Modern*, London 1963, 2.

the locus of vitality and growth, and the equal value placed on the individual's rejection of it in favour of personal self-discovery in some kind of exile.[1] But despite this complexity, a fundamental reliance is still placed upon the human and the moral as the categories within which the problems of personal fulfilment are to be discussed. The evil we have to contend with is describable by rational means. What we are at the mercy of is our own irrational and disordered natures, and the actions which flow from them; we are not faced with evil as a mysterious, indescribable, and transcendental force which lies behind these actions and beyond our conscious awareness at its fullest stretch. To be unaware of our own motives or our own inner weaknesses, to lack self-knowledge and self-criticism, is a moral failing precisely because such self-knowledge is something which, in principle if not in practice, we can achieve. True, we are confined to the limits of our own natures, but these natures are nevertheless not in themselves beyond analysis and description. To say that "the responsibility of tolerance lies with those who have the wider vision"[2] is to assert that this wider vision is not only possible, but is required of us as a moral duty.

Associated with this belief in the ultimate rationality of the moral life—which even George Eliot cannot absolutely consistently maintain[3]—goes an understand-

[1] See C. B. Cox, *The Free Spirit*, Oxford 1963, ch.2, for a useful discussion of this theme.

[2] George Eliot, *Mill on the Floss*, 7, ch. 3.

[3] For instance, when Maggie Tulliver seems to be faced with an insoluble moral dilemma, at the end of *Mill on the Floss*, George Eliot herself is forced to evade the challenge this position entails by making her die in a flood. An "act of God" is necessary in order to bring her struggle to an end, and even George Eliot's art cannot conceal this.

ing of the roots of this life in a whole social and cultural complex of which the individual is only a small part. A profound sense of human society as a single, rich, interlocking system of individual lives, natural environments, and traditional habits and valuations, is part of the humanist vision at its best, and gives it depth and stability. But this vision itself depends upon a capacity, or at any rate a belief in the capacity, of the individual to grasp this system as an intelligible whole. Because of her historical setting, and because of her exceptional range of intelligence and sensibility, George Eliot revealed such a capacity to a degree almost unique in the English tradition. Her works—*Middlemarch* above all—are incarnations of this power to grasp a whole society, and to make sense of it.

The breakdown of the humanist vision reveals itself, then, in two connected ways: first, in the collapse of the humanist confidence in the rationality of our own natures; and secondly, in the incapacity of the modern writer to grasp his world as an intelligible totality. This is the reason why, in the modern age, there has been a double tendency, towards allegory and towards contemporaneity. On the one hand, modern allegories, in giving concrete expression to the uncontrollability and unintelligibility of our own private selves, implicitly accept this uncontrollability and unintelligibility and turn them into art. On the other hand, the typical "contemporary" writer is content to try to make some sense out of one particular segment, or one particular problem, taken out of the social complex in which it is actually set, and then to discuss it. He is, in this sense, less ambitious and less intelligible than his humanist forbears were. He attempts to achieve less, but equally he has thinner material, for the old sense of the inter-connectedness of things is no longer there.

In their different ways Hardy, Conrad, and Lawrence exemplify the transition to this modern dichotomy. Conrad's attempt, in *Nostromo*, to portray a whole social world, and to understand human actions in this total setting, is not a complete success. But it is emphatically not his art, but rather his nerve, that fails him. He does not himself believe in the complete intelligibility of the world he is describing. A radical ambiguity and uncertainty of viewpoint underlies his vision of human character, so that we cannot clearly see or judge his people or their world.[1] There is no settled centre of gravity by which a stable groundwork is established for the reader. Instead of an intelligible order settled by moral valuations implicit in the handling of actions, we find a certain element of irrational mysticism. The fundamental forces at work are unconscious and indescribable except in oblique and symbolic terms. The great episode of the night spent in the boat in the open gulf, despite its power and irresistibility, only *asserts* Nostromo's new strength; it does not reveal its interior source, because this source lies hidden beyond any analysis, and can only be presented through a symbolism which has no clear key. Conrad therefore has to work by vague suggestion, and the power of "objective correlatives" which, though immensely powerful, are ill-defined.[2]

[1] Of course part of what makes Conrad a great artist is that this uncertainty crystallizes the spirit of the age and makes it explicit. Conrad's sensibility is profoundly significant for this reason.

[2] See Douglas Brown, "An Approach to Conrad", *The Modern Age*.

In Hardy, the undefinable antagonism of Egdon Heath towards human growth, and the equally undefinable amiability of the Wessex farmlands suggest a similar movement of thought. But it is above all in the work of Lawrence that the sense of a whole intelligible human world, in relation to its natural environment (as described in the beginning of *The Rainbow*), is explicity shown to have collapsed. The movement from the close-knit Brangwen community in the Erewash valley in *The Rainbow*, to the four isolated individuals searching for fulfilment in the dead world of the alps and the dead sophistication of Dresden, at the end of *Women in Love*, is an epitome of the process of collapse of the humanist vision. After *Women in Love*, Lawrence's search becomes more personal and more irrational. Even *Lady Chatterley's Lover* is only superficially a recovery of the old themes and values. In reality it exemplifies, more clearly than any of the other novels, the tension between the tendency to "contemporaneity"—the treatment of sex as a specific, separate, social problem, soluble in terms of a simple hygienic conjunction of biological appetites—and the allegorical tendency to see it mystically as a hidden and sacred power, approachable only by symbolism[1] and enveloping us with its mystery. Lawrence's development illustrates the evolution of the tension, but he never finally resolves it.

The identification of the typically modern in art with a tendency towards allegory has been argued at length by George Lukács in his book *The Meaning of Contemporary Realism*. Lukács attacks modernism, and its

[1] See Ian Gregor, "The novel as prophecy: Lady Chatterley's Lover", in *The Moral and the Story*, London 1962.

allegorising tendency, from a position of personal confidence in the permanent relevance of what he calls the "critical-realist" tradition, exemplified above all by the great nineteenth-century novelists and, in the present century, by Thomas Mann. In thus attacking modernism, he might seem to be opposing the argument of Stephen Spender's *The Struggle of the Modern*, to which I have already alluded. For Spender's book is a plea *for* modernism, as against the "contemporary" tendency of much twentieth-century art to retreat from trying to interpret the world as an intelligible whole. But in fact, while they approach the problem from opposite sides, their basic assertion is identical: namely, the superiority of an art which tries to understand the world in a comprehensive and intelligible way, over an art that merely deals with it piecemeal (the contemporary) or which rejects it as unintelligible on the purely human level (allegory). Where they differ is in the value given to the particular writers they select to illustrate their arguments.

According to Lukács, modernism originates in the fundamental solitariness of modern man. Because of this view of man as isolated from other human beings, and the consequent absence of any process of personal development by contact with others, either in the present or (and perhaps this is more basic still) in the past, the modernist writer ignores history. Change is only illusory. The "human condition" is, at bottom, eternally the same. It is also eternally meaningless—for meaning is distilled only in historical society, in a context of human communication and of the connectedness of events. Anything in such a world can stand arbitrarily for anything else. To the modernist, nothing is intrinsically orientated towards a meaning or perspective. Anything can happen, for there is no longer any belief in a causal nexus or that inner connectedness which is what we mean by history. The "will" of man is, as in Wittgenstein's *Tractatus,* operative only in a world which has no connection with experience. Modernism is therefore a static, a-historical view of the world.

In modernist writing, a superficial attention to or even obsession with, particular details of the most obvious kind tends to go along with an attenuation of the texture of reality, which takes on the impression of dream or nightmare. No character is capable of becoming representative of anyone beyond himself—he cannot attain that typicality which is characteristic of great realistic art. No action has any significance, for everything is closed in upon itself, and carries no further than itself. There can be no principle upon which to select what shall be put in and what shall be left out of the work, for one thing has as much significance as another, and as much claim to be included. There can be no perspective determining the course of events by leading towards a revelation of new truths or forgotten meanings. Time and space become wholly subjective categories, determined solely by the consciousness which contains them. Inner and outer reality coalesce. This is why the tendency of modernist art is towards *allegory.* For allegory takes as its starting point that things, actions, events have no immanent meaning in themselves. Meaning is something given from outside, by the artist. Meaning transcends the world of things and events. In modernist allegories,

> ... every person, every object, every relationship can stand for something else. This transferability constitutes a devastating, though just, judgement on

the profane world—which is thereby branded as a world where such things are of small importance.[1]

But in admitting the just and devastating character of modernist allegory, Lukács is—rightly, but inconsistently —emphasizing its artistic value, and, in so doing, undermining his ideological objections to it.

Now I am less concerned with the question whether Lukács's strictures on Kafka, Joyce, Virgina Woolf, and other "modernists" are correct, than with the implications of his theoretical argument. It will be clear, from what has gone before, that there is a close connection between the ideology of modernism here presented and certain basic features of secularism, and the "atomic individualism" it involves. The arbitrary character of all symbolism, including language itself, and the absence of any immanent meaning in things or events, are the natural end-products of the secular philosophy of knowledge. The total and uniform subjectification of space and time, which make it impossible to determine the sequence of events, or the spatial connections between them, makes impossible the kind of distinction between *my* bodily perspective and *yours*, between my experience of time and yours, which (I have argued) is the basis of the distinction between the sacred and the secular. Realism becomes naturalism in modernist art, and all sacramentalism is impossible.

This distinction suggests that, just as crucial as the relationship of the work to some "reality" which it is supposed to represent, may be the relationship of the writer to his own work. That is to say, it may be that the capacity of a work to represent and typify, by fusing

[1] Lukács, 42 (quoting Walter Benjamin on German baroque drama).

the particular and the general, is perhaps linked to the capacity of the author, as the lord of his history, to give his work the freedom which it needs to develop its own momentum. There is, I think, in the greatest art, a mystery of creation whereby, despite the fact that the artist is the sole creator of every part of his work, that it is wholly uttered by him, it nevertheless develops its own character, and even stands over against him with its own freedom as a separate world. Thus the danger of allegory is that actions will be given meaning within the structure of the author's perspective at the expense of their immanent meaning, so that the work becomes a contrivance and the symbolism arbitrary. Allegory is liable to draw too much attention to the activity of the author, manipulating his history for a predetermined end behind the scenes. Seeing this, we look back and realise that the freedom of the characters in the picture was after all closely circumscribed—and thus we are forced to revalue the picture itself, so that we find it illustrates, but does not after all reveal, how the world is. But this is not because the story lacks "rounded" characters; for what matters is not the roundedness of the characters, but the freedom with which the laws of the fictional world are allowed to operate.

It is the capacity to depict things, actions, human relationships, both as they are empirically known in themselves and as having a meaning beyond their natural limits, which distinguishes realist art from the merely contemporary. The realist, as Lukács says, offers a structure which is not only particular, and tied to a specific historical setting, but is also representative. His characters and situations are both clearly locatable in a particular moment of time and space, and contain, within themselves, a wider community.[1] Just because they have a locus in history they are able to transcend the limits of that history.

Merely "contemporary" literature, on the other hand, concentrates exclusively upon the historical moment, and excludes the wider meaning. Thus Stephen Spender is right in pointing out that the most characteristic feature of the "modern" movement in literature is that, *pace* Lukács, it attempts to portray the *whole* of modern life. The great modern writers—Lawrence, Joyce, the early Eliot, Virginia Woolf (to name the English representatives of it)—all tried to grapple with the modern world as a single object of thought and response.[2] Their greatest works, or at any rate their output seen as a whole, constitute judgements on the modern world in all its essential elements. Rooted in particular places, and springing from particular experiences and social situations, *Ulysses*, and the *Waste Land*, and *Women in Love* all spread out until they embrace the whole of

[1] Compare L. C. Knights's remark à propos of *King Lear:* "Formal structure is not an end in itself; it is a means of simplifying, concentrating, enriching. When we attend to the play's 'organisation as a work of art'—whether to such devices as the parallel plots and the juxtaposition of scenes or to the power and complexity of the poetry—we find, inevitably, that we are dealing with *meanings* related to one another in a continually widening context." (*Theology and the University*, 213–14). See also Walter Stein's important discussion of this idea in *Theology in Modern Education*, ed. Laurence Bright, OP, London 1965, 68ff.

[2] "Modern" in this sense of Spender's, of course, has almost the opposite connotations from the use I have made of the idea of "modernisation", which is essentially a fragmented approach to the modern world. The great "moderns", in Spender's use of the term, are those who show up, perhaps most clearly, the weakness of mere "modernisation".

modern experience and give it an intelligible unity. The modernist writer is to be contrasted, on the one hand, with those writers who make no contribution to modern experience because they have immured themselves in a detached world of art (like the Georgian poets), and on the other with the "contemporary" writers who see literature in utilitarian terms, as the close analysis of *particular* features of modern life, for the purpose either of analysing it or of simply condemning it. These contemporary writers are, characteristically, "realists" in the sense that they speak of people in definite social relationships which define them; but they are also characteristically unadventurous technically, simply taking up where the "contemporaries" of an earlier generation—Wells, Shaw, Bennett—left off.

Despite the difference in their use of the word "modern", then, Lukács and Spender are agreed as to where the value of the greatest literature lies. It is in the capacity of a writer to grasp, within a particular setting, the whole reality of an age. For what Spender asserts as true of Lawrence or Joyce, as "moderns", Lukács asserts of the great realists: namely, the desire to "portray a social whole".[1] But if Spender is right to emphasize, against Lukács, that the greatest modernist writers do, in their own way, sum up their age as did the greatest realist writers of an earlier generation, it may equally be true that Spender himself misjudges the greatest of "contemporary" writers by failing to see that they too, in their fashion, portray a social whole. I think this is

[1] For instance, while Balzac, in the *Comedie Humaine*, only described his world in a series of segments, each in itself only a particular aspect of the whole, "the greatness of his conception is that the whole is constantly present in the parts". (Lukács, 99)

at any rate true of the most important and characteristic "contemporary" writer of the recent past, George Orwell, who, as a "contemporary" who saw the limitations of his own position, occupies a central place in the modern argument. The discussion of his work which follows may, therefore, be instructive, not only in itself, but as representing a whole movement of thought in contemporary literature.

D. George Orwell

Orwell's work constitutes a remarkably complete, and in its way profound, indictment of the whole of modern life. What is limiting in Orwell is not his contemporaneity, but rather his secularism. He is, moreover, a most illuminating representative of the modern experience, not only because of his obvious sincerity, but because of his self-consciousness of his own position. As he progressed, his concern with the characteristic, and representative, features of modern life became steadily broader in scope. Beginning with an indictment of the British colonial system and its repercussions upon the sensibility of the individual (*Burmese Days*), he proceeded to deal with modern religious experience (*A Clergyman's Daughter*), with the whole system of latter-day capitalism and its hostility to the intellectual and the artist (*Keep the Aspidistra Flying*), the artificiality and collapse of human values in every sphere from the private family to international anarchy (*Coming up for Air*), the disintegration of democracy and the rise of the totalitarian state (*Animal Farm*), and the future condition of the world which would result from all these tendencies (*Nineteen Eighty-Four*). What makes Orwell so distinctively a "contemporary" is not, therefore, the limited scope of his interest or literary ambitions, nor the manner of its treatment, but the presuppositions which lie behind it. It is worth while to consider in some detail the nature of these.

One of the most important things which Orwell did was to expose the connection between language and behaviour. He made a serious attempt to relate what a person says to how he says it; to distinguish between what is spoken and what is being thought, intended, and felt. In other words, there lies behind the political objectives a clearly discernible philosophical presupposition. But Orwell's analysis is based on a certain view of language, which is not without its difficulties. Language, he says, is "an instrument which we shape for our own purposes" rather than an autonomous natural growth. ("Politics and the English Language", *Collected Essays*, 337.) This concept is what lies behind his belief that, by exposing the faults of modern political language, he could do something towards political regeneration. Clarifying expression would make it more difficult to get away with dishonest or foolish thoughts. But unfortunately, Orwell's view of language, clearly stated in "Politics and the English Language", is based upon two almost contradictory ideas. The first ("secular") idea is that words are merely the garment of thought—something selected from a range of possible choices, like an overcoat in an outfitter's shop. It is most fully stated thus:

> When you think of a concrete object, you think wordlessly, and then, if you want to describe the thing you have been visualising you probably hunt about till you find the exact words that seem to fit it. When you think of something abstract you are more inclined

to use words from the start, and unless you make a conscious effort to prevent it, the existing dialect will come rushing in and do the job for you, at the expense of blurring or even changing your meaning. Probably it is better to put off using words as long as possible and get one's meaning as clear as one can through pictures or sensations. Afterwards one can choose—not simply *accept*—the phrases that will best cover the meaning.

The second idea manifests itself in Orwell's belief that to restrict the range of linguistic choice is to restrict the range of possible thoughts: and this is the basis of the theory of "Newspeak" in *Nineteen Eighty-Four*. What is implied by such a procedure is precisely an *inextricable* connection between thought and language— something approaching Marx's view that "language *is* practical consciousness". To tamper with the one is necessarily to affect the possible range of the other.[1]

The real trouble with Orwell's theory is the supposition that the likeness between objects is purely a property of the objects, and is perceivable without any conceptual or linguistic apparatus. With "concrete"

[1] An interesting illustration of the inadequacy of Orwell's first view of language is to be found in Chapter 12 of *Homage to Catalonia*, where he is describing the experience of being shot. "Roughly speaking, it was the sensation of being *at the centre* of an explosion. There seemed to be a loud bang and a blinding flash of light all round me, and I felt a tremendous shock—no pain, only a violent shock, such as you get from an electric terminal: with a sense of utter weakness, a feeling of being stricken and shrivelled up to nothing." What is most noticeable here is the fact that Orwell cannot, in practice, speak in terms of pure sensations at all. He has to use analogies. For there is no sensation definable as *the* sensation of being at the centre of an explosion, no mental picture which could be generally referred to as

objects, especially, we can have a clear and distinct idea of them through bare sense-perception, and it is this fact which makes them so reliable as guarantors of objective truth. They will not deceive us into thinking they are like one kind of thing when in fact they are like another. Behind Orwell's theory of language is the idea that what is "meant" when a person uses a certain form of words is already *present somewhere* in his mind before he gives it expression. But what distinguishes his position, and gives it strength, is the fact that he recognises that it is open to grave perils. His use of the "concrete object", and its visualisability, as a shield against possible deception, is designed to guard us against the dangers.

The idea that one can guard against a deceptive theory by visualising how it might work is one that Wittgenstein used. To understand the relation between thought and expression, he wrote,

> It is useful to consider the relation in which the solutions of mathematical problems stand to the context and ground of their formulation—[for example,] the concept "trisection of the angle with ruler and compasses" when people are trying to do it, and, on the other hand, when it has been proved that there is no such thing. [*Investigations*, 334.]

---

the picture of a man being shrivelled up—let alone shrivelled up to nothing! Orwell has not, as his theory would suggest, described what he visualised when thinking of the sensations involved in the (very concrete) experience of being shot. He has merely perceived analogies and chosen those which seem most apt. Describing *is* just choosing the best analogies. Writing is not a kind of drawing in words. It is saying what the object is like.

If you try to form a picture, or to think out in the concrete, the process of trisection, you soon realise its impossibility: but merely to entertain the idea seems somehow plausible. Orwell's mistake, of course, is to think that, because the act of "visualisation" is what shows its impossibility most clearly, this is what ultimately makes the trisection impossible: that is, that only if I can see the object concretely can I have an absolute guarantee against being deceived. But many purely abstract examples are just as easy to deal with. The contradictoriness of putting together the propositions in the following argument for God's existence:

Everything is caused by something else:
Therefore, there is something which causes everything else,

is just as easy to spot as visualising the trisection of an angle.

An opposite situation is also possible: namely, to be deceived even by the simplest and most direct uses of concrete visualisable objects. In the essay "Politics and the English Language", Orwell diagnoses the corruption of political language as consisting in vagueness, long-windedness, dead metaphor, pretentiousness, and so on. But in *Animal Farm*, where politico-linguistic corruption is actually practised, these are not the most apparent faults. For example, when the pigs break the seventh commandment by sleeping in beds, Squealer explains their behaviour by twisting the very simplest word:

You did not suppose, surely, that there was ever a ruling against *beds*? A bed merely means a place to sleep in. A pile of straw is a bed, properly regarded.

By redefining the word "bed" in this way, Squealer successfully deceives his friends by obliterating a perfectly simple, "visualisable" distinction.

But how can this purely linguistic device affect the world of concrete objects? After all, the very notion of analogy makes ambiguity possible, by extending meanings. It is useless, despite the theory which Squealer's plainly monstrous ingenuity is supposed to vindicate, to hope for a final guarantee against corrupt thought in a precise correlation or tabulation of word against concept. And Orwell knew this. That hope was abolished for ever by the invention of Newspeak. In Newspeak, "Every concept will be expressed by exactly one word." And this very fact constitutes the basis of the linguistic corruption practised in *Nineteen Eighty-Four*.

Orwell imagines all languages as consisting of words which function as the names of objects, and which are learned by some process of ostensive definition. On such a theory, *bed* is a symbol which "stands for" (i.e., names) that class of objects which consist of a spring and mattress supported by four legs. As long as this is remembered, the theory goes on to say, it is impossible to be taken in by Squealer's swindle, because it will be obvious that merely being "a place to sleep in" is not a sufficient criterion for labelling an object "bed".

Obviously this theory of language is based on the Lockeian notion that we learn a word like "bed" by seeing lots of beds and—by systematically not attending to their individual colours, shapes, sizes, and so on— come to notice some common element shared by all of them, possession of which is indicated by calling them each a "bed". We have already seen that this is an incoherent theory. And even if it had any plausibility for "bed", it has none for a word like "science". Thus, in the

C vocabulary of Newspeak there was no word for "science", only words for its particular branches. Hence, science "as a habit of mind, or a method of thought" was abolished, and any possibility of believing that scientific verification could establish the truth about external reality was destroyed. "Science" is now a collective *name* for various particular examples of concrete activity, and as such it is quite unable to provide any basis for the discussion of scientific principles. The very logic of its use has been altered.[1] Unfortunately, Orwell does not see the incoherence of the theory behind this transformation. But he is well aware of its political implications. He sees that a word like "fascism", for instance, is used by unscrupulous people as a kind of collective name for a miscellaneous range of items—say, rubber truncheons, the goose-step, extermination of Jews, Spanish bishops, the Gothic alphabet, autobahns —in order to prevent people from thinking coherently about fascism, and hence opposing it. At the end of "Politics and the English Language" he remarks appositely that

> Stuart Chase and others have come near to claiming that all abstract words are meaningless, and have used this as a pretext for a kind of political quietism. Since you don't know what Fascism is, how can you struggle against Fascism?

It is not surprising to find that it is part of the theory of Newspeak, and especially of its B vocabulary, to

[1] Compare the following from a report on a visit to China (*The Guardian*, 25 May 1961): "We once began a conversation with: 'Suppose a person wishes to change his job . . .' and got the answer: 'Which man ? in what factory ?' There is in fact no answer to anything not now, here, and expedient."

substitute collective names for genuine political and moral concepts. Thus "all words grouping themselves round the concepts of liberty and equality, for instance, were contained in the single word "crimethink". (*Nineteen Eighty-Four.*) The process behind this development is not one of increasing vagueness or greater abstraction: it entails a profound, logical alteration. One cannot ask, What is crimethink?, in the way that one can ask, What is science?—for, unlike "science", which is a method of thought, "crimethink" can cover any thought whatever which the Party wishes to *name*.

It follows from all this that the guarantee of our knowledge of objective reality lies—as I have suggested already in Chapter 2, Section C—in the preservation of a sound logic, not in the experience of "bare sensation" of external objects, even if such an experience were possible. For instance, it is no answer to the suggestion that Negroes or Jews are not really fully human, just to say: Look at them more closely and you will see that they are. It also depends on what kind of objects you are prepared to call "men", and what exactly you mean to imply by this "calling". By unanimously refusing to *call* Negroes "men", we do not stop them from being men; whereas unanimously refusing to call Jones "Jones" is tantamount to his not being Jones. The upshot of Orwell's way of thinking is the idea that by not calling a person anything, his existence can be cancelled; he is simply an *unperson*.

It is because he inherited an incoherent epistemology that Orwell is inconsistent in his account of general terms. Sometimes he seems to think of the word "man" as a kind of collective name. Thus in a review of De Basily's *Russia under Soviet Rule*, he says that

in the past every tyranny was sooner or later over-
thrown ... because of human nature, which as a
matter of course desired liberty. But we cannot be at
all certain that "human nature" is constant. It may be
just as possible to produce a breed of men who do
not wish for liberty, as it is to produce a breed of
hornless cows.[1]

But if it is an *essential* characteristic of human nature
to want liberty, and yet this feature disappears, then the
individuals who come under the concept of human
nature will be changed. No amount of *calling* them
human will make them to be human any longer. This
point is relevant to the very conception of *Nineteen
Eighty-Four*: "Power is in tearing human minds to pieces
and putting them together again in shapes of your own
choosing".

This power is manifested in the Party's absolute
control of the objective world and of the past. These
are the very context in which personality is developed.
Cut off completely from them, a being cannot properly
be conceived of as a person, for the encounter with
reality, and the use of memory, are part of the basis for
personal identity. If control over persons is the Party's
aim, then to reduce its victims to abject automata is to
defeat its own object, for it means abolishing the very
material which it seeks to manipulate.

In *Nineteen Eighty-Four* Orwell's pessimism is so
fundamental that it ends up in logical contradiction; but
in an earlier work ("Looking Back on the Spanish War",
Collected Essays) he does seem to imply that to be
human at all depends on being able to fasten on to

[1] Quoted in John Atkins, *George Orwell*, 254.

certain indubitable objective facts. In past disagree-
ments, he says,

> ... there would still be that body of, as it were,
> neutral fact on which neither would seriously chal-
> lenge the other. It is just this common basis of
> agreement, with its implication that human beings
> are all one species of animal, that totalitarianism
> destroys. [*Collected Essays*, 197.]

But the question here arises, whether, by abolishing
verbal agreement among people, it is possible to destroy
the notion of the one human species; or whether the
notion of a species is based, not upon agreement about
what to call certain kinds of thing, but upon the very
conditions which make the use of language possible at
all. This is a question to which Orwell never seems to
give a satisfactory reply. Thus, there is no indication
how the work of the editors of the Newspeak dictionary
is to be applied to the actual use of words by people at
large. I am not here thinking of the merely administra-
tive problem of how the Thought Police actually control
talking, but the logical problem of how a word-list, like
the Newspeak dictionary, is related to a language-game.
Orwell's theory seems to be that a language simply
consists of its own vocabulary, plus a set of gram-
marian's rules—about inflections, irregular formations,
and so on—which can be varied without reference to
the vocabulary. (See p. 23 above.) Rules, in the
sense of a "language game" with rules, do not exist in
the conception of Newspeak. This is why Orwell thinks
it is possible to reduce the consciousness of people by
restricting their vocabulary: "Every year, fewer and
fewer words, and the range of consciousness always a
little smaller." (*Nineteen Eighty-Four*, 45.) But isn't

this like preventing people from being *able* to play chess just by taking the pieces away? Surely, as long as I have learned the rules of chess (including, of course, the appearance of the pieces—for this is part of the rules), it should be possible for me to play chess 'in my head" with an opponent similarly equipped, provided my intelligence and my memory are good enough? I am not prevented from thinking certain thoughts by not having the vocabulary, but by not having mastery any longer of the rules—including the rules by which words of certain shapes function in the language-game in the way that they do. In fact, *vocabulary consists of these rules*. Hence, the only way to reduce people's consciousness is to make them unable to understand certain rules, or unable to remember them: that is, to make them less *intelligent*. Consider Wittgenstein's example of a tribe who

> measure lengths of a field by striding along and counting the steps. If different results are obtained for the same fields, they think nothing of it! ... The notion of more accurate measurement does not enter into their lives, and so the notion of the *real* length does not either.[1]

It does not follow from this example that, once they have grasped the idea of *real* length, they can be compelled to "not-be-able-to-grasp-it" once more, simply by abolishing the phrase "real length" and destroying all the tape-measures. An intellectual *capacity* cannot be abolished in this way. To attain the objective of Newspeak entails compelling people to forget the rules of

[1] From notes taken at Wittgenstein's lectures, quoted by Norman Malcolm, *Ludwig Wittgenstein: A Memoir*, London 1948, 48.

the language-game, and not to be able to remember them afterwards. But this involves a deliberate personal act of forgetting. Does that make sense? It might have been easy for the Proles to forget how to use abstract or difficult concepts; but with the intelligentsia cooperation in forgetting was required. *Crimestop* "includes the power of not grasping analogies, of failing to perceive logical errors..." (*Nineteen Eighty-Four*, 189.) But not having the power to grasp analogies is different from having the power to not-grasp them. Exercising the power of not-grasping an analogy, or not-remembering a rule, or not-spotting a fallacy, is a contradictory supposition; for it entails having a grasp of what it is you are required not to grasp; otherwise how could you decide not to do it?

What lies at the root of this puzzle is a notion of logical contradiction. Orwell admits there are contradictions in *Ingsoc*. (*Nineteen Eighty-Four*, 169.) Doublethink is the capacity to accept two contradictory beliefs simultaneously and wholeheartedly. But what did Orwell think a contradiction was? Was it something which could not *be* (like the proof of the trisection of an angle)? Or was it a limitation in the human mind, which could be removed by conditioning? On the first alternative, all his efforts to expose the dangers of being able to control thought through manipulating language and using doublethink, were a waste of time. They were based on something which he knew could not happen. But if he accepted the second, epistemological interpretation, then it is relevant to consider his account of how we can be certain of truths about external objects, about the past, and about our own personalities.

For most of the time, Orwell was a philosophising secularist, who insisted that a prelinguistic experience of undifferentiated sensations gives an immediate knowledge of how things are, and so provides the basis of all certainties. The "evidence of the senses" is the final, indubitable guarantor of reality. This position is not consistently maintained, of course, and the idea of attacking reality through attacking language is a kind of refutation of it. But when Winston Smith, in his extremity of confusion, takes refuge in the "concrete evidence" of the photograph of the conspirators, and later in the glass paperweight (*Nineteen Eighty-Four*, 66, 80, 119, and 126), he is surely underwriting Orwell's considered view. "If the past survives anywhere", he says to Julia, "it's in a few solid objects with no words attached to them, like that lump of glass there." It is language alone which provides the Party with its power to corrupt. Get rid of that and you are free. When Winston buys the paperweight, which acts as a symbol of objective truth, he is attracted by its apparent uselessness: but "he could guess that it must once have been used as a paperweight". (*Nineteen Eighty-Four*, 80). Later Julia asks him what it is, and he replies: "I don't think it was ever put to any use. That's what I like about it. It's a little chunk of history they've forgotten to alter." (*Nineteen Eighty-Four*, 119.) Thus, by a piece of half-conscious lying (for he had already been able to guess its use) Winston makes the paperweight a symbol of his certainty about the past, and about his own personal memories. But it is only because he saw it in the first place as being a thing having some possible use—that is, as being a thing of a certain *kind*—that he could conceive of it as being an historical relic. The paperweight's uselessness is significant in the way that any work of art is useless: to be useless is, so to speak, its use. But to see things within a conceptual framework such as this is to see them "with words attached to them": if I did not know the rules for using words like "useless" or "art", I could not form the concept of this object's uselessness at all. There is, after all, no refuge from language, either for the defenders of decency, or for the Thought Police and the Party. They necessarily have language in common—something in common which implies that they are members of the one human species. In trying to destroy this idea they make its truth more obvious.

It is because of his secular empiricist presuppositions —because he thinks he can look upon the objective world as wholly *other*, and himself as a kind of omnipresent camera recording ever more accurately what is presented to him from outside—that Orwell is able to regard *creative* writing as wholly separate from the world of action. During the most vivid moments of recording impressions the creative writer is most truly himself, standing aside as the "saner self" from the dirty work of politics, seeing and understanding it all, but remaining uninvolved.[1] Orwell was not merely the victim of a morbid temperament, but of a deep philosophical dissociation between the observer and the world, between language and thought. This is what makes him such a relevant secularist writer. Orwell's life of exile is an exile from the world of the paperweight and the words which are inevitably attached to it.

This philosophical dualism is not only responsible for Orwell's despair of community; it is also responsible for his rejection of orthodoxies. Ideally, an orthodoxy is simply a reflection of the attempt by man to found his communal living upon a community of thinking—a sharing of thoughts as well as of goods. The opposite of

[1] "Writers and Leviathan," *Collected Essays*, 434.

orthodoxy ought to be solipsism. But for Orwell, the opposite of orthodoxy is common sense—"the heresy of heresies" (*Nineteen Eighty-Four*, 80.) Now words are the instruments of orthodoxy, being the repositories of doctrine. Therefore, "common sense" entails the separation of word from thing. Things stand over against words. They are the foundation and test of truth which can keep us free.

But just as Orwell sees the need to engage in the world's activity, dirty though that activity is, so also he sees that there is a need for orthodoxy as well as for common sense. For only orthodoxy can provide an adequate basis for morality. Of course it is true that a moral attitude which flies in the face of factual evidence is evil. The wickedness of Mr MacGregor, in *Burmese Days*, when confronted by the anonymous slanders against Dr Veraswami, consists in his not looking at the evidence, and in trying to decide *a priori* whether the doctor is the *kind* of man to harbour seditious thoughts. The wickedness of Old Major, in putting to the vote the question, "Are rats comrades?", is that whether a person is a friend or an enemy is a question of his actions and intentions, for which there is evidence to be considered. But Orwell admits morality cannot be constructed simply on evidence—a moral decision is not a matter of assessing the consequences, and assessing the probabilities of this or that result—it is a matter of being under an imperious obligation which cannot be challenged. Moral debate consists in trying to discover where one's obligation lies, not in discussing whether, having found it, one should follow it. One must follow the dictates of conscience, and conscience is often clear and unambiguous, and carries its own authority within itself. Thus Gordon Comstock in *Keep the Aspidistra*

Flying decides to return to the advertising agency, because "when the problem appeared it had brought its solution with it; all his hesitation had been a kind of make believe. He felt as though some outside force were pushing him." (279.) This is a classic example of a moral decision, in Orwell's terms. What makes it so hard to swallow, in this particular case, is that it involves the denial of the whole movement of protest against the capitalist racket which Gordon's own principles entailed. That is to say, for Orwell there can be situations where to do the morally correct thing is, at the same time, to deny the most fundamental needs of one's being. It is this belief in the inconsistency of the human predicament that lies at the basis of Orwell's pessimism. But, unlike many secularists, he refused to brush aside the concept of an absolute morality. For he recognised that

In a society where there is no law, and in theory no compulsion, the only arbiter of behaviour is public opinion. But public opinion, because of the tremendous urge to conformity in gregarious animals, is less tolerant than any system of law. When human beings are governed by "Thou shalt not" the individual can practise a certain amount of eccentricity: when they are supposedly governed by "love" or "reason" he is under continuous pressure to behave in exactly the same way as everyone else. *Hence the unanimity of the Houyhnhms on all subjects.* ["Politics versus Literature", *Collected Essays*, 389.]

But while he sees the need for an absolute moral law (of a negative kind of course—moral *law* for him consists only of prohibitions), he also thinks that to follow it unswervingly could lead to the denial of a person's fundamental needs. There is a contradiction, and absurdity, about the moral universe of man, which cannot be resolved.[1]

But what is so interesting about Orwell is that he did not accept this conclusion without a protest. He did not embrace this absurd world and try to live in it, or make a cult of it, or to affirm its validity in art. On the contrary, he saw that it was an insult to man that must be resisted even though he acknowledged it to be irresistible. There must be an heroic, stoic defiance of this absurd world. For Orwell himself, this defiance consisted largely in a nostalgic retreat to the past, and to the values of a working class which could make sense of the absurdity simply by not noticing it was there (the Proles). But there was also, until the end, an attempt at a rational confrontation as well. The philosophy of the glass paperweight was a kind of last fling in the name of reason, against a contradictory world.

It may seem that I have made too much of Orwell's philosophical presuppositions, and too little of his practical attitudes. But I do not think that the two can be separated. Orwell lived out his conscious beliefs to a remarkable depth, and he recorded the results with an exceptional candour. If we wish to suggest a solution to the absurdity, and despair, to which both his beliefs and his personal experience led him in the end, we can only do so by trying first to understand exactly where the roots of his position lay. The difficulty for Orwell was that he did not discover a philosophy of human community which could remain secure against the erosion of political disillusionment. Emotionally and morally, Orwell remained a socialist, committed to the large ideals of brotherhood and equality. But his philosophy was

[1] See my article "Charity and Commitment", *Slant* 8, vol. 2, no. 1 (February–March 1966), 3–9.

inadequate to secure these ideals. He tried to live in a secularist world, where many others merely adopted its principles academically and remained where they were. The breakdown which resulted from this attempt was not just due to Orwell's own temperamental isolation; it was also due to his honesty in seeing the limitations of his position without being able to transcend them.

Orwell is representative of many people in wanting to preserve the ethic of Christianity while discarding the theology. He is typical, furthermore, in taking that theology to be radically dualistic. While he admits that it is the decay in the belief in personal immortality which lies at the root of all our modern problems,[1] it is clear from his whole position that for him immortality would be the ideal of Charlotte Brontë's Helen Burns; an escape from life. On these terms, it would clearly be immoral to try to recover it. Far better to have the "materialism" of the ordinary working man. This suggests once more that, as in the case of Dickens and George Eliot, the very terms in which the argument is being conducted are inadequate. Before personal immortality can be regarded as a worthwhile hope, the secular dualism and its life-denying emphasis must be overcome. It is here that, today, the temptation to allegory in the novel is strongest. This temptation suggests that perhaps we can show the relevance of an alternative vision of human destiny by the creation of an allegorical framework in which a different set of terms for the argument can be worked out. If the "contemporary" trend in literature has failed to release itself from the secular presuppositions which have hampered it, because it has concerned itself too narrowly with the

[1] See "Looking back on the Spanish War", *Collected Essays*, 206.

immediacies of everyday life, perhaps a return to an older tradition can provide the basis for a renewal in our way of describing that life. In England many hopes for such a return to allegory have been placed upon the works of William Golding. His novels will perhaps form an instructive contrast to those of Orwell from this point of view.

E. William Golding

It is generally agreed that William Golding is the most important allegorist among English novelists writing today. But beyond this agreed judgement it is difficult to find any definite consensus about how his novels should be read. This is not just because of a certain wilful obscurity in his manner of presenting his themes —a kind of sophisticated puzzle-setting which suggests sometimes that the reader is supposed to approach a story with the attitude of one trying to answer a problem in a highbrow weekly paper. It is also because of the problematic character of modern allegory itself. What is the relation of such allegory to the reality it is speaking to us about? We are no longer able to appeal, as in the days of Chaucer or Bunyan, to a widely acknowledged set of norms by which the allegorist can work. The allegorist today has to work without the framework of conventions, or the body of agreed concepts, which form the interpretative channel by which (say) Bunyan's message came over to his readers. For Bunyan, the presence of this system of agreed conventions—the notion of life as a journey, the parabolic manner of presenting moral problems inherited from the medieval preachers, the stock of traditional symbols and theological concepts—made it possible for him to step out of the light, himself, and let the allegory shine for itself. He did not have to intrude, because the framework existed independently of him, and he did not have to be his own guide to the people and places he created. But the modern allegorist has no such advantage. He has to be both the creator of his world and the guide to its history and its pattern of meanings. Golding, of course, knows and takes advantage of this. By deliberately writing for a fairly highly literate public, he can make his patterns in an oblique way, by referring us to snatches of Shakespeare, or Homer, or the bible. He expects us to understand, from a few disjointed remarks, without too much direct help, a sketch of a prisoner-of-war camp, or a naval operation, or the building of Salisbury Cathedral. But, effective though it is, this is only an indirect method of dropping hints and clues, and leaving us to pick them up instead of writing them out in full. It is still not the objective framework which the allegorist of an earlier age had at his disposal. It is simply making use of the assumption that what Golding has read will also have been read by his audience. It is not a living tradition that can be taken for granted.

It is partly this necessary reliance upon a second-hand tradition which causes Golding's work to exemplify, despite its extraordinary exactitude of detailed observation, that tendency towards the "attenuation of reality" which Lukács notes in modernism. (Golding's scenarios and descriptions are not easy to "see" as wholes.) For not only does any allegory, as a form, entail that the meaning of a particular object within the imposed pattern of the whole work is more important than its existence simply in and for itself, but in modern conditions this meaning can only reveal itself by being made part of a *literary* pattern which is at one remove from the world. It is not the contrived character of Golding's novels, as such, that is their limiting feature; for allegory is always a matter of contrivance. It is that they are contrivances invented in a world which has lost the sense of the formality and objectivity of art, and which therefore cannot support, without difficulty, the scaffolding of convention which they need. In this world, imbued as it is with the secularist presuppositions, and lacking the sense of sacramentality, minute descriptions of objects are liable to be taken in a *naturalistic* way. To try to give them an immanent expressiveness, and to make them part of a pattern of symbols, will necessarily seem to involve the author in a retreat from their full reality as things. Golding's descriptions, for all their minute observed detail, are not easy to "see".

That the framework for allegory no longer exists, and has to be rediscovered by each individual, is in effect stated by Golding in *Free Fall*. Indeed, this may be said to be the basic preoccupation of that novel. For allegory rests upon the understanding that there is an inner connection, or interpenetration between two worlds —the world of mere physical causality, or "matter in motion" (to use a Marxist phrase) on the one hand, and the world of personal action, of consciousness in motion, on the other. In this sense, of course, allegory is a sophisticated and intellectualist mode of expression, resting as it does upon a separation of what is, in primordial experience, a unity. *Free Fall* is about one person's attempt to return, at a higher level of understanding, to the recognition of the primordial unity of personal experience. Sammy Mountjoy, at the very end of the story, as he recalls what he saw after having been released from the "cell" which turns out to have been nothing but a broom-cupboard, begins to understand, dimly, what this unity is like. The very fact that a mere cupboard, with a damp floorcloth in the middle of the floor, could have given him such an understanding of his own inner nature that it caused him to see the whole world in a new light—a renewal of the whole process of perception—suggests to him the faint beginnings of the new understanding which he is seeking. (He seeks for the moment when he lost his inner freedom, only because he realises that until he has got back to that point, he cannot be remade, in a new dimension of freedom.) But until he remembers that moment, in the context of all his other experiences, he remains incapable of understanding his life except in terms of two worlds which cannot be united.

All day long the trains run on rails. Eclipses are predictable. Penicillin cures pneumonia and the atom splits to order. All day long, year in, year out, the daylight explanation drives out the mystery and reveals a reality usable, understandable and detached. The scalpel and the microscope fail, the oscilloscope moves closer to behaviour. The gorgeous dance is self-contained, then; does not need the music which, in my mad moments I have heard. Nick's universe is real. [Nick is the schoolmaster scientist who presents, in the novel, the secular view of the world. But over against Nick's world of material regularity and statistical probability is to be poised the world of human action.]

All day long action is weighed in the balance and found not opportune nor fortunate nor ill-advised, but good or evil. For this mode which we must call the spirit breathes through the universe and does not touch it; touches only the dark things, held prisoner, incommunicado, touches, judges, sentences and passes on. . . . [This is the world of Miss Pringle, the embodiment of the religious vision, of the reality of miracles as revelations of the power of God in the world. For Sammy,] both worlds are real. There is no bridge. [*Free Fall*, 252f.][1]

The bridge can only be of a sacramental kind. That is to say, it must consist in the recognition of the immanent symbolism of the objects which surround and support man. Golding attempts to render this immanent meaningfulness in Sammy's experience as he begins after his escape to see the world in a sacramental light. (Chapter 10.) But the sacramentality of things implies a natural pattern of meanings, within which every element has its place, and *Free Fall* fails to establish such a pattern. For the novel is too much involved with the conscious attempt to do so. Sammy's quest is not, really, the centre of interest. It is the pattern which Golding, in telling the story of his quest, makes *for us* that is the true object of the novel. Behind Sammy's attempt to see the pattern for himself, we can see another pattern which Golding himself is creating for our benefit. We know the end towards which he is inexorably pushing Sammy's apparently free exercise of his memory. So Sammy's almost mystical experience (mystical in Wittgenstein's sense, at any rate) consists too obviously of an organised system of planted symbols; fragments of imagery or phraseology picked up from other places in the book, in order to create the pattern which Sammy is trying to discern. We are being tricked into thinking we are watching Sammy freely putting his life together

[1] See also Ian Gregor and M. Kinkead-Weakes, in *Twentieth Century* (February 1960).

in a new way, when we know already that it is just a matter of following the clues that have been planted.

But if *Free Fall* fails because it tries, too directly, to state the sacramentality of the material world—the fiction attempts to become reality—the earlier novels succeed to a far greater degree because they are more obviously self-enclosed. They do not step so decisively out of their own frames. The very abruptness with which each of them starts is evidence of this. We are shot straightway into the story, without any explanation of how the fictional world is to be related to reality.

> The boy with fair hair lowered himself down the last few feet of rock and began to pick his way towards the lagoon . . . [*Lord of the Flies*]. Lok was running as fast as he could. His head was down and he carried his thorn bush horizontally . . . [*The Inheritors*]. He was struggling in every direction, he was the centre of the writhing and kicking knot of his own body . . . [*Pincher Martin*].

In each case, we are told nothing of the time or the place at the outset. We are pitched immediately into action, and the world in which it is taking place only emerges slowly from this context of action. This world usually ends as abruptly as it begins. In *Lord of the Flies*, the social world of the boys is suddenly cut off in mid-career by the totally unexpected, and even arbitrary, appearance of the naval officer. This arbitrariness is not a sign of authorial inefficiency; it is quite deliberate. Just as we step instantly into the world of the novel, so also we step equally immediately out of it. The same is true of the final line of *Pincher Martin*, which, in the midst of a "realistic" last scene which seems to put the action of the novel into a context, pitches us back to the beginning by making us realise that the whole story is concerned with the moment of Martin's death. The self-enclosed character of these earlier allegories enables Golding to suggest the sacramentality which he fails adequately to state in *Free Fall*. But within the limits of the allegorical setting, he does not have to distinguish meanings from objective appearances at all. For in allegory objective appearances merge more and more into meanings, until they are swallowed up altogether. Hence the attenuation of reality towards which allegory necessarily moves.

In Golding's work this progress towards the swallowing up of appearances into meanings is intensified from one novel to the next by a corresponding progress into isolation from the social world, and the attenuation of other human presences. For it is in the world of human communication that objects are shared, and come to possess an agreed, objective reality. Where this communication is absent, objects become more and more the mirror of the individual's purposes and projects as he confronts them in his isolation. In *Lord of the Flies*, there is still a solid material world which is shared by the boys, at least in the beginning. They have a dialogue with objects because they have dialogue with each other. But in *The Inheritors*, where such dialogue is still in the future (as far as the Neanderthal "people" are concerned), and still more in *Pincher Martin*, when the dialogue is for ever past and done with, objects as such tend to disappear into a world of subjectivity. Thus the discovery, which Simon makes in *Lord of the Flies*, that the beast is not the thing on the mountain top— *that* is just an airman's corpse—but is in "us", depends for its validity upon the distinction between human subjectivity and the outer world. True, it is for this discovery that Simon is killed, and to this extent the story is that of a progression into pure subjectivity. And Ralph has increasingly frequent moments of uncertainty, when a curtain comes down in his mind and blots out the distinctions which give him his roots in objectivity. Piggy, the representative of the secular view which denies everything except the agreed observable facts of sense-experience, has to die. The last-minute rescue of Ralph is not an assertion that there is always an unassailable objectivity to be clung to even at the extremity of self-isolation. Golding does not try to cheat himself with an Orwellian reliance on the reality of some purely material object, or some colourless, purely descriptive language. The rescue is simply the ringing down of the curtain upon a drama, an announcement that here, for the time being, is the limit to which the author has chosen to explore the situation. Nevertheless it is true that, in *Lord of the Flies*, so long as there is a society in communication, there is also a world of objects to be recognised and shared. But the beginnings of a later Golding theme are discernible at the very end of Ralph's terror-stricken run from the "savages" who are out to kill him. The objects in the world around him begin to merge into mere subjective impressions. At the same time, his own body ceases to be just himself, and begins to assert itself as an object set apart.

A brown figure showed up at his right and fell away. They were all running, all crying out madly. He could hear them crashing in the undergrowth and on the left was the hot, bright thunder of the fire. He forgot his wounds, his hunger and thirst, and became fear; hopeless fear on flying feet, rushing through the forest towards the open beach. Spots jumped before his eyes and turned into red circles that expanded quickly till they passed out of sight. Below him, someone's legs were getting tired and the desperate ululation advanced like a jagged fringe of menace and was almost overhead. [*Lord of the Flies*, Chapter 12.]

In Golding's works, the subjectivisation of the world corresponds to a retreat into the interior of the purely intellectual being, and hence to a rejection of the body. This becomes simply an object, detached from consciousness. That, for Golding, is the limit of subjectivity. The further one goes along that path, the more objective one's own physical being becomes. The body refuses to acknowledge the tendency which the intellect is following. It is not anything outside, in some quite detached world of external objects, which marks the limit of subjectivisation: it is the very bodiliness of our own nature. But the converse is also true; namely that it is a condition of my recognising the exteriority of the world that I should not be able to think of my bodiliness as something apart from myself. Intellectualism, which moves inevitably towards total subjectivity, is necessarily an inadequate mode of understanding because it cannot accommodate this fact: that this spatial body which I am, is not an object among objects.

In every one of Golding's novels there is a movement towards a sliding apart of the intellectual consciousness from the physical body. Each becomes an object for the other. I have already quoted the first example of this, in *Lord of the Flies*. In *The Inheritors*, the slow extinction of the Neanderthalers is described through the extinction of Lok's capacity to communicate with his companions. Finally he is reduced to a purely animal level. The spark of self-consciousness which their primitive language had given to "the people" is blotted out. But as this happens, Lok himself becomes an object. At the end, he is simply part of a landscape seen by somebody else. He cannot even conceive himself as an object because he has ceased to be able to exercise the concept of "self". The inner division which is entailed by the very fact of self-consciousness has disappeared. Lok has gone beyond bereavement and grief, and has become an undivided brute. Once this has happened, the new race know that they are safe.

In *Pincher Martin*, this process is much more obvious. It is indeed at the very centre of the novel. Like Krook and Smallweed in *Bleak House*, the damned man in Golding's book, who has used people as though they were merely objects, and who dares not trust them as people, is himself reduced to an object in a world of deserted objects. There is no refuge for him in any form of private self-consciousness. He can no longer act a part, for there is no audience. He can no longer speak, for his words do not carry beyond his own mouth. He cannot even escape by going mad, for madness is a kind of transcendence of the world, and he is being reduced to the state of an object in a world of objects. But neither can he escape by becoming an animal, seeking an end of suffering by obliterating the intellect and the will which are the substance of self-consciousness: for unlike Lok he is ineradicably a man, and cannot shed his nature. At each stage of his progress, the isolation of his indivisible consciousness increases; and at the same time the objectivity of his body rises up more and more vividly to torment this consciousness which cannot be rid of it. There is an initial struggle, in which

> ... the man lay suspended behind the whole commotion, detached from his jerking body, [so that] there was a kind of truce, observation of the body. There was no face but a snarl. [*Pincher Martin*, 8.]

Later he manages, as he clambers on to the safety of the rock, to reintegrate himself by rediscovering language, and hence the concept of himself and of the world as over against him.

> He had a valuable thought, not because it was of immediate physical value but because it gave him back a bit of his personality. He made words to utter this thought, though they did not pass the barrier of his teeth.
> "I should be about as heavy as this on Jupiter."
> At once he was master ... [27.]

But the mastery does not last long. Soon the body re-asserts itself as a separate entity, to be seen as just another item among the details which the "centre" sees from inside its own field of vision. He mistakes his hands for lobsters, and is frightened by them [131.] He becomes conscious of the circle of his face as a kind of window from which he peers at the world. [139.] He gives himself an enema, and because it works triumphantly proclaims: "Everything is predictable." [166.] Finally he becomes nothing but a perceiving "centre" and a pair of grasping claws around which the "black lightning" plays "in a compassion that was timeless and without mercy".

In *Free Fall*, a similar process takes place in the dark cupboard which is the place where Sammy finds out about himself. But here the point is made more specifically with regard to the body as a sexual instrument, and the evil consequences of using it simply as such. But in this case there is a release, for Sammy is still capable of an act of will and self-abnegation, and the cupboard door is opened. And as he comes out into the open once again he sees the world transfigured, transparent to its own significance. The huts of the camp

> ... shone with the innocent light of their own created nature. I understood them perfectly, boxes of thin wood as they were, and now transparent, letting be seen inside their quota of sceptred kings. [*Free Fall*, 186.]

The world is now meaningful because it exists in its own setting, not as something to be used or exploited (and so made wholly objective), but as something to be entered into—capable of a dialogue with the man who participates in it.

Finally, in *The Spire*, the distinction between the worlds of "statistical probability" and of moral good and evil is no longer unambiguous. They can be taken apart, but they can be put together again. Jocelin's progress is that of one who has to be torn apart and separated into his constituent elements in order to be made anew, free now from his own deformities.[1] His sins entail that he must be taken to pieces if he is to be made whole again. True, we are not told clearly whether he has fully submitted, as a necessity of his being, and its urge to be

---

[1] Thou hast bound bones and veins in me, fastened me flesh.
And after it almost unmade, what with dread,
Thy doing: and dost thou touch me afresh ?
> G. Manley Hopkins, *Wreck of the Deutschland*,
> Part I, stanza I,

That passage from Hopkins might serve as an epigraph for the whole novel, which ends, like the quotation, with a question mark.

perfect, to the slow dissolution of the unity of his bodily nature. At the very moment of his triumph, when he believes he has saved the spire from falling by inserting the Nail into its very topmost point, he is struck down by a crippling pain. He falls, and as he does so,

> ... his angel put away the two wings from the cloven hoof and struck him from arse to the head with a whitehot flail. It filled his spine with sick fire and he shrieked because he could not bear it yet he knew he had to. [*The Spire*, 188.]

From that point onwards, he has to suffer the slow disintegration of body and spirit which his own realisation of his imperfection demands.

Golding's understanding of the commerce which human life must have with the external world is somewhat like that of Merleau-Ponty. For both of them, the work of the intellect as such is always to separate body from consciousness in an act of rational understanding which undermines the unity of our original experience. But for Golding, however necessary this process is for the development of the human race, it is also tragic. It is a fall from grace. The trend towards an ever greater separation of the conscious subject and its body as object is a trend towards moral and cultural disaster. Only by transcending it, and recovering the unity of experience at a higher level, is it possible to overcome the inadequacy, and indeed the evil, of the human world we know. But despite the virtuosity of his work, and the intuitive understanding of the problems that he raises, how far does Golding succeed in his enterprise? Is the enclosed world of allegory able, in his hands, to give us, living in the real world, the answer to the questions we want to ask? Is he able, finally, to over-come the despair which, in Orwell's hands, resulted from the bankruptcy of the secular philosophy?

I think that the answer must be, No. Granted the return to an explicitly social setting in the last two books, and the greater obliquity of the distinction drawn between the worlds of matter and spirit, of science and morality, there is still a problem raised by the very method Golding uses. It is that he is trying to use the concept of "perspective" in the novel to illustrate for us the "perspective" which exists in history. The process of unmaking and remaking which Golding's characters have to undergo, is not something that just "happens" in his fiction. It is also a reflection of the predicament we have to face in the real world. Its relevance is direct. Golding sees himself not just as a maker of fictions, but as a prophet.

> In my opinion . . . the novelist does not limit himself to reporting facts, but diagnoses them, and his voca-tion has the same value as that of the doctor. To those who are too ignorant or too lazy to know them-selves, I shall continue to say: "Look! Look! Look!"[1]

But the perspective which exists in the novel is governed, not by what is latent at the beginning, but rather by what it is directed towards at the end. In life we discern the pattern only after the events have passed into history; but in fiction the pattern determines what shall happen. As long as the pattern is understood and accepted as being only the pattern of a fictional world that has its own inner laws of development, and into which we enter by accepting for the moment the

[1] *New Left Review*, 29 (January–February 1965), 34f.

validity of those laws through a suspension of disbelief, we can make use of this world, seen as a whole, in the understanding of our own, quite different reality. For the fictional world is an imitation, or projection, of reality. But we can only understand this as long as we do not forget the projectional system which makes it possible. Because there is this projectional system, faith is needed in order to accept this projection and so enter into the fictional world. But allegory dispenses with the projectional system, for it is not an *imitation* of the world at all. It is an oblique *comment* on it. The objects in a true fictional world, like things in reality, have a dialogue with the characters, for they are both objects and carriers of meanings. But in allegory there are no objects, but only meanings disguising themselves in the shape of objects. Reality and truth is where they always have been—in the one, uniform world we know. Allegorical fiction does not challenge the omnipotence and hegemony of the real world. The difficulty about William Golding's work is that it looks so much like fiction that we are frequently taken in by it. The allegorical comment is so oblique, and the exactitude of descriptive detail so dense that we begin to believe in it as a fictional world. But then, suddenly, we discover we have been reading it in the wrong way, and that what we took for a fiction was but an allegory heavily and cunningly concealed. There is a kind of pleasure, of course, to be gained from understanding how the trick is done. But once it has been understood, what remains for our admiration is a divided thing. On the one hand, a marvellously imagined and intricately wrought poetic structure, and on the other an ingenious and searching comment on our real predicament. But what is lacking is that solid, fictional world which the descriptions would reveal to us, and which the interpretation would be concerned with, if Golding were a creator of true fictions and not the cunning allegorist which he in fact is.

The forgoing discussion of two very different modern novelists has been designed to show that the breakdown of the humanist position, and of the critical realism which was its artistic expression, is reflected in literature by the prevalent tendency towards contemporaneity on the one hand and towards allegory on the other. These two fundamental artistic options are, of course, paralleled in the choice which I mentioned at the beginning of this book—the choice, that is, between the secularisation and the modernisation of practical life. The "contemporary" writer, like the political and religious moderniser, is one who takes the empirical social world and its predicament as the starting-point, and who is concerned to analyse it in a specific and limited way. While his concern is analysis rather than practical reform, he is likely to have at the back of his mind a certain implicit, if not explicit social objective. This is obviously true of Orwell, but it is true in a more obscure way of (say) Snow or Sillitoe or John Braine. If, as I have written elsewhere,[1] the post-war literary protest (which is mostly couched in "contemporary" terms) reveals a decline of confidence in any possible alternative world in the name of which the protest is made, nevertheless there is also an element of protest against this decline itself, and the social and cultural conditions which make it inevitable. (The end of *Room at the Top* is perhaps the most obvious expression of this protest.)

[1] *Culture and Liturgy*, 107ff.

On the other hand the allegorist, like the seculariser, is concerned with the interior condition of the individual rather than with any specific area of practical life. His emphasis is on the raising of personal experience to the level of self-consciousness. But he is also aware of the mysterious depths of this consciousness and the inability of the humanist moral categories to account for it wholly. Because of the inadequacy of the categories, the allegorist is forced to turn to technical experiment in order to find adequate means for the expression of his vision, so that, unlike his "contemporary" colleagues, his work is marked by a preoccupation with technical problems, and problems of "style" in the widest sense of that term.

It is clear that while these two tendencies in the literary world reflect the contemporary breakdown, they do not offer any solution to it. That is not, in any case, the artist's role. But in the depth and clarity of their formulations, writers such as Orwell and Golding indicate to us the size and shape of the problem which must be tackled by those whose interest lies in that direction. It is to the discussion of this part of the argument that we must now turn.

4

Rediscovering the sacred

I have already said (pp. 13–19 above) that the philosophical positions marked out by Merleau-Ponty, Wittgenstein, and Marx exhibit resemblances and inner connections with the world-view of religious man as outlined by phenomenologists of religion. In this section I will try to trace these connections, by discussing the work of three writers who have made significant contributions to the phenomenology of religious experience: Lucien Lévy-Bruhl, Gerard van der Leeuw, and Mircea Eliade. The phenomenological analysis which emerges from their work has a remarkable inner coherence, as well as an interesting connection with the philosophical conclusions of the three writers mentioned above.

The main contribution of Lévy-Bruhl is the establishment of the concept of "participation" as being the basic or fundamental mode by which we come to an awareness of ourselves and of the world. Closely associated with this concept—which is surely related, at any rate implicitly, to the insights of Merleau-Ponty —is the insistence that all experience originates in "collective representations" rather than in a purely individual perceptual life. All our experience is socially conditioned long before individualisation becomes possible. But the particular significance of Lévy-Bruhl's work is that it is set in the framework of a "secular" philosophical tradition, and he therefore describes his findings in inadequate terms. Like many thinkers born and brought up in the secular tradition of thought, he is unable wholly to disentangle the results of his research from a system of interpretation which they cannot consistently accommodate. Like Newman, his insight is more satisfying than his logic.

For later scholars, however, like Van der Leeuw and Eliade, the interpretative task was made easier by the absence of any personal commitment to secularist presuppositions; and the result of their work is a far more satisfactory description of the working of the "law of participation", and of the intellectual and social context of religion.

Thus what emerges most clearly from their work is that the religious concept of the "sacred" is not only incompatible with, and inexplicable by, modern secularist presuppositions, but that it is positively suggestive of the phenomenological foundation a contemporary Christianity requires. The notion of the "sacred" forces us to recognise that the church is essentially an extension, into the sphere of self-consciousness, of the human community which is constituted, in the first place, by our bodiliness and by our capacity for language. Grace builds on nature. If bodiliness and language are central elements in the structure of the sacred, and in addition are central to the post-secular philosophy I have already discussed, it is possible to go on to show that they are also the central elements in the structure of the church. Just as it is language which raises our biological species to the level of a properly human society, so it is the Christian structure of sacramental communication, based upon language, that raises human society to the level of a community called by God and structured by his word. Understood in this way, theology can be seen to have its roots in the intellectual concerns of the modern world, and the church's true structure can properly be regarded as the culmination of the social aspirations of mankind.

But two major problems remain. The first is the problem of personal death. For, as I have shown, one of the principal concerns of modern man is with the bringing to consciousness of all the aspects of his own existence. Morality is, for him, the attainment of maturity and self-awareness. But the fact of death seems to negate all this, and to insert a certain absurdity into the very centre of experience. Some way of accommodating, and indeed making sense of death is essential if even a bare outline of a possible future Christian coherence is to be possible.

It is here that the renewed emphasis being placed by Christians upon the bodily basis of all human experience leads naturally towards a positive attitude towards the idea of personal resurrection, and the community of the saints. Death is no longer to be regarded as an escape from the world, or as a passport to a heavenly prize-giving and distribution of good-conduct medals, both of which are rightly felt to be repugnant to the moral conscience of a mature society. On the contrary, death is now seen as a new kind of opportunity for an encounter with a transfigured world. Its evil aspect is indeed already overcome in part in the transfiguration of the world which is taking place in the church here and now. Death is the culmination, not the negation, of our moral striving, and is the supremely personal *action* for which we prepare in life. So far from being an absurdity and a contradiction, death in a truly Christian context is the most personal and characteristic of our undertakings, and gives the final meaning and orientation to our existence.

The second problem is that of distinguishing the true structure of the sacramental, linguistic community of the church from those elements which have invaded it throughout history from alien sources. As I have already said, this is the primary theological problem; and to face it means to come to grips with the meaning and structure of the modern world in which every theological problem poses itself to us. All theology returns, in the end, to the present moment, in which the encounter between God and history, the church and the world, occurs. This is why there can be no escape from a discussion of the immediate commitments and characteristic orientations demanded of the Christian in the contemporary context. But such discussion must always be placed in its historical setting. Neither the ideology of modernisation nor that of secularism does this. Only the radical understanding of Christianity is adequate to this task. The final chapter of this book attempts to indicate in more detail the structure of the argument here sketched out, and to suggest where it should lead us in the future.

A. The "Plain View"?

It is often assumed, tacitly if not explicitly, that the secular view of the world is not just one particular interpretation of reality, but is simply the understanding of reality as it is. The secular view is—as one of its representative periodicals calls itself—just *The Plain View*. This plain view is to be contrasted with any

189

religious view by being free from any positive human interpretation. It is the "scientific" view—that of the detached, impartial observer, whose sole concern is with fact and evidence and rational inference. The religious view, on the other hand, is one which places an interpretation upon facts. Whether rightly or wrongly, religion is concerned with establishing an interpretation of, or with giving a meaning to, the observations of the scientist or empirical investigator. This distinction is not only insisted upon by the secularist; it is often adopted by the "new" Christian too. Thus the Bishop of Woolwich seems to regard the distinction between the statements "the man Jesus was born in Bethlehem" and "God sent his only-begotten Son" as that between a statement of the bare historical fact and a "mythical" interpretation of it. (Of course, in calling it mythical he is not supposing it to be false, but merely drawing attention to the nature of myth as a way of speaking which puts an interpretation on an event, instead of just stating it. In this, he is making a distinction which is elaborated by Bultmann at much greater length.) The "mythical" statement, he says, "represents (in the picture language of the supranaturalist world-view) the theological *significance* of the history". (*The Honest to God Debate*, 266.) In thus separating the fact from interpretation, it is argued, we can preserve the essential meaning of the Christian message without committing ourselves to an expression of it which conflicts with the "plain view" of the secularist.[1]

Now there are two important objections to this line of argument. The first is that, in conceding to the

[1] See too Ronald Gregor Smith, *Secular Christianity*, London 1966, 101ff. and passim; and my review of this book, *New Blackfriars*, 53 (May 1966).

secularist that his view is as plain as he thinks it is, we are making a fundamental philosophical error—the very error which (I have argued) lies at the heart of much that is wrong with secularism itself, namely, the empiricist error. The second is that we are trying to defend a concept of the sacred which is exactly opposite to its original meaning. For, in taking it that the sacred way of thought is essentially an interpretative structure based upon a reality already established independently of it, we are denying its very basis, and raison d'être. These two mistakes are closely interrelated. Indeed, the argument of this book is that, in order to preserve a concept of the sacred which makes sense in the modern world, we need to return to the original understanding of the sacred and to see that, properly understood, it is not only compatible with, but is actually given a new lease of life by, some of the most fruitful elements in contemporary thought. In other words, both the secular humanist's "plain view" and the secular theologian's acceptance of it as valid at a purely factual or scientific level, are typical of an outworn rationalism which is, itself, out of touch with modern developments. The separation of fact and interpretation, and the attempt to keep Christianity at the interpretative level, while abandoning it at the factual or cognitive level, are both products of a secularism which is already on the way out. What is really interesting about the present situation is that the possibility of a renewed concept of the sacred can be seen to be emerging from the struggles of modern thought itself.

In speaking of the "secular" and the "sacred", I am not using these terms in any explicitly religious, let alone theological, sense. While my argument certainly has a theological dimension, I am not yet discussing, explicitly, the possibility of a renewal of the Christian religion in the modern world. In the present context, the terms "secular" and "sacred" are to be understood only at the philosophical level. There can, in this sense, be Christian theologians whose philosophical presuppositions are in fact (though they might not realise or admit it) secularist, and there can be agnostics or even atheists whose philosophy is anti-secularist or "sacred". (It may seem a stretching of ordinary language to call Marx's philosophical ideas "sacred" but in my usage it would not be outrageous. It is one of the characteristics of the present intellectual scene that the wires have become so crossed that it is hard to decide who is on which side in any particular battle.) By a "secular" thinker, then, I mean one whose philosophical presuppositions are inconsistent with a religious view of life; and some Christian theologians must be included in this category. Now such a definition, obviously, implies that it is possible to describe the "religious view of life" phenomenologically, without direct reference to specific philosophical positions. In this section I shall try to show that the modern study of comparative religion and the phenomenology of religion offer us a largely agreed view of what religion in its "essence and manifestation" (to use Van der Leeuw's phrase) really is.

Rudolph Otto's *The Idea of the Holy* was the first really decisive step towards a phenomenological study of the religious way of looking at the world. The work undertaken since the publication of Otto's book in 1917 has led to remarkable synthesis, of which perhaps the most notable elements are the findings of Gerard van der Leeuw and Mircea Eliade. Books such as the former's *Religion in Essence and Manifestation* and the latter's *Traité d'Histoire des Religions* form the basis of a modern concept of religion which can be accepted as objective, as far as such a thing is possible, because of the critical use they make of a vast mass of material from all ages and cultures. It is, at any rate, upon this that I have relied for outlining the religious view of the world which underlies my use of the terms secular and sacred.

Much of the material from which this synthesis has been constructed comes from the study of religion in "primitive" societies. Now it is a fundamental characteristic of the religious outlook, in which the sacred is felt as an ever present reality, that it refuses to take for granted the absolute homogeneity, or uniformity, of the world.[1] Sacred activities are designed to cause a break in the homogeneity of everyday space and time—that is, to help men to understand that in a sacred place, or during a sacred rite, everyday time and space are transcended. Man is transported by myth or rite into another dimension of existence. Now, this sacred dimension, so far from constituting an escape from everyday reality, is understood as a revelation of the ultimate reality which alone gives sense and meaning to the everyday world. The profane is not more, but less, "real" than the sacred. The profane therefore is to be defined as a privation of sacred reality, a condition of relative non-being, or chaos. To think of the sacred as but the human interpretation of an objective world already established by some other purely impersonal, scientific means, is to abandon the original significance of the sacred idea, and to substitute for it something quite different. If, in speaking of the sacred,

[1] Mircea Eliade, *The Sacred and the Profane*, ch. 1 and 2 passim. See also above pp. 64 and 93.

we do not mean something which is more solid and secure than the secular, then we are making a radical departure from the original meaning of the word. This is why any revision of religion which defines the sacred in terms of the secular, as what is left over when all the vital connections have been made, or by reference to a secular "reality" which is accepted on its own terms, is doomed to failure. But we should not submit too lightly. Perhaps a study of what is central to a "primitive" religious view of the world will reveal the possibility of a religious outlook, even under modern conditions of life. (But see note 1 on p. 18 above.)

B. *The primitive mentality: Lucien Lévy-Bruhl*

In the second chapter of his important book, *How Natives Think*, Lucien Lévy-Bruhl put forward his "law of participation" which, he suggested, rules the primitive man's thought about the relationship between himself and the external world.[1] The basis of this law is a belief in "mystic powers" which reside in all things. All things possess, as well as fixed and clearly definable properties, a kind of life. Now this life is a vital energy which can be shared and transmitted to other things. In totemism this idea becomes the dominating feature of a complete religious scheme. The totem animal or thing is not just a "symbol" which, as we would say, represents, or stands for, the group of which it is the totem. Every member of the totem group enjoys his membership because he sees himself as actually partici-

[1] Lévy-Bruhl's ethnological evidence is, of course, obsolete, and his conclusions too simplified. But I am here discussing the relation of his theories to his philosophical presuppositions, not to the evidence now available about "primitive" societies.

pating in the life of the totem. But it is important to notice that the totem is always a particular individual animal or object. It is not just the life of the species in which the member of the totem-group shares. He thinks of himself as participating in the life of some particular, individual creature. It is in the life of this particular creature that his own life is sunk, and to which he is committed. Whatever befalls him is to be attributed to something which happens, first of all, to that particular totem animal, or totem object. The hunter who kills a totem animal may be expected to pay compensation, not just for the killing of the animal, but (much more important) for all the harm that will befall those who are members of it, and whose life is bound up with it. If I am a member of the crocodile totem, then I am able, quite literally, to affirm "I am a crocodile", without qualification. For to *be* myself is to *be*, at the same time, the crocodile of which I, and my fellow clansmen, are members. It is this sharing which provides us with the social solidarity on which our existence as individuals depends.

But totemism is only a highly specialised (and by no means universal) development of a more general notion of the interpenetration that goes on everywhere between things of different kinds. The "law of participation" is universal, but it is especially concerned, of course, with the relation between men and their environment. Everywhere, primitive man

> ... perceives the communication of qualities (through transference, contact, projection, contamination, defilement, possession, in short, through a number of varied operations) which, either instantaneously or in the course of time, bring a person or a thing into

participation with a given faculty. [*How Natives Think*, 99.]

Systematic thought, at the primitive level, is based upon a notion of man's capacity to enter into the reality of the objects which surround him, and of the ability of these objects, with their active life, to enter into him. There is no absolute distinction between subject and object, perceiver and perceived. Neither is there anything absolutely constant about the observed properties which differentiate one kind of thing from another. A man may, for example, be simultaneously here and there, inside his body and outside it, alive and dead, human and animal. What makes this possible, according to the primitive view, is that everything in the world is possessed of occult powers. Nothing is absolutely inert, or "inanimate", and hence simply "objective". Since everything has a certain kind of active life, everything can enter into dialogue with man—for life is power, and can flow from one thing to another.

For this reason, in primitive thought there is no clear distinction between the concept formed by the intellect and the feelings towards the object which disturb the emotions. Primitive man thinks in terms of "collective representations" which are constellations of feelings and concepts intimately combined. It is only at a relatively late stage in human development that, say, the rational differentiation of one species from another can be kept wholly separate from the emotional and religious feelings associated with it.

Now all this presented Lévy-Bruhl with a problem. For, on the one hand, there was the clear evidence that at some stage in his development man was able to experience the world in a way which seemed to make nonsense of the rational categories hitherto accepted by Lévy-Bruhl as basic to all thought. But on the other, it was obvious that men with such a mentality managed to make sense of the world. It was impossible to dismiss this primitive mentality as "pre-human", for it was embodied in language—the very mark of humanity itself. The problem seemed insoluble, to Lévy-Bruhl, within the terms of his own presuppositions. His deep sociological and anthropological insight —influenced by, but outstripping in imaginative understanding, that of Durkheim and his followers—came into direct conflict with his philosophical premises, which were, ultimately, Cartesian. As a sociologist, he insisted (following Comte) that "humanity is not to be defined through man, but on the contrary, man through humanity". That is to say, "the highest mental functions remain unintelligible as long as they are studied from the individual alone". (15.) Language itself was a social reality prior to the individuals who appropriated it in their growth towards adulthood. Thought and language were not the activity of the autonomous individual, and society was neither the mere collection of such individuals nor a collective unity distinct from and set over against them. Hence the collective representations which form the ingredients of primitive thought

... present themselves in aspects which cannot be accounted for by considering individuals merely as such. Thus it is that a language, although, properly speaking, it exists only in the minds of the individuals who speak it, is none the less an incontestable social reality, founded upon an ensemble of collective representations, for it imposes its claims on each one

197

of these individuals; it is in existence before his day, and it survives him. [13.]

As a student of social phenomena, Lévy-Bruhl understood the intricate interconnection between individual and society, and the central place of language, even in the most primitive stage of human progress. But as a thinker in the Cartesian tradition, reared in the nineteenth century, with its implicit belief in the steady improvement of man throughout the ages, he could not allow that the primitive mentality was anything but a crude first groping towards the fulfilment of man's rational powers. He still took it for granted that "our" way of understanding the world (i.e., that of his own culture and tradition) was altogether superior, because more objective and more rational, than that of the primitive man. While he criticised investigators like Tylor and Frazer for their inability to shed their rationalist presuppositions, which rendered them unable to enter into the mind of the primitive world and understand it, he still found it necessary to accept that the "civilised" way of thought was the "true" one. This becomes very clear when he tries to explain the mechanism by which the primitive mode of thought, the "law of participation", was gradually replaced by a more rational intellectualist mode characteristic of "our" stage of evolution. In effect, all he does is to argue that, at a certain stage of development, because of sociological changes, the intensity of the participatory way of thinking dies away among some groups, since it is no longer needed by them. Having rid themselves of this intellectual lumber, the "true", objective way of thinking, which we acknowledge as ours, automatically becomes obvious to them. Once the "contradictions" and "absurdities" of the primitive mentality have been done away with, the self-evident validity of the rational or intellectualist mentality will automatically establish itself. Human progress is vindicated by the fact of our having transcended the absurd (but fascinating) contradictions of the primitive mind.

Lévy-Bruhl suggests that an important element in this mechanism of psychological change is the increasing social specialisation of the "mystic" aspect of experience. The participatory mode of thought is a social necessity, in the first place, and gives solidarity to the primitive community, because it offers a way of controlling the elements upon which man's life depends—the seasonal cycle, the rainfall, and so on. But as these functions become the privilege of specialists—sacred kings, medicine-men, and so on—social differentiation occurs. Some groups will have concentrated upon themselves the whole force of the participatory mode of understanding, and others, by contrast, will be dissociated from it. The first group will continue to see things in the participatory way, but the second will slowly lose sight of it.

[Hence] since the beings and the objects among which the (latter) social group lives are no longer felt to be in direct communion with it, the original classifications by which this communion was expressed tend to become obliterated, and there is a redistribution of a less mystic nature, founded upon something other than the ramifications of the social group. . . . The beings and the objects represented as "containers" of mystic virtue, the vehicles of participation, are inevitably differentiated from those which do not possess this supreme interest for the social group.

The latter are beginning to be ranged according to an interest of another order; their distinguishing features are less mystic, but more objective. In other words, the collective representations of these beings and objects is beginning to tend towards that which we call "concept". [374f.]

Lévy-Bruhl goes on to connect this process of conceptual objectification with a corresponding development of perception.

The attributes we term objective . . . are to the primitive enveloped in a complex of other elements much more important, elements exacting an almost exclusive attention. . . . But if this complex becomes simpler and the mystic elements lose their predominance, the objective attributes *ipso facto* readily attract and retain the attention. The part played by perception proper is increased to the extent in which that of the mystic collective representations diminishes. . . . [Thus] the collective representations more nearly approach that which we properly call "idea"—that is, the intellectual, cognitive factor occupies more and more space in it . . . surrounding nature is seen with less prejudiced eyes and the collective representations which are evolving begin to feel the effect of experience. [375f.]

What is of interest here is the philosophical premisses on which the argument is based. Lévy-Bruhl takes it for granted that the objective, or intellectual, mode of apprehending reality is simply the true mode, which must make itself apparent as soon as the absurdities and contradictions of the primitive mentality begin to lose their grip. Yet, in attaining to this "true" mode of thought we nevertheless lose something of value—something intimately connected with our need for social solidarity and a rootedness in nature. But how can the discovery of truth *entail* the loss of anything worthwhile? Does such a view make consistent sense? What is at stake here is not just the consistency or otherwise of a sociological theory. It is the very rationality of the "plain view" itself. Lévy-Bruhl's philosophical premisses are in question, and the whole edifice he has built upon them. To speak of a mode of thought as rational which is not just of limited value, but actually contradicted by a whole tradition of human experience is itself a kind of contradiction. If the rules of thought are not universally valid, they are not valid at all, and rationality collapses.

In thinking of "rules of thought" Lévy-Bruhl is accepting a particular view of logic: namely, that logical rules are rules which govern the mental processes we set in motion whenever we think. This view of logic is not only unnecessary, but totally incoherent, as I have argued already. (pp. 39ff. above.) Lévy-Bruhl's difficulties are characteristic of the tangles which arise when the "secular" philosopher is faced with an apparently successful and certainly venerable but nevertheless unfamiliar cultural tradition. It cannot be denied, of course, that there are grave difficulties in supposing the primitive mode of apprehension to be tenable. Even if it existed, we could not think ourselves back into it completely. But what Lévy-Bruhl does not recognise is that his own theory of knowledge is itself open to grave objection. He seems to take it for granted first of all, that the intellect, in forming "concepts" simply picks out from the surrounding world some purely "objective" qualities. It does this, characteristically, without paying attention to the emotional and religious feelings which, in the primitive mind, are inextricably mingled with them. The concept, that is to say, is simply a mental representation of certain supposedly objective attributes which the intellect abstracts from the thing. This process of abstraction, based as it is upon the (supposed) perception of the object "as it really is"—that is, as distinguished from all distracting emotive factors—is a process in which the concept arises automatically, once we stop attending to these other factors. Simply by systematically not attending to the complex of other elements, we shall find ourselves with the intellectual concept ready to hand.

There seem to be two stages to this abstractive process. First, we begin to distinguish "perception proper" from the primitive man's "mystic" associations and his attempt to participate in the life of the object. Secondly, within perception itself, a further selectivity of attention results in the mental "idea" or concept with which all our rational and logical thought begins. But an awkward consequence follows from this theory. According to Lévy-Bruhl, the primitive mentality is one that transgresses the basic principles of rational thought —especially the logical law of contradiction. In thinking of himself, for example, as both a man and as a crocodile (in a totemistic way) the primitive man is offending against the fundamental laws of logic. But does this not mean that he is committed to an absolutely contradictory and unintelligble world? Lévy-Bruhl is too honest a student of the subject to shuffle this problem off by simply condemning primitive thought to a forgotten limbo which could safely be ignored by "civilised" man. Faced with overwhelming evidence that primitive man did not seem to be worried by his alleged offences against logic, he found himself compelled therefore to posit what he called a "pre-logical" mode of thought, in which logical laws did not apply.

> Collective representations are regulated by the law of participation and are consequently indifferent to the law of contradiction, and united, the one to the other, by connection and preconnections which prove disconcerting to our reason. [386.] [Yet this disconcerting mode of apprehension] assuredly remains something more imperious and more intense, even among peoples like ourselves, than the thirst for knowledge and the desire for conformity with the claims of reason. [385.]

The religious instinct of man is at the root of this. So the conclusion is inevitable: there must be, even within us, two mutually opposed modes of thought, the one intellectual and rational, the other "mystic" and pre-logical. Thinkers who take, as the starting-point, that "the human mind is always and everywhere homogeneous, that is, a single type of thinker, and one whose mental operations obey psychological and intellectual laws which are everywhere identical" are wrong. Logical laws are relative to a certain level of human development. Its rules are not absolute. We cannot therefore expect the religious mode of thinking to be amenable to logical analysis or regulation. If theology or mysticism is logically self-contradictory, that is only to be expected; for it is a relic of a time when all our thoughts were absurd and contradictory, albeit at the same time rich in social and other values.

Is it possible to avoid this anti-rational conclusion? Two important points must first be made. One is that Lévy-Bruhl greatly exaggerates the extent to which the primitive mentality rejects the ordinary regularities of nature. Indeed, he even goes so far as to say that, to the primitive mind, there are no such regularities. Their world is a Humean one in which "anything may produce anything": "A human being may be born of a boulder, stones may speak, fire possess no power to burn, and the dead may be alive". [377.] But later research has shown that this is by no means true. The primitive is not unaware of the regularities which exist in nature, and which he must make use of if he is to live in, and make sense of, the world. However, what *is* characteristic of the primitive mentality is, according to Van der Leeuw, that in it the judicious and systematic observation of natural processes is not felt to be inconsistent with a "participatory" mode of understanding or with a belief in the omnipresence of occult powers in things. But unfortunately, to make the second point, Van der Leeuw, like Lévy-Bruhl, has also confused us here, by speaking as if this apparent difficulty had something to do with the laws of logic.[1] The basis of this mistake is a psychological theory of logic. Both Van der Leeuw and Lévy-Bruhl speaks as if the laws of logic were laws of psychology, which regulate what can and what cannot be thought. This, as we have seen, is a fundamental error. It is characteristic of the "secular" thinker to hold that the rules of logic are irrefragable laws which govern the processes of inferring, deducing, and so on—which constitute the substance of "our" rational thought. As long as one conceives of logic as a

[1] Van der Leeuw speaks of a "metalogical" mentality in place of Lévy-Bruhl's "prelogical" one. See L. Bouyer, *Rite and Man*, 28, and Van der Leeuw, "La Structure de la mentalité primitive', *Revue d'Histoire et de Philosophie religieuses*, VII (1928), 1–31.

branch of psychology it is impossible to avoid the conclusion that a totally different notion of how the world is organised (such as the primitive mentality reveals) must entail a different logic for its systematisation. Or rather—since logic has always claimed to be the most universal set of rules for governing the processes of reasoning that it is possible to conceive—the conclusion is inescapable that in the primitive world logic does not apply at all.

But this conclusion is itself an offence against the very logic in the name of which Lévy-Bruhl was able to call the primitive mentality contradictory and absurd. For if logic was the most general of all conceivable rules about thought, then it was strictly inconceivable that there could be a mode of thought which did not come under its jurisdiction. Lévy-Bruhl did not attempt to meet this difficulty. He merely presented his case, and left us to deal with it as best we could. As a piece of imaginative reconstruction of the primitive mind, his work was a great advance on anything hitherto produced. But its implications were self-contradictory. Only a different way of understanding logic itself could resolve the difficulty—the formal way. I have already mentioned what this involves in discussing the inadequacy of empiricism generally. (See above pp. 32–41.)

C. Participation as a way to the world: Gerard van der Leeuw

As I have already said, later scholars have been able to make more coherent sense of the "law of participation" than Lévy-Bruhl was able to do, because they are relatively free from the false logical presuppositions implicit in a specifically secular outlook. Of these phenomenologists of religion, Gerard van der Leeuw is especially important, and has made one of the outstanding contributions to the subject's development. Despite his worries about the "metalogical", he makes much good sense out of the facts concerning participation in the religious mind,[1] and these connect remarkably closely with the phenomenological analysis of our modern experience as discussed by such philosophers as Husserl and Merleau-Ponty. What is relevant here is to mention those elements in Van der Leeuw's study of the religious mode of thought which are relevant to the discussion of modern experience.

First of all, to the religious mind the world is not something apprehended as simply a given, wholly external environment. For Van der Leeuw, as for Merleau-Ponty, in a real sense, we make our own world. "Out of his own particular environment everyone constructs a world for himself which he believes himself able to dominate." Man's path to the world, therefore, "is neither that of contemplation, nor reflection, nor presenting himself as a subject and so forming a 'substratum', but of existing as oriented *towards* the world".

One consequence of this primitive mode of experiencing the world is that the distinction between man and material objects is very fluid. There is no absolute break between animate and inanimate nature (though there are regularities which are obvious enough and which are perfectly reliable in themselves). Because there are no altogether autonomous natural laws, there is no distinct concept of the supernatural either. These categories do not apply, in the religious world. It is possible to influence the world, not only by making use of its regularities, but also by making use of the

[1] G. van der Leeuw, *Religion in Essence and Manifestation*, ch. 82 passim.

206

occult powers which pervade it. One way of doing this is the *magical* way. Magic, Van der Leeuw insists, is in no sense a kind of primitive science or technology. It rests upon the determination to dominate the powers and make them serve man. Thus, if one believes (as is asserted of "primitive" mentality) that "when one rows, it is not the rowing that moves the boat, but rowing is only a magical ceremony by which one compels a *daemon* to move the boat",[1] one is not positing any distinction between nature and the supernatural. One is merely trying to dominate the environment by using a feature which is pervasive throughout the world. But this world towards which man is orientated by his very existence, is nevertheless felt as superior to, and often crushing, man with its overwhelming powers. Magic is a protest by man against his enslavement to this over-bearing world. It is a way by which he tries to transcend his own predicament. But he achieves this only at a price: namely, that of defying, and even denying, the power of the world towards which his existence carries him. He has to take the world into himself. In the use of magic,

> Man does not trouble himself about "reality": he dominates it creatively, since he immures himself against it; he erects a kingdom internally, a divine service in his own soul. [549.]

And when he does this in a situation in which magic comes up against some fixed and unchallengeable obstacle to its own efficacy, severe mental tension results. (Sometimes this may even go so far as schizo-phrenia—a reduction of the world to complete sub-

[1] Nietzsche, *Human, All Too Human*, I, 117–18. (Quoted by Van der Leeuw, 547f.).

jectivity. Only God can make the world to be exactly as he wishes.)

The magician, then, is one who tries to create a world which, even if it be subjective, is nevertheless pliant to his own will. The *mythical* attitude is the exact opposite of this. Here man tries to throw himself into the world, now seen as eternal, static, unchangeable. (Myth is concerned with some place and time in which every human aspiration and movement is seen *sub specie aeternitatis*.) By projecting his own subjective tensions and will into a mythical world—that is, a world indubitably set apart from man in his immediate concerns—he is able to come to terms with himself and his environment.

> Primitive man has created a world for himself which, although it is for us only a product of imagination, implies for him a very concrete reality; but he thus elicits from his own soul all the possibilities that he has experienced. He peoples field and forest with the figures of his desires, his dread, his hope and his woe. [552.]

Magic and myth are contrasting ways of dealing with the problems raised by man's own participation in the world, his orientation towards it which defines his own self in relationship to the environment. They indicate a certain dissatisfaction with the "law of participation" and a need to rise above it. In this sense they represent the beginning of a new, intellectual, approach to experience. But they also reveal the beginning of a corresponding social breakdown. Thus Lévy-Bruhl rightly notes that

> . . . where the participation of the individual in the social group is still directly felt, where the participa-

tion of the group with surrounding groups is actually lived—that is, as long as the period of mystic symbiosis lasts—myths are meagre in number and poor in quality.[1]

But he goes on to suggest that perhaps myths can be regarded as

> ... the products of primitive mentality which appear when this mentality is endeavouring to realize a participation no longer directly felt—when it has recourse to intermediaries, and vehicles designed to secure a communion which has ceased to be a living reality. [Lévy-Bruhl, 368.]

That is to say, myth is an attempt to make *intellectually* explicit something formerly felt to be expressible only in life and action. It is both an approach to and a retreat from the world as directly experienced.

The very process which creates a world apart, in which man's possibilities can be realised, leads to a conceptualisation and intellectualisation, which in time begins to rob active experience of its immediacy. Finally it may reduce a lived religion to the merely literary mythology of a religion which has gone dead. The development of our concepts of the act of *naming*, both of people and of things, illustrates this point clearly. For archaic religious man, to whom the concept of a personal god is still indistinct, the act of giving a name to the basic religious experience—that is, experience of a power which exercises a will over him—helps to

[1] L. Lévy-Bruhl, 368. Lévy-Bruhl, under the influence of Durkheim, emphasizes here the concept of participation only in a social sense. Later scholars, notably Van der Leeuw, reinforce this idea with the more profound one of participation in the divine action of which the myth speaks.

> ... give an outline of this experience and to delimit it from other experiences. ... For the Name is no mere specification, but rather an actuality expressed in a word. Thus Yahweh creates the animals and leads them to Adam; he says something to them, and that is their name. [Van der Leeuw, 147.]

The name in this sense is primarily adjectival, assigning

> ... a definite form and some settled content, and is therefore by no means any abstraction. ... That is why man longs to know the god's name; for only then can he begin to do something with his deity, live with him, come to some understanding and—in magic —perhaps even dominate him.

It is only because they have names that the gods can become figures in myth for "myth is nothing other than 'dual experience of the form', that is the experience of the god encountered anew, but henceforth indirectly, structuralised, and endowed with form". But according to the modern philosopher,

> We give names by fiat and there is no right or wrong about the procedure. A thing is introduced to me by its proper name, and thereafter I can refer to the same thing by using that name: but the name tells me nothing about the attributes of the thing.[1]

If this last point about myth as suggestive of social breakdown is true, then it has an important bearing upon the use of the notion of myth by theologians like Bultmann and other "de-mythologisers". As has already been mentioned (pp. 189–91 above), the argument has often been that myth is an interpretative structure erected

[1] P. Geach, *Mental Acts*, 69.

upon a foundation of "fact" established, or capable of being established, quite independently of it. But the study of myths themselves seems to suggest that this view is mistaken. Myths are concerned, not with the creation of meanings which give a human orientation and interest to the objective facts, but with the recovery of meanings which have been, or are in danger of being, lost. They do not therefore give a meaning where none before existed; they simply recover meanings which were there from the beginning, embedded in the very structure of human experience—that is, in the participatory way to the world which primitive man developed. Myth then is part of a movement towards the renewal of the integrity of this participation. It is intrinsically concerned with the union of the object with its human significance, which the law of participation asserts; not with the maintenance of the distinction. It remains to be proved, and is by no means obvious, that it is possible to remove the myth and retain the facts; for it is not here that the distinction is to be drawn.

It is not merely a question for the historian whether myth has arisen as a way of recovering a meaning that has been lost. It is also a matter of the very nature of myth, as a unique and indispensable way into the world which we cannot do without. In order to understand this it is necessary to take the argument a stage further.

D. Participation in creation: Mircea Eliade

The psychology of religious man suggests the hypothesis that our fundamental mode of being in the world may be "participation". But so far this idea has been given very little positive content. It is now time to show, in more detail, the reality of the "sacred", in which

religious man participates and into which—I am argu-
ing—it is now possible for modern man once more to
enter meaningfully. In particular, the role of the community in this conception needs to be given more depth.
The scholar who has done more than any other to give
content to the nature of religious experience is
undoubtedly Mircea Eliade. Most of his work centres
on a number of basic themes which he has distilled from
an immense scholarship into a clear-cut survey in his
short popular work, *The Sacred and the Profane*. A
number of points from this and other works are of
special importance for the present purpose.

It has already been noted (see p. 64 above) that the
sacred involves a notion of the discontinuity of space
and time. By contrast with the modern, scientific,
"desacralised" view, religious man thinks of the world
as being capable, in itself, of revealing a dimension of
space and time which is not that of everyday. The
sacred space of the consecrated ground, or house, or
temple, and the sacred time of the festival and of the
mythical narration—both represent this capacity of the
world itself to manifest the sacred. (Nor do the occult
powers which the world manifests exist of themselves;
they are rather the manifestation of the power which
belonged to the ancestral or divine beings which
founded the world, and gave it its very existence and
order, in the beginning of things.)

Rituals and techniques for the consecration of space,
whether they have the simplicity of the sacred pole
of the Achilpa (round which the ground is sacred) or
the complexity of Solomon's temple, are concerned with
the construction of an order and an orientation within
what is otherwise felt to be formless chaos. The profane

world is essentially structureless. (It is often the work of the dragon which lives in the shapeless waters of chaos.) To consecrate a space within this formlessness is therefore to create a world, an intelligible order and a habitable structure, for the pursuit of a common life. But this process of consecration is not its own justification. What makes it a sacred activity is that it puts man into close relationship with the original creative order. In living in the sacred place, man is living within the orbit of the gods. His entrances and exits mark the transition from the profane to the sacred—that is, divinely creative—order. The act of consecration is thought of as making man a sharer in the primordial work of the world-founding powers.

The sacred space is not only created; it is also given. Thus in order to give access to the order of the world-founding powers, it is necessary to situate the sacred space in a place especially close to "heaven"—that is, to the focal point of reality. Hence sacred places tend to be either on mountain tops, or to be thought of as at the centre of the world, forming the *axis mundi* around which all life revolves. For the sacred is the secure centre; it is the real, the unassailable, the eternal.

Because the consecration of space is a participation in the work of founding the world, it constitutes a return to the beginning. Hence, in itself, it marks a discontinuity in time as well as space. It takes man back to the origins, the time of the creative powers of the gods or the ancestors. Hence also, rites and recitations of the community's history, which form an essential part of its religious life, themselves consecrate the time in which they take place. The time of the festival, the time of the mythical remembrance is itself a sacred time, which is marked by a change in the rules of life. The great sin is to forget the primordial time of the beginnings in which life was established as intelligible and orderly, either by neglecting to recall it or by departing from what is established as the means for re-entering into it. Thus, initiation ceremonies are primarily designed to take the initiate back into the primordial time, in which he is remade by the gods, and so constituted a complete person. Childhood is a time of relative unreality. For to be a person, fully, is at the same time to be made sacred and to be given a place in the community. But the community is a prior reality, into which the initiate enters in order to become himself. So, in entering the community, the individual is also entering into the life of the gods, the life of reality itself. The community is a manifestation of the creative community of the world-founding powers, and is necessarily sacred.

The myth of the beginnings, therefore, not only tells of the community of the gods; it also, by that very fact, has an important role in the founding of the community and in its preservation. It is a link between the two worlds, of the primordial divine reality and of the human counterpart. In speaking of the community of the one, it makes a reality of the others. It is, in this sense, a sacramental narrative, which enacts what it tells.

The consecrated space—house or temple or altar—is a model of the cosmos which the gods have made. To make it sacred is to do what they did at the beginning—that is to say, found the world. Not only is the sacred place at the centre of the cosmos, therefore; it is designed to manifest the essential features of the cosmos. To live or worship in it is to be in the world.

But if the sacred structure is a microcosm, so also is the human body. Man inhabits a body, as he inhabits a house; and in consecrating his body he makes it to be a miniature cosmos, an ordered thing. Perhaps his spine is the axis round which the world turns, just as the mountain on which the building stands, or the cross-roads where it is sited, or the pillar which holds it up, represent an *axis mundi*. But conversely, the house or temple is a kind of body, and its parts are organically connected.

But it is not only in these fundamental features of life that man puts himself into contact with the gods, and with the sacred realm they inhabit. For everything —objects, words, tasks, relationships—is capable of becoming a "hierophany". This is not to say that everything is felt to have a sacred quality immanent in itself, but—on the contrary—that there is a dimension within which everything can be considered as sacred because it goes beyond itself. The fundamental demand of the religious man is to make everything real, to put everything in its right place, to banish insecurity and evanescence and decay, and to prevent that sliding backwards into chaos, which is the tendency of every unconsecrated thing in the world.

The point which needs to be emphasized in this account is that the "sacred" is unintelligible if we think of man simply in his individual setting, confronting the world. The religious mentality, orientated towards the sacred, is necessarily a communitarian one. To exist is to be one of the tribe. To exist fully, as an adult, is, furthermore, to be fully participant in a community which manifests, in its own life and common activity, the creative reality of the world-founding powers. The ritual separation from family and friends of the person undergoing initiation is designed to release him from the power of unreality with which his life hitherto has always been contaminated; and so to make him capable of the greater life of the community. He becomes an individual by becoming a participant.

It is easy here to concentrate too much on the external, physical aspect of the sacred, and too little on the fact that everything is felt to be orientated towards the human community as its point of reference. In his suggestions about Christianity, in the course of his analysis, Mircea Eliade sometimes falls into this mistake. The results are illuminating for the present purpose. First of all, in regard to the Christian idea of sacred space, he writes that any church

> ... shares in a different space from the street in which it stands ... the threshold that separates the two spaces also indicates the distance between two modes of being, the profane and the religious. [Eliade, 25.]

For him the Christian church building seems to be simply a Christian version of the Jewish temple. It is a sacred space which brings us into contact with the divine. No doubt, at the back of his mind, there is not only the thought that the church is a symbolic structure, full of sacred emblems, designed to reveal in its design and decoration the Christian fact, but that the focus of attention in it is the really present Christ, brought sacramentally to the altar and residing in his tabernacle. In this sense, it seems to be suggested, the Christian church fulfils, completely, the aspirations and hints of the religious instinct of archaic and pre-Christian man as exemplified in the ideas and actions already described. But such a view is radically mistaken. There is, for Christianity, no need to have a sacred building at all. The church building may be a useful teaching device, if it is adorned with symbolic features which present the Christian message.[1] But it is not a temple which houses the Christian God. Indeed it is a central feature of Christianity that, with the advent of the risen Christ all temples are now abolished. Christ himself is the new temple, which is not made with human hands. The presence of God is now not actualised by the consecration of a physical space, but simply by the consecration of the community. It is true that in the eucharist, Christ in his very substance is made present. But his real presence is not just a physical location, but a location in and for the assembly of those who are gathered together for the celebration of his mighty work of redemption.[2] Christ's presence is to his people, not to physical things; and this presence is the medium in which the community communicates with him, and hence with itself, and so makes itself to become the very body of Christ. Christ's body is, literally, in heaven; but it is sacramentally on earth, as the "ecclesial reality" which is at the centre of life and gives it meaning and orientation.

If, according to the primitive conception of the sacrality of man, my body and yours are microcosms of the whole sacred world, in Christianity this is made

[1] See my *Culture and Liturgy*, 86ff.
[2] See Herbert McCabe, OP, "The Real Presence", *Clergy Review*, XLIX, 11 (November 1964); and my own article, "The Ministry of the Word", *New Blackfriars*, 47, (November 1965), 545.

true, literally, by the consecration of the people. Just as they are physically present to each other and so, as members of an animal species, capable of a mutual membership of each other; so, as members of the distinctively linguistic human community, they are capable of communicating this participation in a more complete way.[1] But, to speak of the physical body—that is, the body as open to perception—is not necessarily to speak of the mere organs and mechanisms as the physiologist thinks of them. For as Newman realised,[2] it is the body understood as a unity, not as the totality of parts, that we first of all perceive. Long before the physiologist can get to it, the physical body is a manifestation of the power for action (see pp. 54f. above). Christ's body was, and indeed in its risen life is, the supreme example of this manifestation of power. The body of Christ is given to us to make our bodies truly sacred—that is, truly present and complete—by means of the eucharist.

Thus, for Christianity, the sacred space is not that of the consecrated building, but rather the space which is created by the presence of the members of the community to each other. In the first place, this space is that of the liturgical assembly; for it is to this assembly, as such, that the reality of Christ is given. But the effect of this presence, and the sacred space which it creates—

[1] For an expansion of this point see pp. 94ff. above.

[2] "In knowledge we begin with wholes, not with parts. We perceive men, each individually being a whole. Then we take to pieces, or take aspects of, this general and vague object that is before us. The idea of unity is prior (in order of thought) to the idea of wholeness, or totality. [—that is, the idea of a sum of the parts.]." From an unpublished note on "Abstraction" by Newman, which is preserved in the Birmingham Oratory, and quoted by A. J. Boekraad, *The Personal Conquest of Truth*, 187ff.

the place of the "circumstances", those gathered around the celebrant—is not wholly confined to the liturgical time or place. This is because the liturgy is essentially a mode of communication, the work of a linguistic community. As such it has no clearly defined spatial limits. There are no walls delimiting or controlling the space created by those gathered together around Christ. But one can go further. *All* communication, by virtue of its sharing in the medium by which the liturgy exists (language) is to that extent sacred, and creates a certain space. Every dialogue, every human encounter, consecrates the space in which it occurs; and this is so not only in the physical sense (so that the ground the beloved walks on becomes, somehow, holy) but also in the conceptual sense. There is a conceptual space, an intellectual playground in which people communicate, which is also sacred because it shares the linguistic character of the liturgical consecration.

All dialogue is "sacred" because it shows forth, to a greater or lesser extent, the divine creativity of *the word*, and brings about an articulated structure of meaning and a social structure of human presences into which the divine presence can be inserted. That is to say, it brings into being the church; and the church is the locus of this dialogue which brings about the presence of Christ. It is the ground on which the religious language-game is played. That is its essential character as seen from the human side. It is where the language of religious encounter and the sacramental communication of the creative word are carried on. This process of communication *is* its structure.

Surely we have here a fruitful hint for the recovery of a properly religious understanding of the nature of the church as the Christian community in the modern world. For if the church is based on the human word, it is also the case—to put it another way—that it is called together by God's word. First called on Mount Sinai, and then later by Christ the incarnate word, the people of God are reconstituted by the dialogue of the liturgy or ministry of the word at every eucharistic celebration. In this dialogue a social structure is created to which Christ can be made present. (As we have seen, the presence of Christ is always a presence to a human community, through which it is made present to the individual. See pp. 222ff. below.) And to say this is to recall that, for religious man, the *word* is creative power. Language is not just the secular instrument we use for describing and recording experience. It is a pervasive medium which structures that experience and expresses the social dimension of our being, and so helps to "give us" the world. Thus, if my utterance of human words makes present the community whose words they are, and so enables me to act as the representative of that community, so much more does God's utterance of his word, in the life, death and resurrection of Christ, make present his life and make Christ the representative of the people of God. But what links God's word and man's is that, just as man achieves himself in the appropriation of the common language and so makes a community out of a mere species-life, so Christ appropriates this community life and makes it into himself. In the eucharist especially, we come to share Christ, each of us appropriating him wholly to ourselves, just as at the human level we each come to possess the whole of the language which we share. In the eucharist, and even more in the coming life of glory,

the bodiliness which still divides us is finally transformed to become not a principle of division but one
of union.[1]

[1] Christianity "affirms that no one of us can achieve his destiny in isolation from his neighbour, nor indeed from the whole
of the rest of creation. For 'the body', to the Hebrew way of
thinking, is the symbol of solidarity, not, as it had been in
Greek and Western thought, the principle of individuation. It
is what binds man together in the bundle of life, not what marks
off or isolates one man from the next. And that is why the New
Testament connects the resurrection of the body, not with the
moment of the individual's death, but with *the last day*, when all
the relationships of nature and history shall finally have been
knit up, no longer in their present solidarity of sin and death,
but into the new solidarity of life, the body of Christ's glory."
(J. A. T. Robinson, *On Being the Church in the World*, 39f.).

5

Sacred and secular
in theology

So far I have discussed the church from the side of purely human experience. Human bodiliness and human language are, in this respect, the basis of the church's structure as a human community. But of course, this is but a preliminary to the discussion of the theological ideas of the church, intelligible only by faith, as a community which is "in Christ" and as a community of *grace*, vitalised by the power of the Holy Spirit. It is to these ideas that we must now turn directly.

A. The Christian community "in Christ"[1]

The basic idea of the community which is "in Christ" is that of the permanent sacramental presence of the risen Christ to his people. But this idea needs to be related to what I have already said of the essentially linguistic structure of the church as a human community. The connection has to be established between linguistic communication and sacramental communication. This is best understood by a discussion of the

[1] Part of this section is reproduced from my article, "The Church: A Radical Concept of Community", *The Committed Church*, 253–79.

eucharist as the communication of Christ's presence. Just as the eucharistic meal is not a sharing out of Christ, but is a meal in which every participant receives the whole person of Christ into himself, so that it is no longer he who lives merely, but Christ lives in him; so the community which is constituted by the sacraments is a congregation united not just by a common purpose, or a common way of life, but by a common sharing in the one personal life of Christ. Just as Christ recapitulates, in his own person, the entire community which he has redeemed, so by virtue of his belonging to Christ each person, in his measure, recapitulates the life of Christ and also, because Christ *is* the Christian community, he also recapitulates the life of that community. He bears the whole church within himself as Christ did. Hence each Christian bears a double burden. On the one hand, he carries the human species into which he is born and the community which he appropriates in his language; and on the other he carries the Christian community which he appropriates by faith and the sacraments. But these two communities which meet in him are not two quite distinct entities, let alone opposite armies in some interior battle—though things can arrive at a stage where a battle has to be fought. On the contrary, the meeting of the two communities in the person of the individual Christian is an encounter between two aspects of his very own nature as a human being. He offers, in his own person, a place where Christ is able to carry on his work of reconciling all things to himself. So the individual is not an autonomous creature to be set over against the human community, or "society". On the contrary, it is only from the united complex which is "me", as I and others experience it, that those abstractions can be dissolved out. But once abstracted, they can easily become more monstrous realities than I am; then they create nothing but a conflict interrupted by the uneasy peace of compromise and acquiescence.

The task of the individual in the church, at a time when the bankruptcy of this "stop-go-stop-go" war of individualism has become inescapable, is to enter once more into himself, in the first place, and to understand that he is both more complex and more fundamental than the prevailing analysis suggests. He is himself, whether cleric or lay or religious, the locus of a reconciliation which is not an adjustment of the available checks and balances, but the rediscovery of a different picture of community. He will find that he is, himself, the intersection of God and the world, of Christ and his temptations. He will not see himself primarily as a citizen of the city of God, whose duty is to make forays into the enemy-held territory. He is himself on both sides. His very unity as an irreducible person is the guarantee that the war is, in any case, phoney—a distraction from the main task of self-awareness. But this discovery of the phoney character of the war between the Christian community and the world is, itself, only the supreme example of a process which must go on in every social—which is to say, every human—activity. To reconcile all things to oneself is not just the task of Christianity in its explicit form. It is simply the human task as such. The political, the economic, the intellectual demands are, in the end, resolvable only at this level of re-entry into oneself which is, at the same time, a new openness towards other people.

Now this idea is not to be understood in a purely personalist sense. It does not imply an openness to some abstraction called "the other person" shorn of his concrete social attributes—his job, his class-position, his habits, manners, accent, education, culture, and the rest of what makes him to be himself. Such a personalism is a false oversimplification, which seeks to evade the social, political, and economic issues by concentrating on some shadowy Cartesian ego. What is needed is not this, but rather a recognition that the private and the public, the personal and the political, the autonomous and the conditioned, the interior and the institutional, are all abstractions, jostling each other in the phoney war. The resolution of this war is not the victory of either side, nor yet a negotiated peace, but simply the discovery that it is itself only a dream. What is needed is that we should wake up, once more, to practical consciousness; and this, as Marx saw, is the same as coming to understanding a different and perhaps unfamiliar language.

But here we come up against an unresolved problem in modern theology itself. In the theology of the church, as the Vatican Council's *Constitution on the Church* shows, the emphasis today is, undoubtedly, on the communal character of the work of Christ. But in moral and, even more, in social thought the old dichotomy of individual and society seems to persist. While the speculative theologians have been busily reconstructing the communal life of the people of God, those who have been more concerned to refurbish the image of the Church as a champion of individual liberty have tended to emphasize the autonomy of the individual conscience. But there is a tension between these emphases which has not yet been resolved.

Pacem in Terris, for all its assertion of freedom in the modern world, still seems at times to rest upon the old individualistic theology. It begins with an assertion of the individual's rights and duties more reminiscent of Jefferson and the United Nations charter than of Schillebeeckx or Rahner. Society is thought of as a means to man's perfection, rather than as the ground of our very existence as human beings. By means of our living in society,

> ... men can share their knowledge of the truth, can claim their rights and fulfil their duties, receive encouragement in their aspirations for moral goodness, share their enjoyment of all the wholesome pleasures of the world, strive continually to pass on to others all that is best in themselves, and make their own the spiritual riches of others. [*Pacem in Terris*, para. 36.]

This passage makes it clear that, to the authors, society is no more than a system of extrinsic relationships between individuals conceived of as autonomous in themselves. Community is a means rather than an end, something useful for our complete perfection; but it seems that, at a pinch, we could do without it. This view is one that goes better, in theological terms, with the old idea of the liturgy as just the public, official worship of the church, than it does with the modern view of the liturgy as the very basis of the church's existence as a visible community in the world. The discrepancy marks the distance which still remains between the theology of the church which has been achieved by speculative thought and biblical rediscovery, and the application of these concepts to the church's position in the modern world. It is in the idea of the individual as one who, because he is a member of a community which defines his very being, re-presents that community in his speech and action, that a theo-

226

retical solution can be found to the perplexity of our modern experience.

This idea of the individual as re-presenting the life of the community which defines his being provides a basis for the intelligibility of the life of the Christian community as a life which is "in Christ". For it is now possible to see that faith is not in the first place some interior, hidden, personal relationship to God, or even to Christ. It is the life of the Christian community *in* which I share. Since the Christian community's life is structured by the presence of Christ, my life in that community is a life "in Christ". It is true that this truth is only intelligible to faith; but then faith itself is something which goes on "in Christ". Belief in Christ is a life carried on in Christ, much as, on the old physical theory, light waves were something that went on in the ether. The waves could live only if there was something for them to live *in*. Similarly belief in Christ can only live if there is something for this belief to live *in*. The ether was not a material object existing in the world apart from the waves that were in it. On the contrary, the life of the waves alone showed *what* it was they were in. Similarly, when I say: "I believe in Christ", I mean that Christ is the ether in which my life of faith subsists. But Christ is present in the world only as long as the life of faith of Christians makes this to be so. The life of the Christian community, then, is what my faith is *in*.

But what does this mean? Obviously there is a difference between encountering the life of faith of the Christian community and just meeting Christians, over cups of tea. Even in a totally Christian society there would be a distinction between encountering the church, as such, and being introduced to some, or even all, of

227

the people who constitute it. For the church, being a new and divine creation, springing from Christ, cannot be identified with the old creation simply of man as such. So it is the church as a distinct social reality discernible within society that we have to be able to encounter. And this is only possible if we hold that this distinct social reality has its own distinctive and encounterable life. And this is what the liturgy is. The liturgical life of the assembled faithful is what makes the church to be a distinct social reality. The whole structure of power and authority in the church exists for the pursuit of this liturgical life, which is its very raison d'être.

Thus, "I believe in Christ" means "I am in Christ and therefore in possession of the grace to believe". (Belief *that* Christ is God, rose from the dead, and so on, is of course the precondition for belief *in* him.[1] Faith can exist only in the church, just as, on the old theory, waves could exist only in the ether. Faith without, or apart from, the church—apart, that is to say, from the socially encounterable and distinct liturgical life of the Christian community—is as inconceivable as observable waves which are not *in* anything.)

Another way of describing the difference between belief *that* and belief *in* is to say that, in the former case, language is being used in a descriptive way, whereas in the latter it is used in a performative way. This distinction is precisely the difference between the historical and the mythical (in Eliade's, not in Bultmann's, sense of the term). To put it more generally, it is the distinction between the profane and the sacred ways of using language. For the profane, or historical, or

[1] For an elaboration of this point, see my article "Faith, Creed, and Community", *Clergy Review*, XLIX, 9 (September 1964), 529–39.

228

"secular", purpose of language is to make statements of fact, to communicate facts to others, to argue towards conclusions in a rational fashion. It depends for its very existence upon a profane conception of factuality (which, at its most extreme and exclusive, becomes the philosophy of a Gradgrind). But the sacred use of language is that by which man, as the language-bearing species, is enabled to participate in the life and power of the world around him, and to manifest this power in a living utterance. In this sense, the sacred use of language is the medium of communication between man and God, which transcends the communication between men at the level of fact and argument. In the sacrament of baptism, in which the initiate is asked what he wants of the church and replies "faith", the transition from profane to sacred language is achieved for that person. Having crossed the threshold he is now given the power (which is the power of God) to utter the sacred word, and so to participate in the power of God which is the very life of the linguistic community of believers. The liturgy, in all its phases, is sacred language in action, making really present the power of God in the world, by creating a community which shares in it. For God's power in the world is nothing but this Word, which is shared by the community at the level of complete personality—that is to say, both as animal, in the physical nourishment of the eucharistic meal, and precisely as human in the sharing of the divine language which is also God's Word. Ultimately, there is no distinction between the liturgy of the word and the liturgy of the sacramental meal. Both are equally liturgies of the Word; both are equally founded upon the power of God uttered in a word.

B. The Christian community: power, grace, and control of the world

At this point we need to turn to the second of the theological bases of the church's structure—the concept of the community of grace. For grace is, properly speaking, only another term for God's power over the world. The notion of grace—indissolubly linked as it is with the sacramental structure of the community of the faithful—needs to be revitalised by the recognition that it is essentially power. Grace is not a "spiritual" and purely interior working, but rather a living energy, which is always liable to manifest itself in the world unexpectedly, especially in the lives of those "filled with the Holy Ghost". Grace, however, is not a gift of power given privately to the individual. It is first of all given to the church, and mediated to the individual through his incorporation into the community in the sacraments of baptism and confirmation. But the church, like a language, is not something quite distinct from the individuals who share it. Grace is mediated, or transmitted, to the individual *in* the church, and by his fellow members. The Christian is a grace-bearing, power-giving creature. And he is enabled to be this because, especially in the eucharist, he participates in Christ, and shares his power. This is the fundamental meaning of the real presence. It is a kind of supreme fulfilment of the notion of participation which is to be discerned, darkly, in totemism. Grace is the infecting, cleansing, possessing power which makes possible the real unity of every Christian with the person of Christ, who is his living "totem" and who constitutes not just the symbolic head, but the reality and life, of the community which comes under his sway. This is the basis of the unity of the church; for we are all members one of another, members of the same Christian "totem-group", and each of us can thereby say: "it is no longer I who live, but Christ who lives in me."

Now it will be objected at this point that while the belief in occult powers may be a basic element in pre-historic religious consciousness, one achievement of religious thought during human history has been the refinement and systematisation of this crude conception. This is no doubt true; but the important point to consider is, what form this process of refinement has in fact taken, and what are the genuine and what are the spurious forms of it. To put the matter very roughly, the prevailing interpretation which has been put upon this process, perhaps especially by Western thinkers, has been in terms of "spiritualisation". Beginning from a crudely "materialistic" view of power as a kind of fluid force, man has slowly come to see that true power is not of this kind at all. Power is either an intelligible and controllable element in nature, open to scientific investigation, or it is a "spiritual" power which properly belongs to immaterial and invisible beings who reside in a world apart, and who use their power to cause extraordinary events in the world only because of the relative crudity of man's understanding. As humanity progresses, miracles and wonder-working become less important; for now man has begun to grasp the concept of a power which is purely "spiritual"—that is to say, is to be understood more on the analogy of our purely mental processes than on the analogy of our total activity. The principal work of this power, or of the "gods" who wield it, is the founding of the world. It is not their task to supervise its day-to-day running, continually at work behind the scenes. Control of the world is man's task, to be achieved by the evolution of correct ideas about the laws of nature and their application by technical expertise. Religion is not concerned with this control of the environment, but with the worship of the purely other-wordly beings who live apart from it. It is therefore concerned more with understanding the other world than with this one, which is of relatively little importance to the religious man.

In Christianity, the links between the two worlds have been conceived of in terms of *prayer*—which is man's "spiritual" ascent towards the divine—and *grace* —which is a kind of immaterial "mercy" which, in the divine condescension to the human, is able in an ineffable way to affect the "soul" and give it sustenance. So man lives by two parallel, but distinct systems. On the "material" plane he lives by taking in material food; on the immaterial plane, he lives by taking from the divine world immaterial food, which is absorbed by the immaterial part of himself. It is true that, in the sacraments, the link between the bodily and the spiritual has always been *asserted*. But in practice, even in the Catholic tradition, the connection between the grace-giving power and the bodily activity has, in popular thought, been very tenuous. The bodily activity of the sacramental rite has been thought of as, so to say, initiating, or releasing, the grace-giving power. It has also been recognised as having a rich symbolic value, representing the immaterial power in visible and material form. But representation has, very largely, not been taken literally; it has not been felt as *re-presentation*. The sacramental life of the church, seen as a dramatisation of the "spiritual" life in visible terms, has emphasised the gulf between the reality and this dramatisation, rather than linking the two together. Grace has been "spiritualised" to the point at which its root in the primitive idea of sheer power has all but been forgotten. It has become simply a latent or hidden potentiality which is never actually manifested in the world.

For example, the lives of the saints are no longer seen as public manifestations of such power (except in implausible legends, which may preserve some of the original conception, but only at the expense of reducing the credibility of their subjects[1]). Saints are now seen as moral examples. Their actions are motivated by "love", conceived of as an interior surge towards God and other people, responding to, and actualising, the purely potential energy of the grace they have received. This love is manifested primarily in the conscious, self-aware following of the path of "duty" or "obedience". The *power* of the saints, as such, is discounted (except by the incredulous). The great "spiritual" writers tell their followers to take as little notice as possible of any actual manifestations of power which may take charge of them in a quasi-physical sense. It is part of any "progressive" attitude to pour scorn on those crudities of popular superstition, even though they may be the only manifestation left of the fundamentally religious acknowledgement of a power which is real, and active in the world. It is easy to see why this dilution of the power of sanctity has come about. For centuries now there has been no framework in which the notion of a power manifesting itself as such in the world could

[1] English tradition is rich in this kind of legend. Perhaps the outstanding example is the Anglo-Saxon poem on the life of Guthlac, who spends most of his time overcoming hordes of surrounding demons. See R. K. Gordon (ed.), *Anglo-Saxon Poetry*, 284–309.

make sense. Any recovery of the sacred must be largely concerned with the construction of such a framework.

The "spiritualisation" of religion is popularly thought of as a central feature of the Christian tradition. Certainly, from the manifestation of the power of Yahweh in the burning bush, or from the top of Mount Sinai, it is a far cry to the thirteenth chapter of the Book of Wisdom, with its scorn for those who have vainly imagined

> ... either the fire, or the wind, or the swift air, or the circle of the stars, or the great water, or the sun and moon, to be the gods that rule the world ... if they admired their power and their effects, let them understand by them that he that made them, is mightier than they: for by the greatness of the beauty, and of the creature, the creator of them may be seen, so as to be known thereby. [Wis 13 : 2–5.]

It will rightly be said, of course, that the "spiritualisation" in evidence here, under Greek influence, is simply part of a polemic against a decadent Canaanite perversion. But the fact is that, just as the author of Wisdom wishes to distinguish the manifestation from the reality behind it, so too, in primitive religion, it is the power, and not the thing itself, which is the object of awe and the subject of religious attention. The Wisdom polemic against idolatry is not, itself, an argument against primitive religious consciousness, but a protest against something which is itself a departure from the primitive understanding. And, in fact, the sense of the reality of power is by no means replaced by a more "spiritual" conception in the main stream of Judeo-Christian religion. After all there is a continuous history of power manifesting itself, from the traditions concerning the exodus, the death of Uzzah who foolishly stretched out his hand to touch the ark of the Lord on its way to Jerusalem (2 Sam 6), the prophetic call of Isaiah whose lips were "cleansed" by the burning coal (Isaiah 6), and many other Old-Testament instances, to the pouring out of the Holy Ghost at Pentecost and the action of the "faith and power" (*kharis* and *dunamis*) of St Stephen and the other early saints and martyrs. As Van der Leeuw says, the "grace of God ... should not be understood as friendly disposition or mercy, but as power that is poured out and absorbed". (35.) Yet very little of this conception comes through the theological filters we have set up between genuine religious experience and our own "spiritualised" (that is, secularised) philosophy.

The most obvious outward characteristic of power, both in its primitive setting and in such developed religious awareness as we find in the New Testament and the acts of the early Christians, is its unpredictability. It is the exact opposite of the orderly behaviour of the world as we find it in normal circumstances. The Spirit blows where it will, just as the *mana*, or luck which inheres in a person, or a tree, or a weapon, may come and go without warning and cannot be brought under control. The distinction we ought to draw between the concepts of Christianity, as understood in the biblical and apostolic periods, and those of simpler societies, is not that the one is crude and materialistic and the other sublimely spiritual. In both cases, the object of religious awareness is beyond this kind of categorising. The truth is that, in the course of human development, the distinction between those elements in the world which are capable of being brought under prediction and control, and those which are, of their

235

very nature, not subject to such control, has been progressively clarified. This is the real significance of the reaction of the Wisdom literature to the idolatry of the surrounding religions. For the Wisdom writer, it is absurd, a patent confusion, to suppose that a mere artefact should have the power which, as it is, only belongs to the creator of the world.

> Unhappy are they, and their hope is among the dead, who have called gods the works of the hands of men, gold and silver, the inventions of art, and the resemblances of beasts, or an unprofitable stone, the work of an ancient hand. [13 : 10.]

According to Wisdom, it is far more absurd to regard the things man has himself made—that is, things over which he obviously has complete control—as having power, than it is to see such power in nature. Certainly those who make natural phenomena into gods are mistaken; but at least their mistake lies in the right direction. There is a *prima-facie* reasonableness, from a religious point of view, in thinking of the "natural" world as divine; for it is uncontrollable, at any rate in its fiercer and more hostile, and perhaps also in its most outstandingly beautiful manifestations.

Can we see here religion at a half-way stage of human development? At an earlier stage, power was just as likely to be found in artificial as in natural phenomena. Indeed, the distinction between the two scarcely existed.

> The early handworker ... particularly the smith, wields a power which he certainly knows how to employ, but of which he is nevertheless not the master; and thus we can realise why the smith's work is regarded as sacred in many parts of Africa and

Indonesia. . . . In the grips and blows of the tools, then, there dwells not only the strength of arms and legs, but also a specific power residing within the implements themselves; and this explains why tools are always made after the same model, since the slightest deviation would injure the potency.[1]

[1] Van der Leeuw, 40. In speaking of the development of tools Ernst Fischer (*The Necessity of Art*, 28) furnishes an interesting example of a sound Marxist analysis which is defeated by alien, empiricist assumptions. He rightly associates work and language closely together. (See p. 74 above.) In doing this, he tries to show how the making of similar tools gave man general concepts. Firstly man makes "occasional" tools, and for these no term is necessary, for each is its unique self. But if "standard" tools are evolved, then a specific term is needed (Fischer calls this a "name", which might be right if interpreted in a "primitive" sense, but is certainly wrong if interpreted in the modern sense—for general terms are certainly not names). But the systematic imitation of the standard tool brings about a new conception. "All the imitations, made to resemble each other, contain within them the same prototype . . . Man can take any of the imitations instead of the original hand-axe because all of them serve the same purpose, produce the same effect and are similar or identical in their function . . . Thus the first abstraction, the first conceptual form, was produced by the tools themselves: prehistoric man 'abstracted' from many individual hand-axes the quality common to them all—that of being a hand-axe; in so doing, he formed the 'concept' of a hand-axe." Here, Fischer has left out the important element which gives Van der Leeuw's analysis its intelligibility, and has substituted for it a purely "modern" theory of conceptual abstraction which is identical with that of Locke and suffers from all its defects. Instead of seeing that what links the imitation to the prototype is the *power* which resides in the one and is transmitted to the other by the exactitude of the copy, Fischer puts forward a purely conceptual scheme, in which the "quality of being a hand-axe" takes the place of the living power residing in the tool itself. To suppose that this "quality" is something which resides in the tool is simply the logical consequence of a theory

But to man at a later stage of development, the controllability of artefacts became manifest, and the distinction between the human and the natural, as objective and over against man, established. The realm of religion, therefore, became more specific. The sacred was no longer, for the Wisdom writer, identifiable with the world as a whole; it was not even the world of natural phenomena. The world of sacred power was now identified exclusively with the transcendent creator. But, at the same time, the natural world—with whose beauty the gentiles were so struck that they took its various features to be gods—is certainly a quasi-revelation of the divine, or sacred, order. The natural world speaks to us of the Lord, even though it is not itself sacred.

However, this process of narrowing down the realm of the sacred, through the elimination of those elements in the world which man discovers to be predictable and subject to control by technique, cannot stop here. There may be a prolonged stage at which it is reasonable to believe that, although it is possible to know how one's own tools will behave, one cannot know how the weather, or the sun or the stars above it, will behave. These at any rate are still the domain of power in its unpredictable spontaneous life. Whether the sun will

---

according to which concepts are atoms of pre-linguistic thought released in the act of merely perceiving the object that is before the senses. And since it is, by definition, a quality distinct from all the distinguishing features which mark this hand-axe off from that, it is necessarily (and contradictorily) inaccessible to the senses; for all that can be perceived is this or that hand-axe, each in its unique particularity. The primitive concept of a power, or energy, residing in an axe, on the other hand, is perfectly intelligible, although it is no doubt false. Here is an example of a writer whose fundamentally valid insight is contradicted by his "secular" presuppositions.

rise tomorrow, or the spring return next year, or the seeds grow in the ground, is by no means certain; there, at any rate, uncontrollable power rules. And so these things must be assured as far as possible by the appropriate rites and the recitation of the appropriate myths. Such is the position in the main phase of agricultural culture. But man is eventually able to discover a pattern even within the apparent spontaneity of those events, and arrives at a concept of a transcendent power, which may not itself be subject to predictable law, but which nevertheless regulates the various apparently unorganised events within its orbit. The task of religion in such a situation is to put forward a life-ideal conforming to the power which rules the world, whether it is sublimely uninterested in particular events (as in China) or is continually striking into the affairs of men (as in Israel). On the one hand, the aspect of unchangeability and regularity which, everywhere, is seen as pertaining to this power is liable to turn man towards the idea of fate and of his subjection to the stars. It is also likely to suggest to him concepts of time as a regular and recurring sequence, which lead towards the effort to calculate and measure which, in its train, brings the advance of science and the increase of man's control over his environment. On the other hand the aspect of spontaneity and intervention leads towards an increasing emphasis on man's subjection to an uncontrollable environment, and so to the deepening of a religious awareness which is always liable to degenerate into superstition and mechanical observance.

The beginning of a conflict between the scientific spirit and the religious outlook is apparent, then, even at this stage in human affairs. The recent history of the Western world is simply the intensification of this already latent tension. As man's control has increased, so his religious horizons have been narrowed. As he has begun to understand the causes of natural phenomena, especially those events which seem most unpredictable, they have been taken away from the realm of the sacred and incorporated into the profane, purely human world which has emerged. The sacred becomes associated in the popular mind with a world apart, a "heaven" beyond experience. God exercises a providence over men, but hardly over the rest of creation. He speaks to us, not in external events or public occasions, but in the recesses of the "soul"—which is thought of as inaccessible to the prying eyes of the scientist or the sceptic. The sacraments of Christianity become just *occasions* of divine help. It is a purely "spiritual" help they give, and this has to be appropriated, translated into moral terms, to be of any effect. A few phases in human life may, for a time, still be considered specially subject to the divine concern. Births, marriages, and deaths in particular may be allowed a place of honour in the advertising columns of the newspapers. While the weather is generally favourable, we assume that it is carrying on according to its normal laws, but in times of drought, storm, or flood, or at harvest, we may still try to influence it by public prayers and ceremonial. The insincerity of these procedures is obvious to everyone. For the fact is that all the time, in every sphere of knowledge, human control is increasing and the concept of the sacred, the unpredictable, is being whittled away.

Many religious thinkers, appalled by this situation, have tried to return to a pseudo-primitivism which is little more than a hopeless demand for the turning back of history. Thus Chesterton tried to bully himself and his readers into a religious frame of mind by striking arguments, like this one:

> A man walking down a lane at night can see the conspicuous fact that as long as nature keeps to her own course, she has no power with us at all. As long as a tree is a tree, it is a top-heavy monster with a hundred arms, a thousand tongues, and only one leg. But so long as a tree is a tree it does not frighten us at all. It begins to be something alien, to be something strange, only when it looks like ourselves. When a tree really looks like a man our knees knock under us. And when the whole universe looks like a man we fall on our faces.[1]

That may be, as Van der Leeuw says, a genuine description of religious awareness; but it is hardly relevant to us today. We *cannot*, any longer, see the whole universe in this way, or convince ourselves that such an experience is permanently valid.

Others, more optimistic about historical developments, have found it necessary to go to the opposite extreme, by jettisoning the basic concept of religion—that is, the acknowledgement of the power which is to be found in the world—and to reduce Christianity to a highly self-conscious ethical personalism which has scarcely any roots in religious awareness as traditionally understood at all. The scriptural manifestations of power have to be explained away as simply the "myths" or conventions of an earlier age, the "sanctity of life" becomes merely a moral attitude generally to be adopted but not to be accepted as an overwhelming demand, and the ideas of heaven and hell—which traditionally are

[1] G. K. Chesterton, "Science and the Savages", *Heretics*, 152.

simply the two opposite sides of the one unbearable but inescapable presence of God's power[1] are rejected as absurd, and even sadistic. Such a Christianity, deprived of most of its truly religious elements, but at the same time expressed in the jargon, and pervaded by the emotions, of a traditional sacramental community, is hailed as a great break-through for religion in this secularised world.

These reactions to the modern predicament are understandable and significant. Each in its way attempts to preserve something essential to the religious world-view. If the one is a reassertion of the reality of God's grace, majesty, and sheer power, and of his providence as subject to no scientific law or calculation, the other recognises that the conceptualisation and interiorisation of religion which has marked man's historical course is inevitable and is, indeed, part of our growth in under-standing. History moves relentlessly towards the ever more complete control of the environment by man, for his own needs and purposes. And it also moves towards an ever greater degree of self-awareness, and the elimination of all privileged "religious" corners in either private or public experience. Today a wholly "profane" world is already visible on the future horizon, at least for the Western industrial nations, and probably for everyone. The question therefore arises whether there is any place for the "sacred" in this profane world. And even if there is, why should we bother to try to find it? Are we not just as well off without it? What is lost by the elimination of the sacred? If God is essentially un-predictable power, and such power has been discovered to be an illusion, is not God dead? And even if he is

[1] As William Golding, in *Pincher Martin*, makes very clear.

lurking in a few unexplored corners, is such a lame God worth having?

That conclusion is, I think, too drastic. It leaves out of account certain elements in our ordinary experience which cannot be accommodated within a purely "secular" framework. As I have tried to show, there is a kind of participatory understanding which is still required if we are to develop a philosophy adequate for the facts at our disposal, and this is an understanding which can be shown to have a recognisable connection with the religious belief in power and man's participation in the world which possesses it. I have already suggested the epistemological outline of such a philosophy. The anti-empiricist philosophical argument which I have put forward implies the necessity for a concept of the reality of the natural species, and of the sharing of this reality among its individual members, which is fundamentally a development of the religious beliefs in the sharing of occult power. (See pp. 95 and 223 above.) It is a legitimate intellectualisation of the idea that things really are similar to each other, and belong in the same kind, not just because we say they are, or because some unmediated perception "sees" they are externally alike, but because they really share a common nature. This "common nature" is but the intellectual taming of the power which the primitive man thinks of as a fluid force within things.

Of course, by contrast with this primitive mode of thought, the realist philosophy of participation is both more exact, in the sense that there is a precise definition of boundaries, and less exciting. It involves a sharper distinction between living and non-living things, and between different kinds of predicates. But it belongs, despite this, to the world of the genuinely religious. It is closer to the religious mentality than it is to the intellectualism and nominalism of the "secular philosophy". Of course, it has proved a difficult philosophy to hold, because the temptation to oversimplification is strong. On the one hand, there is the tendency towards atomism and individualism—the theory that only particulars actually exist, as realities in the world—and, on the other, towards the theory (which naturally goes with this) that what unites all similar things is some one common feature which runs, like a thread, through them all.[1]

But the fact that a philosophical position is difficult to hold against such temptations is no argument against its validity. In a world of increasing complexity and human control, it is only to be expected that the distinctions between truth and error, between the specious and the profound, will be hard to draw. We should not be surprised to find that, as the human capacity for handling intellectual problems increases, the solutions become more complex. The very process of historical advance which the secular thinker tends to emphasize, should lead us to be suspicious of any easy and obvious solutions. Religion, like everything else, will naturally become more complicated and subtle, and make greater demands on our intelligence. It is a mistake to hope that, in the religious field, we shall always be able to find some haven of simplicity, away from the pressing demands of the world for an ever-increasing concentra-

[1] Wittgenstein, in *The Blue and Brown Books*, 87, pinpoints this error in the following striking way: "What ties the ship to the wharf is a rope, and the rope consists of fibres, but it does not get its strength from any fibre which runs through it from one end to the other, but from the fact that there is a vast number of fibres overlapping."

244

tion of intelligence, of knowledge, and of the capacity to discriminate. A religious world-view which is complex and demanding is today more likely to be true than one which is easy to grasp. We cannot evade our responsibility for the intellectual progress we have made. We have to accept that the "sacred" can no longer be maintained as a constellation of concepts and feelings about some *part* of the world which surrounds us, and which is inviolably protected from the intrusion of the profane. There can, from now on, be no permanently privileged corners reserved in our world for the exercise of a specifically "religious" experience as we have traditionally known it. To this extent, those who see the development of the profane spirit of science as destructive of the "supernatural" as popularly conceived are right. But unfortunately, in England and America at any rate, this rejection of the traditional popular version of Christianity has been very largely carried out within a system of ideas and values which are not only foreign to the genuine traditional theology, but are incapable of yielding anything more coherent in its place. (Indeed, part of my argument is that we need to return to traditional theology, in order to understand what has gone wrong with "popular" Christian attitudes. It is not Thomism which is to blame for the incoherences, but the absence of a proper understanding of St Thomas's philosophical presuppositions.) Briefly, the rejection which has become associated with many avant-garde thinkers (including avant-garde theologians) is largely based on a liberal individualism which is now being effectively undermined on all sides—philosophically, sociologically, and psychologically. The empiricist assumptions of this individualistic outlook lurk everywhere beneath the appearance of a communitarian theology. In place of these, we need to grasp once more, but in a new way, the idea of the human community which lies behind the religious experience of mankind. For, just at the moment when the "sacred" as a special realm within human experience has begun to collapse, it is now possible to see that, so far from having been thus eliminated altogether, the sacred is now open to us in our very experience of the human community itself.

All human experience has, as its base, the fact that we constitute a community. We are not created on what Elton Mayo called a "rabble hypothesis"—though, as he discovered, in his study of the workings of modern industry, most of us have hitherto assumed that we are.[1] But this fact, which has begun to be made apparent once more in the philosophical work of Wittgenstein and, in a different way, by Merleau-Ponty and even Marx, has hardly begun to re-establish itself in the popular Christian mind—though it is beginning to re-establish itself in the work of some Catholic theologians of the *aggiornamento*, especially in their doctrine of the church. What is needed more urgently than anything else is a process of translation by which the concepts and values which theology has begun to take for granted can be made available in the analysis of the wider problems, so that the experience of the sacred as the fundamental bond of the community can be made manifest just at

[1] This hypothesis declares that: (1) national society consists of a horde of unorganised individuals; (2) every individual acts in a manner calculated to secure his self-preservation or self-respect; (3) every individual thinks logically, to the best of his ability, in the service of this aim. (Elton Mayo, *Social Problems of an Industrial Civilisation*, Boston 1945.) See my *Work and the Christian Community*, 34 for a brief discussion of this hypothesis in its relation to the Christian approach to industrial work.

the time when, in its traditional setting, it is having to be abandoned.

But here, as I have hinted earlier (see pp. 138ff. above), we are faced by one very important difficulty. This is the problem of death, and the absurdity it seems to introduce into the very heart of this attempted renewal of the idea of the Christian community. For surely death negates the whole idea of community, not merely by its extinction of life and action, but—even more importantly—because it is so unilateral. "Each of us dies alone", as Sir Charles Snow insisted in his Rede lecture. (The isolation of death represents, for him, a positive value; for it offers that sense of the "tragic" which is a proper counterbalance to the danger of a facile optimism on the part of scientists like himself.[1]) The supreme test of a theology for the modern world, then, is death, and the kind of sense that can be made of it. On the one hand, the immoral idea of an immortality which exists merely as a reward, or compensation, for the trials and achievements of life, must be rejected as repugnant to the whole moral sensibility of a society which seeks maturity and understanding for their own sake. On the other, some kind of eternity seems to be required to complete, and give final meaning to, the struggle for maturity and understanding itself. The question therefore poses itself: Do the insights of contemporary philosophers or theologians offer any help in the solution of this difficulty?

C. Death and resurrection

Perhaps the most natural way of conceiving death, as something other than mere extinction, is to look

[1] I have discussed the inadequacy of Snow's view in *Culture and Liturgy*, 94ff.

upon it as the crossing of a threshold into an altogether different world. Throughout my argument, the idea of a threshold or boundary has been more or less constantly at work. We cross from the secular to the sacred world by crossing a threshold which marks the division of sacred space from profane space, and we enter a kind of permanence within experience when we leave behind, in myth or rite, the duration of profane time. In the experience of art, similarly, we cross a threshold into another world, and this gives us a premonition of sacred reality by offering us another kind of world —that of the imagination. Death too is surely the crossing of a boundary to a new world. But it is a boundary which we cannot cross within experience as we normally understand it. For death is a boundary, not in the sense of a line drawn between two territories, but in the sense of the end of a life. As the work of Merleau-Ponty made clear, all experience lies within a field of presence. This field of presence is simply my life. "Our life has no end in just the way that our visual field has no limits."[1] Everything that can be seen must lie within this field, and there are no visible things outside it (in this sense it has no boundary; *everything* that can be in it is already within its range).

But there can, in another sense, be an end of seeing. The darkness of sleep or blindness is neither within nor beyond the visual field. It is simply the absence of the visual field. Similarly, death is not within life, nor is it beyond life in the same line of development. It is the end of life, the end of all fields of presence. This is what Merleau-Ponty means when he says that the feeling for eternity is hypocritical. For, in his sense of the term,

[1] Wittgenstein, *Tractatus*, 6.4311.

eternity feeds on time, which is to say, on the field of presence, and death is simply the end of this presence. Personal immortality as the continuation of life across a threshold is therefore a contradiction. Immortality can only mean, as Wittgenstein also saw, the experience of the present, with the kind of permanence which the present has. The "next world" can only be a misnomer. If eternal life means anything at all it *can* only mean a different kind of presence in this one world.

Christians tend to think of the resurrection of Christ as the first crossing of this threshold. The Christian hope and consolation in the resurrection then becomes the kind of hope one has from seeing the first member of a queue go through his ordeal successfully. As we see him do so, we realise that we too can hope to emulate his success. If he can do it, so can I. Clearly this picture of Christ's death and resurrection will not do. For the essential thing about the resurrection of Christ is that by it he is made present to us, fully and even bodily, in the sacraments—especially the eucharist. That is to say, he has not crossed a threshold before us; he has brought what we had thought of as the end of our field of presence, the end of our life, *into* that field, so that now it has no end—for everything is present. In other words, what before seemed to be darkness and negation— simply the absence of the field of presence altogether —has now been transformed into a "darkness visible", a positive mystery which is at the same time experienced within our field of presence. The "threshold" of death was always, then, a delusion. There was no threshold, because there was nothing on the other side of it. Precisely what we had thought of as a threshold with nothing beyond it (so that we had to dream dreams of something beyond it, which were always merely reproductions of what we have already experienced—feasts, the music of harps, the unity of the fire and the rose) now reveals itself, in the resurrection, as a part of our life. It becomes something we can taste, and so it becomes ours. The dreams were *true* after all. The "death of me" is transformed into *my* death. Death is my act, something I *do*, a positive realisation of my whole life. (Martyrdom is simply this: making, out of the mere negativity of death as an ending, a personal action, something to be embraced.)

Thus what had seemed to be unattainable, because it lay beyond a boundary which, of its very nature, had nothing beyond it, is now part of our ordinary experience. What comes after death is already present to us, in life. Christ's resurrection joins heaven and earth,[1] not in a spatio-temporal sense, but in the sense that God has become accessible to our field of presence. In Christ, he is already within the scope of our life-experience, and cannot be banished from it. But our life is lived within the sphere of the cosmos, and if it is this one life which persists after death, then the sphere of this persistent life —heaven (or hell)—cannot be regarded as a "place" beyond the cosmos.[2] (Only God is "beyond" the cosmos.

[1] "Nox in qua terrenis caelestia, humanis divina iunguntur" ("the night on which heavenly things are joined to earthly and divine to human")—from the Exsultet of the Holy Saturday liturgy.

[2] This notion of the cosmos is difficult. Perhaps the following paragraph from an article in *Herder Correspondence* (April 1965) summarising the thought of Fr Ladislaus Boros on the Last Things is suggestive of the right way of approaching it: "In death man enters into a new mode of relationship to cosmic reality as his soul ceases to animate his body. Losing its intrinsic and constitutive relation to the restricted portion of matter which it has informed as its body (and which is part of the whole

His presence to us *is* heaven). For just as all my experience lies within the one field of presence which is my life, so also all my experience lies within this one cosmos which is the locus of all experience. Humanity—including the humanity of Christ—is intrinsically geared to the cosmos, just as it is intrinsically geared to the body. Body and cosmos are complementary. There can no more be a resurrection and life outside the cosmos than there can be sight outside the visual field. Hell and heaven can, therefore, only be different ways of experiencing this one cosmos, transformed by Christ's resurrection, transfigured by God's power.

> Hell is not . . . a special place but the same world in which the blessed live also in their happiness. God cannot create a bad place any more than anything else bad. It is the reprobate who is out of place, a misfit, out of his element. The damned live unhappily in a universe that is transparent to God.[1]

(Satan, in the Book of Job, lives side by side with the angels before God.) The work of Christ is not to transform men by separating them from the one setting in

[1] Boros, *Herder Correspondence* (April 1965).

---

material universe) the soul does not become acosmic, 'out of the world'. It retains its constitutive ordination towards matter and stands in wider relation to the cosmos in its entirety, pancosmic, open to it in some way analogous (but only analogous) to the way in which the angels are cosmic principles, and essentially related as spiritual persons to the cosmic order". The latter point is, no doubt, what lies behind St Thomas's distinction between God as the one necessary being who has his necessity from himself, and the angels, who, though they are necessary beings, in the sense that they cannot not exist, are nevertheless only derivative, and are part of "creation".

which they can exist, but to transform them *in* that cosmic setting. If human community is a dialogue with the world, a commerce with objects which support and give life to men, then the community of heaven is a dialogue in the presence of God between resurrected humanity and a cosmos transfigured to meet man's new condition.

It follows from all this, of course, that this transfigured cosmos *is* the sacred world. The break between sacred and profane, of which I have spoken in various contexts, takes its meaning from this understanding of death and resurrection. Because the transfigured life, and the transfigured cosmos, are already realised, albeit only partially, in experience, the sacred is not just "another world", nor is it a corner in this world. It is the sacrality of the transfigured life which Christ's work has brought about, and which is sacramentally realised now in the world—especially in the liturgy. The liturgical assembly *is* the sacred, since in it the world is already transfigured, because the resurrected Christ is present to it. Here we actually experience what we took to be on the other side, beyond experience.

But it is essential to this mystery that Christ's resurrection be a true coming to life again of the man Jesus. For as we have seen, there is no human experience which is not that of a person, which is to say of a body. Human community entails, as its basis, a community of bodies—not bodies as mere objects, but bodies as expressive, in action. It is as necessary for an encounter with Christ to be a bodily encounter as it is for any other human encounter. If it is not a presence of bodies in actual contact, or within the field of the senses, it must at any rate be an encounter which has a "family continuity" with such experience of encounter.[1] (There is no such thing as a purely spiritual encounter.) That is to say, it depends, at the very least, upon there having been bodily encounter in the past, and there being the possibility of bodily encounter in the future. For without this future possibility of encounter, there can be none in the present. (There can be no human community with a corpse. There can be commemoration of the departed spirit, and there can be prayer; but not encounter.) These possibilities are necessary, from the side of man, but also from the side of Christ. Heaven must be a community of bodies—Christ's body and ours. The church is his body, and the eucharist is his body, only because his body is encounterable in heaven. The church militant is continuous with the church triumphant, the eucharist is continuous with the heavenly banquet. We are already on the other side of death. What remains is to make death our own, and the world ready for the coming transfiguration.

This may sound too easy, and to make light of the problem of the survival of the disembodied soul. But the point is that the problem of the disembodied soul is precisely the problem of how such an entity could have experiences. I am not pretending that there are not difficulties about this idea (though they are reduced if we insist that such an experience is only an interlude made possible because the soul has been the life of the particular body which it once animated, and which it will certainly animate again). But it is important to see that the difficulties are philosophical, and not religious. For,

[1] This expression is borrowed from R. Harré, *Theories and Things*, 58. Any set the members of which are (a) overlapping in some feature, (b) such that the beginning- and end-members of the set are not overlapping, is a set showing family continuity.

at any rate in the Christian view, it is only because we are unprepared for death that there is any interlude between giving up the body and taking it up again in glory. If we fail to make death our own, by omitting to prepare for it in life (by "mortification", which means "making dead" as Fr Herbert McCabe has reminded us (*The New Creation*, 198), then the interlude between this life and the transfigured bodily life becomes a problem and a worry—the problem and worry of "survival" and of preparing for the new life of heaven. (That is the problem of purgatory.) But in perfect life there would be no such interlude at all. Sleep is terrible only because it can be given a content—dreams. But dreams draw all their terror from past experiences which we can still recall, although we can now no longer control them. The life of a disembodied soul can only be borrowed from the life of the person who has died. The terror of its experiences comes from the recollection of a life it dared not forgo. But if all desire to cling to that life has been given up, and the bodily mechanism which is necessary for memory has gone, then there will be no content to the life of the soul, and therefore *for it* no interlude. (Here surely is the deepest meaning of the doctrine of the bodily Assumption of our Lady.) If there were no experiences between the moment of death and the moment of resurrection then, *for that person*, there would be no waiting for eternity, however long *we* might watch his body disintegrating in the grave.

This means that not only is the fear and worry of the "interlude" something of our own making. The very fact of there being an interlude at all is of our own making as well. It is not just a fate to resign ourselves to, a consequence of some "fallen condition". It exists solely by virtue of our own orientation to the world and what we make of it. It follows that all our moral growth must properly be directed towards this culminating, personal act of dying. It is here that George Eliot's concept of a moral growth which has no end must, finally, prove inadequate. It can make no sense of death. For death is our supreme moral achievement, the flowering of our personality. The way I enact my own death is not merely a reflection of the way I acted towards my world, and towards other people, in life. Life is not just a training for dying. My death is the supreme *expression* and *actualisation* of my human maturity; it is the flowering of my moral sensibility, the unfolding of my potentialities in so far as I have allowed them to unfold. Death makes me a complete person. (It does not just *need* the greatest possible love to die for a friend, as though dying for a friend is undertaken as the proof of my love in the eyes of the world. To die for a friend is to *do* something for him, to make myself over to him completely; and hence, in such an act, love is manifested, not as a kind of proof, but for its own sake.) Death is the achievement of my full self-consciousness, the furthest stretch of my powers for life. This is why there can be no retreat from death back into oneself, not even into madness (as Pincher Martin realised). There is nothing to be discovered that has not been revealed by this action. At death I must remain what I am, for there is nothing more to be done. From that moment I simply am what I am.

This view of death is the only one which makes possible a reconciliation between the humanist's concern for a continuing growth in all our human powers —in moral freedom and responsibility, in awareness of self and others, in the sharpening of sensibility—and the fact of death as an end of growth. The humanist is right to look at the escapist death offered by conventional Christianity, which is simply a gateway to a reward in the next world, as a moral monstrosity. Certainly, if immortality is just an escape or a compensation, it makes nonsense of the moral and intellectual drive towards a greater grasp of life which we know as the most significant feature of our present condition. But it is also true that, if death is merely an end, it makes a nonsense of this striving. The "immortality" conferred by posterity, and the "growing goodness of the world" to which we have contributed is no answer to it. Such "immortality" offers us only a metaphor, where nothing short of a reality will satisfy.

It will be objected here that, to think of death as the bringing into experience—that is, into the field of presence—of something that is, of its very nature, beyond all experience is a contradiction. But this is to beg the question. For just as the church makes present the risen Christ in the world, so it makes present the fact of death. The Christian dies daily. His acts, done "in Christ", are not just rehearsals for the final act of dying; they are truly parts of it. We begin to die as soon as we are alive. Just as the liturgical assembly is a real presence, here and now, shadowy but real, of the community of heaven, so the acts of the individual who is joined to this community, in Christ, are joined to Christ's death in a shadowy but nevertheless real way. Our growth in moral responsibility is not merely directed towards the final action; it is part of a single process which flowers in it. There is only a contradiction in the idea of making death a part of our everyday experience if it is assumed from the start that death is an end, in the way that the cutting off of the plant is an end. If death is not an end—that is, if our life is endless in the way that the field of vision is without limits—then there is no such thing as an end in this sense of the term. There is only a renewal, after sleep, of the same field of presence—which is to say, of the same bodily person.

This is where Christianity can give a new intelligibility to the problem of death. For, on the secularist's principles, death is the supremely unintelligible fact. It cuts short the very process of growth into self-knowledge which is the driving force of the humanist morality. The whole emphasis which, rightly, is given by the humanist to the growth towards self-knowledge as the supreme moral endeavour, implies that there can be no absolute natural end. Maturity is of its nature a moral aim rather than a moral achievement. It is the very antithesis of the humanist ethic to be satisfied with any achieved growth. There is always more to be done. Yet surely death makes nonsense of this fact. For there *is* a limit to what we can do, and our growth seems to be towards annihilation, not completion. Of course, there can be a kind of heroism in the acceptance of this fact; but it is a heroism of defiance, not a heroism of understanding. It does not bring death into the orbit of the intelligible, but simply banishes it as irrelevant precisely because it is beyond intelligibility. Such heroism may be morally better than the acceptance of death as a price to be paid for a purely "spiritual" reward. (For that is a subhuman as well as an unintelligible idea, based as it is upon the consignment of the body to destruction, and hence upon the destruction of the human as such.) But the heroism of defiance is inadequate by the very standards of the humanism which suggests it. It marks the collapse of the whole movement towards human control. Only when death has been made intelligible, as a right and proper part of the humanisation of life, can the humanist begin to feel that his purposes are attainable.

It is here that Christianity can offer some tools of understanding. For it claims to show that there is a way in which death can, and indeed has, been brought into the orbit of the intelligible. Death is not a threshold into a bodiless immortality (which would be sub-human) nor a cutting short of the moral growth which it is the task of humanity to foster, but precisely a completion of humanity itself. The fact that this completion must come as a gift, and not as something which naturally lies at the end of a journey (as a terminus lies at the end of a railway line), is unacceptable only on the presupposition that such a gratuitousness is itself intrinsically unintelligible. But the very paradox of a growth which, while it is for ever open to further development, at the same time entails the idea of completion as its aim (for it is a growth *towards* something), is in any case equally unintelligible. The morality of humanism therefore entails the very gratuitousness which it explicitly denies. What it envisages as that towards which moral growth is directed, *must* lie beyond the limits of the very capacities it acknowledges as exhaustive. The meeting of grace and nature is already implicit in the natural growth which it has been the achievement of the humanist moral vision to validate. By showing that this meeting of nature and grace has already taken place, in the life, death, and resurrection of Christ, Christianity is able to offer an intelligible, even if incredible, perspective in which the humanist moral vision can be freed from its own intolerable paradox. The fact that, to most people, the Christian perspective is incredible is relatively unimportant. For the first thing that is demanded is a perspective which *is relevant*. Only if Christianity first appears to offer a concept which is meaningful can the possibility of its being true be even raised. It is a waste of time canvassing irrelevancies, even if they are true. Or rather, if they are irrelevant, they cannot be true. For Christianity's first claim is precisely to universal relevance.

The relevance of the Christian concept of death is that in it, death becomes something I enact, as a person who is in control. It is not consigning the body which I am to oblivion, but consigning it to the possibility of its own completion from beyond itself. That this completion (or "glorification") seems incredible to the humanist is due, not only to limited moral vision, but to his entanglement with a secularist philosophy which cannot fully support it. He cannot fully trust his own instinct. The Christian is simply a humanist who has learnt to trust the ground upon which he stands.

Seen in this way, the "supernatural" claims of Christianity become at least relevant to the humanist's deepest concern. To do away with them, so far from helping Christianity to come to terms with humanism, renders it incapable of offering just that perspective which the modern world requires in order to release itself from its own intolerable paradox. It is because the best in contemporary humanism entails a gratuitousness which it cannot envisage, that there can be a mutual endeavour between believers and unbelievers to discover the meaning of the world they have both inherited. It is in the working out of this endeavour that the challenge to modern man lies.

Conclusion

1. The concern of this book, as I said in the Introduction, has been to give some intellectual underpinning to the "radical" approach to Christianity in the modern world. If it has been an involved and difficult argument, this is partly because of a lack of clarity and an immense intellectual complexity in the subject itself. That complexity must emerge from any serious attempt to discuss the religious problem in our kind of society. Nevertheless some clarification and possibly some further development is necessary in order to see the intellectual argument in its proper perspective.

We are faced today by the unique historical possibility of a totally humanised and controlled world. The old distinction between the sacred and the profane in terms of the unknown and mysterious and unpredictable, on the one hand, and the known and the controllable on the other, is fast disappearing. The world may soon present to us a wholly humanised environment, in which there is no corner left untouched by man. Everywhere human meanings and human modifications will confront us. We shall see nothing but the reflection of ourselves. (Dickens has shown us the disastrous moral and spiritual consequences which can follow from this process when controlled by a purely secularist vision.) Unfortunately, this humanisation of the world has taken place, histori-

cally, under the auspices of a particular intellectual outlook which I have called the secular philosophy. I am
aware that I have sketched the outlines of this philosophical outlook extremely baldly, and without most
of the nuances which make it interesting. But I believe
nevertheless that, in the very broadest terms, the analysis
I have offered of it is correct, and that it is still, despite
many variations, a distinctive and powerful intellectual
current in our culture. (One reason for the discussion of
Orwell in philosophical terms was to show that the
secular philosophy, in almost its pristine clarity, is still
a possible and in some ways attractive intellectual option
in the middle of this century, and that it has influential
adherents.) Yet it is equally clear that there is no necessary logical connection between the secular humanisation
of the world, even as undertaken by the West, and the
particular philosophy which, in fact, has shaped it so
decisively. Further, the movement of secularism itself
has begun to reveal the poverty of the philosophy which
at first encouraged and promoted it. This is where the
crisis of modern culture is deepest. It has found its own
philosophical basis crumbling without having any more
solid foundation to replace it.

It is at this point, of course, that Christians are ready,
and indeed are often only too eager, to step in. Only
by a return to Christian values, and a Christian philosophy, can the rot be halted, they assert. This assertion
is not so much false as premature. For the fundamental
problem to be solved, whether it be couched in terms of
a return to Christianity or in terms of a new kind of
secularism, is that of making sense of our experience in
the new setting. It is this which the very humanisation
we have brought about demands of us. If the world is
to be one of increasingly human control, the problem is

that of finding an intellectual basis upon which to understand the meanings which this world offers us. This is the first priority—not the imposition of Christianity or any other "-ity" or "-ism", but the discovery of a new kind of intelligibility. At its best, the attempt to secularise Christianity is of course just such a search for intelligibility. It is not merely a tailoring of the gospel to suit a new age, but an attempt to understand the world by the transformation of the old Christian categories which once afforded a basis for understanding it, but which can do so no longer. Now it is easy, as an academic exercise, to refute the arguments used so far by the Christian secularisers—who are after all only fumbling at the very edges of a vast problem. Professor Mascall, in his book *The Secularisation of Christianity*, has demonstrated how easily this can be done, but also how little has been achieved when it is completed. For the question remains (and it is one which Professor Mascall does not properly answer): How are we to tackle the problem of modern secularism in order to make it intelligible to ourselves? This is not just a matter of offering the old answers, and expecting the new world to take notice of them. It is the much more radical problem of coming to grips with an historically new situation: the total humanisation of our life.

The humanisation, or secularisation, of the world has involved two closely connected revolutions: the technical, and the moral. It is because the two are closely connected, not by logic but by history, that the subject is so immensely complex. For it is quite possible to welcome the technical revolution and reject the moral revolution, and vice versa. The technical revolution is that process by which we have achieved the capacity to control and subdue the natural environment, so that the whole world is almost laid at man's feet for him to do as he likes with. The moral revolution is much harder to trace out in a clear-cut way. Roughly it consists in the substitution of values such as vitality, maturity, self-knowledge, and personal freedom for the older values of duty, obedience to moral law, self-abnegation, and submission to the inherited social tradition. Because it is possible to affirm the moral revolution while deploring the technical revolution, and vice versa, the range of responses to the secularisation of the world can be enormously wide. *Modernism* may be typically regarded as the affirmation of both revolutions as mostly or wholly good. Whether it is described in terms of approbation—as by Snow—or in terms of disapprobation—as by Lawrence—modernism in this sense is a characteristic response to our world. But it is not the universal, or even the typical, response. Equally typical are the pessimism of the radical humanist who rejoices in the secular morality while condemning the impersonal brutalisation of the technical revolution, and the optimism of the authoritarian technocrat who rejoices in the technical marvels of the age while yearning for condemnation of its moral anarchy. Finally, there is the total pessimist, to whom both revolutions are a disaster from which our culture is never likely to recover. But all these responses are inadequate in various ways, for they fail to consider in sufficient depth the nature of the connection between the two revolutions. They depend upon a certain dissociation of moral from social and technical problems, and think of each as autonomous in its own sphere.

This dissociation is itself a natural product of the secular philosophy, according to which morality is the concern of the individual with his personal choices.

Society is over against this as an impersonal force which cannot be controlled. It is a constant theme of moralists in the liberal tradition to assert that the only refuge from the evils of the technical revolution, and the social forces it has released, lies in a renewal of individual life. Until the individual is brought to a moral maturity equal to the technical maturity which our society has achieved, we cannot, it is said, begin to solve the modern problem. Society and its energies are beyond the realm of human control. There is a technical revolution, and there is an individual response; but there can be no fruitful social revolution, as such. For all that we can expect from any social revolution is a situation in which the methods of impersonal technical control are applied wholesale to human beings. This is totalitarianism; and it is intolerable. Now, because traditionally we have been brought up to analyse the situation in these crude terms, there *can* be no solution which brings the two together. Individual despair and socially uncontrolled technical exploitation therefore proceed hand in hand, and moral individualism is offered as the only way of escape from the pressures of economic and technical domination. The concept of a social revolution as such —that is, a change in our ideas of society in the direction of the humanisation and democratisation of social energy —is ruled out by such an analysis as this. Yet clearly it is just this conception that we need if we are to match the humanisation of technique and the humanisation of individual moral life with a corresponding humanisation of social life. For it is in social life alone that the technical and moral revolutions have their context and meaning.

The secular philosophy has, as its natural political product, individualistic utilitarian liberalism. Its social philosophy is necessarily thin and negative, consisting largely in the denial of social claims. It is here, in the consequent ravages of the technical revolution and of the uncontrolled capitalism which it has engendered, that the poverty of the secular philosophy is most apparent. But this is only the visible part of the secularist iceberg. Beneath it lies a deeper problem of a philosophical character—the problem of the philosophical exploration of our experience of the world and of ourselves. It is at this level that I have tried to discuss the possibilities of an alternative to the secular philosophy. Only when these are made explicit, or at any rate when some indication has been given of the direction in which to look for a solution, can we begin to solve the visible problems of creating a secular world which is tolerable for human beings—that is, a world which is dominated neither by impersonal technique nor by individual ambitions, but by an awareness, which is realised in our institutions, of the social dimension as such.

If this is the central problem which faces Western culture, then it is only in this context that Christianity is likely to be found even relevant, let alone true. Unless Christianity can show that it has some special insights to offer in the solution of this problem it will have failed. For it is just here, in the humanised world, that man has to find himself. Hence, to assert at this point that his true salvation lies elsewhere is, at this deepest level, sheer irresponsibility. Indeed, if that is what Christianity is about, then it is plainly false and certainly immoral. But to say this is not to assert—as those who want to debate the issue within the constricting terms of the secular philosophy tend to suggest—that the "supernatural" claims of Christianity are irrelevant. Both the Christian and the humanist are here in danger of prejudging the real issue. For the problem is one of discovering meanings, not one of applying ready-made meanings to a known situation. It is precisely in the search for a valid and fruitful way of understanding the problem that the difficulties lie and the answers (if any) are to be found. What Christianity *means* is as much in question here as everything else. (The deepest "ecumenism" is this common search for an intelligible meaning, and it applies to Christians and to unbelievers alike.)

2. I have tried to argue that in the work of Merleau-Ponty, Wittgenstein, and Marx we have the beginnings of a coherent, modern, non-secular way of understanding our experience. (That this part of my book is difficult, tentative, and vague is to be expected. For we are all trying to explore an unknown territory, in which many mistakes will be made.) But it is not enough to provide a purely philosophical framework for a new Christian theology—this philosophical framework has to be related to practical life.

In my Introduction I said (see p. 2 above) that one of my purposes was to give some intellectual underpinning to what I called the "radical" concept of Christianity, as distinct from the views of the "secularisers" and the "modernisers". It is now time to see whether anything more can be said about Christian radicalism than was possible at the outset. I hope that in the course of my discussion I have been able to give some body to the brief descriptions given, at the beginning, of both the secularist and the modernist approaches to the problems which confront a Christian in the twentieth century. But since I described the radical alternative as an attempt to bring together the positive merits of each, while rejecting the limitations, it is perhaps necessary to suggest in a more direct way what such a radical position entails.

Both the seculariser and the moderniser are basically concerned with the same problem—that of "making the Christian religion intelligible and acceptable to twentieth-century civilised men and women".[1] Now, perhaps this is just where the radical differs from them. For he is not primarily bothered about whether Christianity is acceptable to other people. His first concern is to see whether, as a twentieth-century person, he can make sense of it for himself. Radicalism is not, in any sense, an apologia. The radical has no stake, intellectually, in the maintenance of the Christian religion, except as a means whereby to understand himself, and *his* world. His religion simply *is* his understanding of these things.[2] If he wishes to persuade others of its truth, this is because, as one human being to another, he is concerned to bring his own understanding to the common stock of wisdom. Naturally, because he believes—as any rational person must—that one truth cannot contradict another, he hopes that his understanding of the world in Christian terms will help others to make sense of their situations. He of course believes that, once properly grasped, it must do so. For the radical believes in the human community as one body, and therefore that any truth which one person has proved, in his intellectual life and on his pulses, must be of value to others in their search for truth. But he holds that the world has already developed beyond the point at which any minority institution, however venerable, can reason-

[1] E. L. Mascall, *The Secularisation of Christianity*, 107f.

[2] Of course, as the burden of my argument has made clear, this does not mean that the individual can make sense of his own experience in isolation from the rest of the human community.

ably claim, or expect, to be heard and acknowledged as authoritative just by virtue of the claims it makes for itself. We are now in a world in which all claims to teach have to be vindicated by the sincerity, intelligence, and moral integrity of those who make them; or rather, this is the climate which the modern world has, rightly, begun to see as the best for the future development of civilisation.

Naturally, in the face of such a demanding test, we are all failing. We still tend to take as authoritative the claims of scientists, entertainers, politicians, journalists, and even, occasionally, clergymen, when they offer no rational foundation for our credulity. But at least we recognise that this *is* a failing, and that it points to an inability, as yet, to achieve the full exercise of human powers which we know is possible. To the radical Christian, this climate feels right. He does not particularly regret it when a bishop or even the pope is shouted down on some issue over which he should not have spoken. For ultimately the interest of Christianity is not bound up with that kind of authority, or that image of the teacher's role in the world.

But the radical Christian does not, on this account, proceed to abandon the whole concept of a teaching community, and strike out on some individualistic path of his own. For he finds that a community in which (among other things) teaching and learning, the search for self-knowledge and an understanding of the world, are pursued in common, through visible social structures which give the opportunity for the ordered exercise of different gifts and functions, is necessary for his own purposes. As a critic of himself and of his own world, his purpose is "the common pursuit of true judgement".[1] Nor does he try to create, from scratch, such a community in an ideal setting, for he recognises that the process of learning and understanding can only be fruitful if it takes account of the past as well as of the present—that is to say, if it is based upon a tradition which is alive. For he sees that there can be no genuine community of learning and understanding except one which is, in a sense, already in existence and living its own life. This is why the radical rejects the "secular" tendency to throw overboard the empirical society of the given church. He agrees with the "moderniser" that this community is all that we have, and that without it there can be no articulated structure of tradition. But unlike the moderniser, he does not therefore limit himself to some concept of what is "practicable" within the church as at present constituted. He looks at its structure in the light of a theoretical analysis and is prepared to make distinctions and priorities on this basis, and to let them form a springboard for action. He sees that the church is not just the institution that we know, and that how it is to be changed depends largely upon the language we use to describe it. Therefore the discovery of a language which describes it in a way which is faithful to its own essential nature, but which is also intelligible to himself, is an urgent and practical problem.

The radical's disagreement with the secularisers, on the other hand, is that they have misunderstood the nature of the modern world which they are trying to interpret in a Christian sense. That is to say, as I have tried to indicate in the course of my discussion, the philosophical basis which they have tended to take as

[1] T. S. Eliot, "The Function of Criticism", *Selected Essays*, 25.

typical of modern thought, and with which they have tried to reconcile the Christian idea, is not the central or fruitful concept which they have taken it to be. So, far from succeeding in understanding the modern world, and its crucial forms of thought, they have chosen as characteristic of it aspects which are of relatively little value, or which have no longer any potency for further development. The nature of these ideas, and the nature of the alternative concepts which I believe to be more fertile, have already been indicated in my discussion of the "secular philosophy" and of the ideas of Merleau-Ponty, Wittgenstein, and Marx. I do not wish to pursue in detail here the ways in which any particular "secular" Christian thinkers have adopted false or inadequate positions.[1] The purpose of this discussion is rather to clarify a line of thought which seems to me to be more fruitful, and also more self-consistent, than the "secular" philosophy which has been and still is a powerful intellectual force in Western culture.

I said at the outset that one of the characteristic features of a radical position was that it implied some kind of theoretical picture of the future. The kind of society towards which we are trying to move, not just in the immediate short-term, but in a more distant perspective, is important for the radical because it is the basis of the discriminations he wants to make about the characteristics and trends of the present. Since, as I have said, the central preoccupation of Christianity is the understanding of ourselves in the context of our common life, and not just as autonomous individuals,

[1] For such a critique of Christian secularism, see my review of Ronald Gregor Smith's *Secular Christianity* in *New Blackfriars* 53 (May 1966).

the exploration of the idea of the Christian community, and in particular of its future development, must be in the forefront of any Christian effort. But it is impossible to pursue this idea in isolation from its own context, which is that of the modern world. Ideas drawn from current social and political theories have always been used by theologians to construct a picture of the church for their own times, and our own age is no exception to this. (It is one of the dangers of the moderniser's approach, beginning as it does with the "given" community he finds, that it tempts him to analyse its weaknesses in terms of itself, instead of in terms of its relationship to the surrounding world which supports it. He tends to use an old-style language, and out-of-date concepts, because they have been of service in the past, and have been hallowed within the community he is examining. Wilsonian socialist modernism is full of nineteenth-century working-class slogans, and papal documents are still couched to a great extent in "Vaticanese".)

What is required, therefore, for the radical position, is an understanding of the church in contemporary terms, not just in order to produce a streamlined image, but in order to make possible a genuine understanding of itself. Since the radical position is one which accepts the notion of a structured Christian community, with traditional authority and historical continuity from Christ as its very foundation, the first priority is therefore to examine this conception in terms of contemporary processes of learning and understanding.

The claim of the church which most scandalises the modern man is its claim to teach authoritatively. This is partly because he feels—often with some justice—that this claim is not only arrogant in itself, but is made by people who have no more—and often less—competence, understanding, and integrity than those they are addressing. But if that were the only objection, then the moderniser, whose concern is to clean the image and to remove the blemishes, would be right. There is a deeper scandal, however, which rests upon an objection to the whole idea of a claim on the part of one human group to *teach* the rest of humanity how to think and behave. The fact that, in the case of the church, this claim is made in the name of God and not in its own name makes no substantial difference to the scandal involved. Until this particular scandal has been removed, the content of what the church wishes to say will not be heard, and certainly not understood. Indeed, it will not even be noticed. Now it is important here to point out that all theological language is borrowed from our experience of the world. The word "teach" is no exception. What imagery is evoked when somebody says, either in attack or defence of the church, that its role is to teach? This question is hardly ever asked. When bishops or controversialists insist, for any reason, that the task of the church is to teach, they tend to assume that it is obvious and indeed self-evident what this means, and that the only question that matters is whether it is true. So the old controversy about the authority of the church goes on around this issue, when the important question—namely, what does it mean to say that the church's role is that of a teacher?—is passed by. But in point of fact, the concept of teaching is by no means a clear one. I have tried elsewhere[1] to suggest some of the ways in which the idea of teaching has

[1] *Culture and Liturgy*, 173–7.

been falsified in the course of the church's history. Here it may be more useful to try to offer some more positive concept in order to replace that which has prevailed so far.

The image of the teacher, from which the dominant thinking of Christians derives, is that of the school-master—and the not very enlightened schoolmaster at that. The teacher is one who has a textbook in one hand and a ruler in the other. He reads from the book, expecting that, after a long enough period of listening, the class will remember, and (he hopes) understand, what he has read to them. If the class does not respond, or pay attention, he can rap on the desk for silence, demand a hearing on the ground of his authority, beat the lazy or the sceptical in order to bring them into line, and even (as a last resort) send the rebellious out of the room. He can even send them to the headmaster for a pep-talk, or an order for expulsion.

Now, it is a picture of this kind which lurks at the back of the minds of most of us when we come across some official reassertion of the authority of the church to teach. The word "teach" itself carries this connotation with it—not necessarily because teachers are normally like that (though certainly the kind of teaching that is done in schools must, eventually, have its effect upon the way theologians or bishops use the word in a theo-logical context) but because that is the picture which our culture, in various ways, still presents to us. Because the word has this connotation, whatever may be the subjective intention of its user, this use of it is bound to carry over into the minds of the listener. Only when teaching as a part of our cultural life is so transformed that this imagery is no longer part of its normal signifi-cance, will it be possible to speak of the church as

273

"teaching" with authority while not giving a false impression of what this means. (This is one of those cases in which the language forces us, even against our wills, into a certain path. It is part of the fact that the language we use shapes the kind of experience we have, and the general interpretation we put upon it. Until teaching has become something different, it will not, in general, be possible to talk with real point or clarity about the church as a teaching body. The interaction of theological language and the culture of the surrounding community is important in just this way.)

It is probable that the changes which have already taken place in the teaching process have had an impact upon the climate of doubt and discomfort which is experienced when some pronouncement is made about the need to reassert the teaching authority of the church. For those who have been influenced by the revolution in teaching methods at the earliest stages of education, or who have as students and adults been taught in a mature seminar fashion, are likely to feel with embarrassment the impact of an older and more insensitive tradition as it comes through to them in the lofty dogmatism of an ecclesiastical pronouncement. This is not teaching as they have come to understand and respect it. It is indoctrination, not education. (The more the specifically Christian schools are brought up to date in their teaching methods, the more acute will this embarrassment become.)

A radical Christian is committed, as I have said, to the same ideal of moral and intellectual maturity as is the seculariser. It follows from this that the model which he must adopt in thinking of the church as a teaching community must be suited to this adult ideal. It is to the notion of the seminar, not to that of the class-room or the lecture-hall, that we must look for our analogies. The class-room suggests immaturity, the lecture-hall impersonality and one-sidedness. It is in the seminar, where the teacher's role is that of catalyst, the crystalliser of the thoughts of the group, that a suitable context can be found for a new theological exploration of the concept of the teaching church, and of the bishop as "tutor" to his "students". The initiative may come from any member of the group. Discussion is free-ranging and uninhibited. But it is not without direction. For the tutor's task is to give a sense of direction; to point out the ideas which have been forgotten, the emphases which are out of balance, the facts which have been misstated or misused, the arguments which are invalid or lacking in evidential support. His authority for doing this lies partly in his position as the acknowledged and appointed tutor, and partly in his superior knowledge of the subject and skill in handling its difficulties. His authority is not given to him by the group; but in order to maintain the credibility of his position, he must continually vindicate his authority by the evidence of his competence, his sensitivity to the interests of the students, his capacity to stimulate them to new ideas, and his general awareness of the context in which the group's work is being carried on. He must be both a traditionalist and a contemporary, living at the edges where new life comes into being, on the boundaries between past and future.

This, I suggest, is the best model available for the structure of a human community which is dedicated primarily to the exploration of experience and the increase of self-awareness. It is on this structure that the other teaching processes—the imparting of facts, the supervision of experiment, the conducting of research—

all focus; for it is here that the creative work of a learn-ing *community* is carried on. Indeed since teaching (as opposed to proclaiming) implies learning as its other term, the very concept of a teaching church implies that of a learning church. The two cannot be separated; for they are simply the opposite sides of a single process of self-exploration by the whole people of God. As Abbot Butler has said in reviewing Hans Küng's *Structures of the Church*: "We shall have to think again about any distinction between *ecclesia docens* and *ecclesia discens*. These are, perhaps, rather two aspects of a single entity."[1]

The main point at which the seminar analogy is relevant is the liturgical assembly. The articulation of the assembly-structure, and in particular the distribution and character of the different roles within it, is to be thought of in these terms. But the extent to which the liturgical dialogue fulfils its task of constituting the community at each gathering depends to a great extent upon the kind of dialogue which goes on in the time when the community, as a visible body in action, is in abeyance. There is a natural relationship between the activity of the liturgical assembly and the activities of its members, in their various roles, outside it. It is in this outside activity that the model of the seminar is most apt. For it is here that the concepts which are put to use in the liturgy are freely explored and learned by the community together, and in cooperation with other people who are not necessarily part of the liturgical assembly at all. It is here that the celebrant takes off his liturgical robes and becomes a tutor, authorised to teach.

[1] *The Tablet* (11 September 1965), 997.

The picture which the radical Christian has of the teaching church for the future is one in which the seminar analogy has replaced that of the class-room. It is with this objective constantly in view that he discriminates between right and wrong ways of encouraging the renewal of Christianity here and now. It is not that the radical view is contemptuous of tradition. On the contrary, it is essential to the radical that he can establish the validity of the view of tradition which is implied in his criticism of the degeneracy which marks the Christian community as we know it today. But tradition, for the radical, is a living thing. What counts is tradition insofar as it is alive now, or is recoverable in the future.

> What might have been and what has been
> Point to one end, which is always present.
> [T. S. Eliot, *Burnt Norton*, I.]

The teacher, insofar as he is one to whom a tradition is committed, and on whose shoulders its preservation and future life rest, must be a person whose understanding of tradition is always geared to the needs of the present (for there is no other moment for which he has any responsibility), and who interprets it in the light of the present. Not only must he be one who is steeped in tradition, but equally he must be one alive to and engaged in the life of the present; for it is at the point of reaction between the two that his work of teaching is to be done.

If we take the model of the seminar as that which is most fruitful for the future understanding of the church's teaching mission, we see at once how thin and superficial are the moderniser's concepts of renewal. For the moderniser thinks only in terms of "consulting the faithful", or of improving technically the means of communication by which the dialogue between hierarchy and laity can be effectively pursued. These things are indeed necessary, but it is the picture of the future for which this dialogue is to be carried on that is the important thing. For to the radical, the achievement of this ideal is the criterion by which he judges the work of renewal that he is prepared to support in the present, and he is not to be diverted from it by ingenious solutions to problems which, for him, appear futile and illusory. This is because it is only in such a context as the "seminar" that the church has any fundamental relevance for him.

He is not concerned with the preservation, or even the reform, of the ecclesiastical *apparatus*, except marginally. What matters for him is that he is already committed to membership of the seminar which life in the modern world impels him to join. Seeing that this is where the fruitful and creative work is going on, he is waiting for the time when the church can bring itself to join in properly. He sees that before it can do this, it must first of all undergo a good deal of practice in the conducting of "seminars" with its own people, and educate itself to the maturity which is demanded of it by the world. Until it has achieved that level, the radical Christian will have to live an uncomfortable existence, trying to maintain effective communication with both sides in a complex and unsatisfactory world.

Bibliography

This bibliography is divided into three sections. In section A are listed the source books—the works of classical and modern philosophy, the novels, and the works on the sociology and anthropology of religion—which I have discussed and commented on in some detail in the text.

Section B lists other books cited or quoted in the text, while the third and last section, section C, lists other books which I have consulted in the compilation of this book and which may prove of some assistance to readers wishing to follow up any of the ideas I have alluded to.

A. Source books

Chapter 1: The secular philosophy: empiricism

BERKELEY, George, *The Principles of Human Knowledge* (1st ed. 1710), ed. T. E. Jessop, London (1937).

HOBBES, Thomas, *Leviathan* (1st ed. 1651), ed. M. Oakeshott, Oxford (1946); and in Everyman's Library (1914).

HUME, David, *Enquiry Concerning Human Understanding* (1st ed. 1748), ed. L. A. Selby-Bigge, Oxford (1902, reprinted 1951).

LOCKE, John, *Essay Concerning Human Understanding* (1st ed. 1690), abridged and ed. R. Wilburn, Everyman's Library (1947).

—— *Two Treatises of Civil Government* (1st ed. 1690), ed. P. Laslett, Cambridge (1960).

Chapter 2: The end of secularism

MARX, Karl, *Karl Marx: Early Writings*, ed. and trans.
T. B. Bottomore, London, C. A. Watts and Co. Ltd
(1963).
—— *Karl Marx: Selected Writings in Sociology and Social
Philosophy*, ed. and trans. T. B. Bottomore and ed.
Maximilien Rubel, London, C. A. Watts and Co. Ltd
(1956), and London, Penguin Books Ltd (1963).
—— and ENGELS, Friedrich, *The German Ideology*, ed.
R. Pascal, London, Lawrence and Wishart (1938).
MERLEAU-PONTY, Maurice, *The Phenomenology of Percep-
tion*, trans. Colin Smith, London, Routledge and Kegan
Paul (1962), French original Paris, Gallimard (1945).
WITTGENSTEIN, Ludwig, *The Blue and Brown Books*,
Oxford, Blackwell (1960).
—— *Philosophical Investigations*, trans. and ed. G. E. M.
Anscombe and Rhush Rees, Oxford, Blackwell (1958).
—— *Tractatus Logico-Philosophicus*, trans. D. F. Pears
and B. F. Guinness, London, Routledge and Kegan Paul
(1961).

Chapter 3: Sacred and secular in fiction

(Dates in this section are those of first publication.)
BRONTË, Charlotte, *Jane Eyre* (1847).
CONRAD, Joseph, *Nostromo* (1904).
DICKENS, Charles, *Bleak House* (1852).
—— *Dombey and Son* (1846).
—— *Little Dorritt* (1855).
—— *Our Mutual Friend* (1864).
—— *Pickwick Papers* (1836).
ELIOT, George, *Adam Bede*, (1859).
—— *Middlemarch* (1871).
—— *Mill on the Floss* (1860).
—— *Silas Marner* (1861).

GOLDING, William, *The Inheritors*, London, Faber and Faber (1954).
—— *Lord of the Flies*, London, Faber and Faber (1955).
—— *Pincher Martin*, London, Faber and Faber (1956).
—— *Free Fall*, London, Faber and Faber (1959).
—— *The Spire*, London, Faber and Faber (1964).
LAWRENCE, D. H., *The Rainbow* (1915).
—— *Women in Love* (1920).
—— *Lady Chatterley's Lover* (1928).
ORWELL, George, *Down and Out in Paris and London*, London, Gollancz (1933).
—— *Burmese Days*, New York, Harper Bros. (1934).
—— *A Clergyman's Daughter*, London Gollancz (1935).
—— *Keep the Aspidistra Flying*, London, Gollancz (1936).
—— *The Road to Wigan Pier*, London, Gollancz (1937).
—— *Homage to Catalonia*, London, Secker & Warburg (1938).
—— *Coming Up for Air*, London, Gollancz (1939)
—— *Animal Farm*, London, Secker & Warburg (1945).
—— *Nineteen Eighty-Four*, London, Secker & Warburg (1949).
—— *Selected Essays* London, Penguin Books, (1957).
—— *Collected Essays*, London, Secker and Warburg (1961).

Chapter 4: Rediscovering the Sacred

ELIADE, Mircea, *The Sacred and the Profane*, New York, Harper and Row (1961).
—— *Traité d'Histoire des Religions*, Paris, Payot (1949).
—— *Myths, Dreams and Mysteries*, London, Harvill Press (1960).
LÉVY-BRUHL, Lucien, *How Natives Think*, London, Allen and Unwin (1926).
VAN DER LEEUW, Gerard, *Religion in Essence and Manifestation*, London, Allen and Unwin (1938).

B. Works cited and quoted in the text

ALDRICH, Henry, *Artis Logicae Compendium*, Oxford (1961); ed. John Hill under the title *Artis Logicae Rudimenta*, Oxford (1821).

ANSCOMBE, G. E. M., *An Introduction to Wittgenstein's Tractatus*, London, Hutchinson (1959).

ATKINS, John, *George Orwell*, London, John Calder (1954).

AYER, A. J., *Language, Truth and Logic*, London, Gollancz (1936); and, with new introduction, Penguin (1956).

BAYNES, T. S. (trans. and ed.), *Port-Royal Logic*, Edinburgh, (1861⁵).

BOEKRAAD, A. J., *The Personal Conquest of Truth*, Louvain (1955).

BOUYER, Louis, *Rite and Man*, London, Burns and Oates (1963).

BRIGHT, Laurence, OP (ed.), *Theology in Modern Education*, London, Darton, Longman and Todd (1965).

―― and CLEMENTS, Simon (edd.), *The Committed Church*, London, Darton, Longman and Todd (1966).

BUCHDAHL, Gerd, *The Image of Newton and Locke in the Age of Reason*, London, Sheed and Ward (1961).

CHESTERTON, G. K. *Heretics*, London (1905).

COULSON, John (ed.), *Theology and the University*, London, Darton, Longman and Todd (1963).

COX, C. B., *The Free Spirit*, Oxford University Press (1963).

DAICHES, David, *Middlemarch*, London, Edward Arnold (1963).

DAVIS, Charles, *The Study of Theology*, London, Sheed and Ward (1962).

―― *The Making of a Christian*, London, Sheed and Ward (1964).

EDWARDS, David L., *The Honest to God Debate*, London, SCM Press (1963).

EVANS-PRITCHARD, E. E., *Theories of Primitive Religion*, Oxford University Press (1965).

FISCHER, Ernst, *The Necessity of Art*, London, Penguin Books (1963).

FREGE, G., *Translations*, ed. P. T. Geach and Max Black, Oxford (1952).

GEACH, Peter, *Mental Acts*, London, Routledge and Kegan Paul, (1957).

GORDON, R. K. (ed.), *Anglo-Saxon Poetry*, London (1927).

GREGOR, Ian, and NICHOLAS, Brian, *The Moral and the Story*, London, Faber and Faber (1962).

HARRÉ, R., *Theories and Things*, London, Sheed and Ward (1961).

HAWKINS, D. J. B., *Crucial Problems of Modern Philosophy*, London, Sheed and Ward (1957).

LUKÁCS, Georg, *The Meaning of Contemporary Realism*, London, Merlin Press (1962).

LUKASIEWICZ, Jan, *Aristotle's Syllogistic*, Oxford University Press (1951).

MALCOLM, Norman, *Ludwig Wittgenstein: A Memoir*, Oxford University Press (1958).

MANSEL, H. D., *Prolegomena Logica*, Oxford (1851).

MASCALL, E. L., *The Secularisation of Christianity*, London Darton, Longman and Todd (1965).

MAYO, Elton, *Social Problems of an Industrial Civilisation*, Boston (1945).

McCABE, Herbert, OP, *The New Creation*, London, Sheed and Ward (1964).

—— "The Validity of Absolutes", *Commonweal*, vol. 83, no. 14, New York (1966).

MILLER, J. Hillis, *Charles Dickens: the World of his Novels*, Cambridge (Mass.), Harvard University Press (1958).

MUNBY, D. L., *The Idea of a Secular Society*, Oxford University Press (1963).

NIETZSCHE, Friedrich W., *Human, all too Human*, trans. H. Zimmerman and P. V. Cohn, London (1910).

OTTO, Rudolph, *The Idea of the Holy*, London (1923).

POPPER, Karl, *British Philosophy in Mid-Century*, London (1957).

ROBINSON, J. A. T., *On Being the Church in the World*, London, SCM Press (1960).

RYAN, Columba, OP, "The Traditional Concept of Natural Law", *Light on the Natural Law*, ed. Illtyd Evans, OP, London, Burns & Oates (1966).

SMITH, Ronald Gregor, *Secular Christianity*, London, Collins (1966).

SPENDER, Stephen, *The Struggle of the Modern*, London, Hamish Hamilton (1963).

WICKER, Brian, *Culture and Liturgy*, London, Sheed and Ward (1963).

—— *Work and the Christian Community*, London, Darton, Longman and Todd (1964).

—— "Newman and Logic", in *Newman Studien*, Folge 5 (1962), pp. 251–68.

FORD, B. (ed.), *The Modern Age*, London, Penguin Books (1961). (Penguin Guide to English Literature, vol. 7.)

Ideas and Beliefs of the Victorians, London, Sylvan Press (1949).

C. Other Works Consulted

AARON, R. I., *John Locke*, Oxford (1955).

ALLEN. Walter, *The English Novel*, London, Penguin Books (1954).

—— *Tradition and Dream*, London, Phoenix House (1964).

ANDERSON, Perry and Others, *Towards Socialism*, London, Fontana (1965).

ANSCOMBE, G. E. M. and GEACH, P. T., *Three Philosophers —Aristotle, Aquinas, Frege*, Oxford, Blackwell (1961).

AQUINAS, St Thomas, *Summa Theologica*.

AYER, A. J., *The Problem of Knowledge*, London, Penguin Books (1956).

BARON, S. H., *Plekhanov: The Father of Russian Marxism*, London, Routledge and Kegan Paul (1963).

DE LA BEDOYÈRE, Michael, (ed.) *Objections to Roman Catholicism*, London, Constable (1964).

BENNETT, Joan, *George Eliot: Her Mind and her Art*, Cambridge University Press (1948).

BERGER, Peter, and PULLBERG, Stanley, "Reification and the Social Critique of Consciousness", *New Left Review* 35 (January–February 1966).

BLACK, Max, *A companion to Wittgenstein's Tractatus*, London, Hutchinson (1959).

BLÖCHLINGER, Alex, *The Modern Parish Community*, London, Geoffrey Chapman (1965).

BOROS, Ladislaus, *The Moment of Truth*, London, Burns and Oates (1965).

BRAITHWAITE, R. B., *An Empiricist's View of Religious Belief*, Cambridge University Press (1955).

BRANDER, Laurence, *George Orwell*, London (1954).

BROTHERS, Joan, *Church and School*, Liverpool University Press (1964).

BROWN, J. A. C., *Freud and the Post-Freudians*, London, Penguin Books (1961).

—— *The Social Psychology of Industry*, London, Penguin Books (1954).

BULTMANN, Rudolf, *Existence and Faith*, London, Hodder and Stoughton (1961).

BURNHAM, James, *The Managerial Revolution*, London, Penguin Books (1945).

BUTT, John and TILLOTSON, Kathleen, *Dickens at Work*, London (1957).

CAMERON, J. M., *The Night Battle*, London, Burns and Oates (1962).

CAMPBELL, George, *The Philosophy of Rhetoric*, London (1776).

COCKSHUT, A. O. J., *The Imagination of Charles Dickens*, London, Collins (1961).

CONGAR, Yves, OP, *Lay People in the Church*, London, Geoffrey Chapman (1959).

COPLESTON, F., SJ, *A History of Philosophy* (7 vols.), London, Burns and Oates (1946–63).

—— *Contemporary Philosophy*, London, Burns and Oates (1956).

—— *Aquinas*, London, Pelican Books (1955).

CORNFORTH, Maurice, *Dialectical Materialism*, 3 vols., London, Lawrence and Wishart (1952–4).

COX, Harvey E., *The Secular City*, London, SCM Press (1965).

CRONIN, J. F., *Cardinal Newman—His theory of Knowledge*, Washington (1945).

D'ARCY, M. C., *The Nature of Belief*, London, Sheed and Ward (1931).

DAVIS, Charles, *Liturgy and Doctrine*, London, Sheed and Ward (1960).

DISRAELI, Benjamin, *Sybil* (first published 1845), (1926).

DURKHEIM, Emile, *Elementary Forms of the Religious Life*, (2nd French ed. 1912), Glencoe (1947).

DURRWELL, F. X., CSSR, *The Resurrection*, London Sheed and Ward (1960).

DUTT, Clemens (trans. and ed.), *Fundamentals of Marxism-Leninism*, Moscow, Foreign Languages Publishing House; London, Lawrence and Wishart (1961).

ELIADE, Mircea, *Birth and Rebirth*, London, Harvill Press (1958).

—— and KITAGAWA, Joseph M., *The History of Religions*, Chicago University Press (1959).

ELIOT, T. S., *Selected Essays*, London, Faber and Faber (1932).

ENGELS, Frederick, *Dialectics of Nature*, London, Lawrence and Wishart (1940).

—— *Anti-Dühring*, Moscow, Foreign Languages Publishing House (1954); London, Lawrence and Wishart (1955).

—— *Letters*, (Marx and Engels) in *Selected Works* vol. 2, Moscow, Foreign Languages Publishing House (1949); London, Lawrence and Wishart (1950).

FORD, G. H. and LANE, L. (edd.), *The Dickens Critics*, Ithaca, N.Y. Cornell University Press (1961).

FORSTER, John, *The Life of Charles Dickens*, London (1873–4).

FRANKFORT, Henry and others, *Before Philosophy*, London, Penguin Books (1949).

VAN GHENT, Dorothy, *The English Novel*, London, Harper Torchbooks (1961).

GRIFFIN, James, *Wittgenstein's Logical Atomism*, Oxford, Clarendon Press (1964).

HALÉVY, Elie, *The Growth of Philosophical Radicalism*, London, Faber and Faber (1928).

HARDY, Barbara, *The Novels of George Eliot*, London, Athlone Press (1959).

HARVEY, W. J., *The Art of George Eliot*, London, Chatto and Windus (1961).

HEPBURN, Ronald, W., *Christianity and Paradox*, London, A. and C. Watts (1958).

HOGGART, Richard, *The Uses of Literacy*, London, Penguin Books (1958).

HOLLIS, Christopher, *A Study of George Orwell*, London (1956).

HOLLOWAY, John, *The Victorian Sage*, New York (1965).

HOUGH, Graham, *The Dark Sun*, London, Penguin Books (1961).

HOUSE, Humphrey, *The Dickens World*, Oxford University Press (1941).

JAMES, E. O., *Comparative Religion*, London, Methuen (1961).

JARRETT-KERR, Martin, *The Secular Promise*, London, SCM Press (1964).

JOHNSON, Edgar, *Charles Dickens, His Tragedy and Triumph*, London, Gollancz (1953).

KAMENKE, Eugene, *The Ethical Foundations of Marxism*, London, Routledge and Kegan Paul (1962).

KENNY, Anthony, "Aquinas and Wittgenstein", in *Downside Review* (Spring 1959).

287

KETTLE, Arnold, *An Introduction to the English Novel*, 2 vols., London, Hutchinson (1951–3).

LEAVIS, F. R., *The Common Pursuit*, London, Peregrine Books (1962).

LEAVIS, F. R., *The Great Tradition*, London, Peregrine Books (1962).

LECLERCQ, Jacques, *Christ and the Modern Conscience*, London, Geoffrey Chapman (1962).

LENIN, V. I., *Materialism and Empirio-Criticism*, London, Martin Lawrence (*Collected Works*, n.d., vol. XIII).

LOVEJOY, Arthur O., *The Great Chain of Being*, New York, Harper & Row (1960).

LUNN, Arnold and LEAN, Garth, *The New Morality*, London, Blandford Press (1964).

MACINTYRE, Alasdair C., *Difficulties in Christian Belief*, London, SCM Press (1959).

—— and FLEW, Anthony, *New Essays in Philosophical Theology*, London, SCM Press (1955).

—— (ed.), *Metaphysical Beliefs*, London, SCM Press (1957).

MARCUS, Steven, *Dickens: From Pickwick To Dombey*, London, Chatto and Windus (1965).

MARX, Karl and ENGELS, F., *Manifesto of the Communist Party* (1848) Moscow, Foreign Languages Publishing House.

—— —— *Letters* (with Engels) in *Selected Works* vol. 2, Moscow, Foreign Languages Publishing House (1949); London, Lawrence and Wishart (1950).

MASCALL, E. L., *He Who Is*, London, Longmans, Green (1943).

—— *Existence and Analogy*, London, Longmans, Green (1949).

MEYNELL, Hugo, *Sense, Nonsense and Christianity*, London, Sheed and Ward (1964).

MITCHELL, Basil (ed.), *Faith and Logic*, London, Allen and Unwin (1957).

MUNZ, Peter, *Problems of Religious Knowledge*, London, SCM Press (1959).

MURRAY, Henry A. (ed.), *Myth and Myth making*, New York, George Brazziler (1960).

NEWMAN, John Henry (Cardinal), *The Idea of a University*, London (1852).

—— *Apologia pro vita sua*, London (1865).

—— *Oxford University Sermons*, London, Rivingtons (1845).

—— *An Essay on the development of Christian doctrine*, London (1845).

—— *Autobiographical Writings*, London, Sheed and Ward (1956).

—— *The Grammar of Assent*, London, Longmans, Green (1891).

NOWELL-SMITH, P. H., *Ethics*, London, Penguin Books (1954).

PLEKHANOV, G., *Selected Philosophical Works*, vol. I, London, Lawrence and Wishart (1961).

—— *In Defence of Materialism*, London, Lawrence and Wishart (1947).

—— *Art and Social Life*, ed. A. Rothstein, London, Lawrence and Wishart (1953).

PLUMB, J. H. (ed.), *Crisis in the Humanities*, London, Penguin Books (1964).

RAMSEY, I. T., *Religious Language*, London, SCM Press (1957).

REES, Richard, *George Orwell—Fugitive from the Camp of Victory*, London, Secker & Warburg (1961).

RHYMES, Douglas, *No New Morality*, London, Constable (1964).

RICHARDSON, Alan, *University and Humanity*, London, SCM Press (1964).

ROBINSON, J. A. T., *Honest to God*, London, SCM Press (1963).

—— *Christian Morals Today*, London, SCM Press (1964).

—— *The New Reformation*, London, SCM Press (1965).

SCHILLEBEECKX, Edward, OP, *Christ the Sacrament*, London, Sheed and Ward (1963).

SILLEM, Edward, *Ways of Thinking About God*, London, Darton, Longman and Todd Ltd (1961).

ST JOHN-STEVAS, Norman, *Law and Morals*, London, Burns and Oates (1964).

STENTON, Doris Mary, *English Society in the Early Middle Ages (1066–1307)*, London, Penguin Books (1951).

SMART, Ninian, *Philosophers and Religious Truth*, London, SCM Press (1964).

SNOW, C. P., *The Two Cultures and the Scientific Revolution*, Cambridge University Press (1959).

STRAWSON, P. F., *Individuals*, London, Methuen (1959).

TANNER, Tony, *Conrad: Lord Jim*, London, Edward Arnold (1963).

TAWNEY, R. H., *Religion and The Rise of Capitalism*, London, Penguin Books (1938).

TEILHARD DE CHARDIN, Pierre, *The Phenomenon of Man*, London, Collins (1959).

THALE, Jerome, *The Novels of George Eliot*, New York, Columbia University Press (1959).

THOMAS, Edward M., *Orwell*, London and Edinburgh, Oliver and Boyd (1965).

THOMSON, G, *Aeschylus at Athens*, London, Lawrence and Wishart (1946²).

—— *Marxism and Poetry*, London, Lawrence and Wishart (1945).

TILLICH, Paul, *The Shaking of the Foundations*, London, Penguin Books (1962).

TILLOTSON, Kathleen, *Novels of the Eighteen-Forties*, Oxford University Press (1961).

VATICAN COUNCIL II, *De Ecclesia—The Constitution on the Church*, London, Darton, Longman and Todd (1965).

VIDLER, A. R. (ed.), *Objections to Christian Belief*, London, Constable (1963).

WALGRAVE, J. H., OP, *Newman: le Développement du Dogme*, Tournai (1957). Translated into English as *Newman the Theologian*, London, Geoffrey Chapman 1960).

WARD, Wilfred, *Life of John Henry Cardinal Newman*, 2 vols., London (1912).

WELDON, T. D., *The Vocabulary of Politics*, London, Penguin Books (1953).

WETTER, *Dialectical Materialism*, London, Routledge and Kegan Paul (1958).

WILLIAMS, Raymond, *Culture and Society 1780–1950*, London, Penguin Books, first published by Chatto and Windus (1958).

—— *The Long Revolution*, London, Chatto and Windus (1961).

WHATELY, R., *Elements of logic*, London (1868⁹).

WHITELEY, C. H. and WINIFRED, M., *The Permissive Morality*, London, Methuen (1964).

WINCH, Peter, *The Idea of a Social Science*, London (1958).

WOLLHEIM, Richard, *F. H. Bradley*, London, Penguin Books (1959).

ZENO, P., OFM CAP, *John Henry Newman—Our way to Certitude*, Leiden (1957).

Index of subjects

Principal page references and titles of books referred to are in italics.

as a common world, 56
ordinary language, 73–4, 80, 82, 84
as picturing reality, 74–6
elementary language (Wittgenstein), 74ff.
as the limit of my world, 76
language-games, *84ff.*, 160, 219
form of the community, 85ff., 95
Orwell's theory of, 152ff.
relation to politics in Orwell, 152ff.
in Lévy-Bruhl, 197ff.
as shared by members of the community, 220
sacred and profane uses of language, 229
see also CHURCH (as linguistic community); LOGIC; MARXISM; SECULAR PHILOSOPHY

Language, Truth and Logic (A. J. Ayer), 70
Leviathan, 43
Lévy-Bruhl, *194–205*
law of participation, 186, 195–6, 198
collective representations, 186, 196, 203
mystic powers, 194
totemism, 194–5
incompatibility of sociological and religious theories, 197
language as a communal activity, 197–8
nineteenth-century rationalist presuppositions, 198

socialisation of mystic powers, 199
conceptualisation and abstractionism, *200ff.*
logic, 201ff.
exaggeration of primitive mentality, 18*n.*, 194*n.*, 204

Linguistic analysis, ix, 2
Liturgy
as communication, 219
eucharistic, 220
as official worship, 226
as making the church encounterable, 228–9
Locke, *Essay Concerning Human Understanding*, 26ff.
see also SECULAR PHILOSOPHY; IDEAS
Logic
psychological (secular) theory of, 23, 39
syllogism in Aldrich and Aristotle, 39–41
Aristotle's syllogistic, 49*n.*
Newman and Logic, 41*n.*
mathematical logic and Wittgenstein, 71
in Orwell, 157–8, 162
logical contradiction, 162
in Lévy-Bruhl, 201ff. (Abstractionism)
see also NAMES; LANGUAGE; SECULAR PHILOSOPHY

MAGIC, 52, 57*n.*, *207ff.*
Mankind, solidarity of, 5
see also SPECIES
MARXISM, 9, 10, 13, 66–7, *88–97*, 171

in de-mythologised theo-
logy, 210
Naturalistic fallacy, 45, 47
Natural law, 44
in Hobbes and Locke, 46–7
in Newman, 46–7
in primitive mentality, 206
Nature
sovereignty of nature in
George Eliot, 105ff.
relation to the human world
in *George Eliot*, 112ff.
human nature in Orwell,
158
natural world as revelation
of God, 234, 238 (Book
of Wisdom)
New Left Review, 13, 182
"Newspeak", see ORWELL
New theology, viii
Newton, 32 and *n.*, 68, 72
Principia, 32*n.*
Nominalism, see SECULAR
THEORY OF LANGUAGE
Novel, *102–85 passim*
development of, 16
use as documentary evi-
dence, 16
as prophecy (William Golding), 182

ORWELL, GEORGE, *151–169*
as a "contemporary", 151
relation of language to
politics, 152ff.
and the secular philosophy,
151ff.
theory of language, 152, 156
"Newspeak", 153, 156
language and objects, 153ff.
Homage to Catalonia, 153*n.*
Animal Farm, 151, 155

logic of general terms, 157ff.
logical contradiction, 162
Nineteen Eighty-Four, 151,
153, 163ff.
creative writing, 164

PARTICIPATION, LAW OF, 57*n.*,
67, 186, 194ff., 205, 208
in Mircea Eliade, 211ff.
necessary for a religious
outlook, 243
see also LÉVY-BRUHL
Perception
secular theory of, 22, *24–32*
passivity of observer, 24
solipsism, 25
phenomenology of, 18, *48–
68*
and conceptualisation, 51–
53
visual field, 50, 60, 63
Newman's theory of, 218
and *n.*
see also MERLEAU-PONTY
Phenomenology, ix
of perception, 48–68
of religion, 186–9
see also MERLEAU-PONTY
Philosophical   Investigations
(Wittgenstein), 72, *81–
88*
acts of will, 81ff., 154
Port-Royal Logic, 37*n.*
Power
occult powers, 231
and increasing human con-
trol of the world, 231ff.
spiritualisation of, 230ff.
and the idea of reality of the
species, 243
in tools, 236–7 and *n.*

Presence (of Christ),
  to people not to things, 217
    and *n*., 218, 219, 222
  as a basis of the Church,
    222ff., 227
  see also CHRIST
Principia (Newton), 32*n*.
Psychology, 3
  Gestalt, 48
Purgatory, 254

RABBLE HYPOTHESIS (Elton
    Mayo), 43 and 246*n*.
Radicalism, 13
  and sociology, 13*n*.
  and Christianity, *260–78*
Realism in literature, 150ff.
  see also MEANING OF CON-
    TEMPORARY REALISM
Reification, 13*n*
Religion, 17–18
  phenomenology of, 18 and
    n.
  in primitive societies, 193
  spiritualisation of in Wes-
    tern societies, 231–47
  and human control of the
    world, 231–47
  conflict with scientific out-
    look, 239ff.
  reduced to ethical personal-
    ism, 241ff.
  necessarily complicated,
    244
*Religion in Essence and Mani-
    festation* (van der
    Leeuw, 192, 205ff.
Resurrection, 10, 19, 220–21,
    247–59
  of Christ, 249–50, 258
  a true coming to life of the
    man Jesus, 252

Retinal image, inversion of,
    59–60
Rite and Man (L. Bouyer),
    204*n*.

SACRAMENTS as communica-
    tion, 222ff., 232
  see also CHURCH
Sacred, the, 17, 53, 69,
    186–221
  as the real (in contrast to the
    secular, or profane
    "chaos"), 193–4, 212ff.
  participation in founding
    the world, 213
  as communitarian, 215
  dialogue of persons as
    always sacred, 218–9
  narrowing of concept of
    sacred in modern soc-
    ieties, 238ff.
  once more accessible in the
    community today, 246
  see also MIRCEA ELIADE;
    VAN DER LEEUW;
    SECULAR PHILOSOPHY;
    LANGUAGE;   SPACE;
    TIME
Sacred and the Profane, The
    (Mircea Eliade), *212–
    221*
Saints
  lives of, 233
  power of, 233
Secular philosophy, *14–17*,
    21–47
  dissatisfaction with, viii
  and politics, 4
  theory of society, 4
  collapse of, 16
  Lockeian empiricism, 21

300

301

Time (*cont*).
  sacred time, 65, *212ff.*
    breaking the homogen-
      eity of profane world,
      193, 212, 213ff.
    as the beginnings of the
      world, 214
*Theology and Modern Educa-
    tion*, 149*n.*
Tools, 236–7 and *n.*
Totemism, 194–5, 230
Tractatus Logico-Philosophicus
    (Wittgenstein), *68–88*,
    140, 248*n.*
  positivistic interpretation
    of, 70–71
  on what can be shown but
    not said, 72, 78
  as a secular book, 72
  elementary language, *74ff.*
  atomic facts, 75
  the empirical self in, *77ff.*,
    80
  world as independent of my
    will, 78–80
  see also WITTGENSTEIN
Tradition, Catholic, 12, 277

VAN DER LEEUW, *205ff.*
  man and the external world,
    206ff.
  metalogical mentality, 204*n.*
  myth and magic contrasted,
    207–11
  myth as an intellectual
    explanation, 209
  naming as a sacred action,
    209–10 (see NAMES)
Vatican Council
  and modernisation, 6
  Constitution on the Church,
    7
  irrelevant to modern agnos-
    ticism, 11
Visual field, 50, 60, 63
  in Wittgenstein's *Tractatus*,
    79

WISDOM, Book of, 234, 236,
    238
Word, creativity of, 219–21,
    229
  see also LANGUAGE

Index of names

Eliade Mircea (*cont.*)
187, 192, 193*n*., *211–21*,
228
Eliot, George, 17, 103, *105–
118*, 119, 120, 124, 127,
134, 135, 136, 137, 138,
139, 140, 141 and *n*., 142,
168
Eliot, T. S., 1, 67, 123*n*., 149,
269*n*., 277
Engels, Friedrich, 91*n*., 94*n*.
Evans-Pritchard, E. E., 18*n*.

FISCHER, ERNST, 237*n*.
Frazer, J. G., 198
Free Fall, 171–4, 179
Frege, G., 35 and *n*.

GEACH, P. T., 35*n*., 38*n*., 39*n*.,
69*n*.
Golding, William, 17, *169–
184*, 242*n*.
Gordon, R. K., 233
Gradgrind, Thomas, 22, 229
Gregor, Ian, 144*n*., 173*n*.
Guthlac, 233*n*.

HALL, STUART, 12*n*.
Hardy, Thomas, 143, 144
Hard Times, 134
Harré, R., 253*n*.
Hawkins, D. J. B., 71*n*.
Heidegger, Martin, 2
Hill, John, 37*n*.
Hobbes, Thomas, 42, 43, 45,
47, 89, 107
Homer, 170
Hopkins, G. Manley, 180*n*.
House, Humphry, 105*n*.
Hume, David, 24, 70, 71, 204
Husserl, 34, 35 and *n*., 206

Inheritors, The, 174, 177

JEFFERSON, 226
John XXIII, Pope, 11
Joyce, James, 147, 149, 150

KAFKA, FRANZ, 147
Kinkead-Weakes, M., 173*n*.
Knights, L. C., 149*n*.
Küng, Hans, 276

LAWRENCE, D. H., 143, 144,
149, 150, 263
Lear, King, 122
Leeuw, Gerard van der, 18
and *n*., 186, 187, 192, 204
and *n*., *205–11*, 235, 237*n*.,
241
Lenin, 4
Lévy-Bruhl, Lucien, 18*n*.,
53*n*., 57*n*., 131, 186, 187,
194–205
Little Dorrit, 122, 123, 133,
134, 135, 139
Little Gidding, 1
Locke, John, 24, *26–34*, 37*n*.,
42, 43, 44 and *n*., 45, 47, 49,
70, 73, 89, 156, 237*n*.
Lord of the Flies, 174, 176
Lukács, G., 117*n*., 144, 145,
147 and *n*., 148, 149, 150
and *n*., 170
Lukasiewicz, Jan, 40*n*.

MALCOLM, NORMAN, 161*n*.
McCabe, OP, Herbert, xi,
47*n*., 217*n*., 254
Mann, Thomas, 145
Mansel, H. D., 34 and *n*.
Marx, Karl, ix, 4, 13, 15, 17,
48 and *n*., *88–97*, 153, 171,